4/16/08

Greetings to
Dave Harrison

"Jim Chet"

"I'm Chet"

The autobiography
of Chet Krause
as told to
Arlyn G. Sieber

Designed by Elizabeth Krogwold

Contents

Forward

Chet Krause is one of those people you remember meeting for the first time. I distinctly remember my introduction to him. It was early on the morning of Tuesday, September 2, 1980 – my first day of employment with Krause Publications.

As instructed, I reported to the office of Cliff Mishler, who at the time doubled as the company's executive vice president and publisher of its numismatic division. Cliff was on the phone as I walked into his office, and this 50-something guy was leaning up against some cabinets in Cliff's office. He was casually but smartly dressed in a short-sleeved shirt and slacks. His arms were folded across his chest, and he was holding some papers in one hand.

As I approached the door, I hesitated when I saw Cliff on the phone and another person in the office. But the guy leaning against the cabinets waved me in, smiled at me, held out his hand, and said, "Hi. I'm

Chet." I shook his hand, told him my name, and then thought to myself, "This guy looks like the bookkeeper."

I had known about Krause Publications for several years by then because my brother subscribed to *Old Cars*. I shared his automotive interests and looked at his copies of *Old Cars* regularly. I had also attended a couple editions of the Iola Old Car Show and Swap Meet, including the one immediately preceding my interview and then employment with the company in 1980.

I had applied for an advertised editorial position with the company prior to the car show that year and in response got the standard form letter stating my application had been received and so on and so forth. Weeks, if not months, went by and I did not hear anything more. "So much for that," I thought. But then in late July, I got a call from Cliff and an interview was scheduled. A short time after the interview, I got another call from Cliff offering me the job on the *Numismatic News* editorial staff.

Today, I realize why I had to wait weeks, if not months, for that interview. It is said that Iola divides its year into two segments – "before car show" and "after car show." For example, "That will have to wait until after the car show." Or, "We better get that done before the car show." Apparently, filling that *Numismatic News* editorial position in 1980 was an "after-car-show" task.

I accepted the job – not that it was a big decision to do so – and moved to a new community for the second time in my life. The first time occurred when I was only 18 months old, so my move to Iola was really the first major change in my life.

In the course of tying up loose ends at my old job, finding a place to live in a new community, moving, and then starting a new job, I never stopped to think how Krause Publications came to be called Krause Publications. It did not occur to me to ask during my interview, and Cliff did not volunteer it.

And my introduction to Chet was certainly of no help in that regard. It was not "I'm Chet Krause, president of Krause Publications." When I walked into Cliff's office that morning, it was not a perfunctory introduction by Cliff after he got off the phone and a perfunctory hello from Chet as he moved on to much more important business. And it certainly was not – heaven forbid – "Mr. Krause."

No, it was just a simple "Hi. I'm Chet." After that, I was left to my own devices to figure out who Chet was, which I did eventually. In subsequent years, it would amuse me whenever a newer employee would address him as "Mr. Krause." I always knew what the response would be: "I'm Chet," he would tell them firmly but politely.

I never would have imagined from that simple "I'm Chet" how big of an influence this man would come to have on my life.

He was my employer for many years; he was my confidant and counselor at times; he was my traveling companion on many business trips; he was my breakfast or lunch or dinner companion many times on those trips; he was my host for a Green Bay Packers game on one occasion; and he was a guest at my wedding.

I spent 12 years working on the editorial staff of Krause Publications' numismatic division before I transferred to the position of public-relations coordinator. A major reason why I made the move was because I enjoyed telling the Chet Krause and Krause Publications story. If it were fiction, the story would be riddled with clichés: Raised as a simple farm boy, a small-town carpenter hits on a business idea, achieves great success with it, and turns philanthropist in his later years. But it is not fiction, and it is not a cliché. It really happened, and the story of how it happened is told on the pages that follow.

I continued with Krause Publications and its successor in various executive-support and editorial roles until January 2006, when I resigned. I wanted to enjoy an early semiretirement, pursue some freelance work and personal projects, and spend more time with my family. (Yes, I know. Everybody who quits a job says they want to spend more time with their family. But I really did, and I really have.) Chet left the company several years prior to my resignation.

I never would have imagined from that simple "I'm Chet" introduction how big of an influence this man would come to have on my life.

I thought my days of telling the Chet Krause and Krause Publications story were over, but I was wrong. On a pleasant day in May 2006, I was headed down Main Street in Iola on my morning constitutional, and I met Chet coming out of the car-show office. He told me that his family was encouraging him to write his autobiography and asked me if I would help him with the project. We met a couple of more times that month and discussed the project further. We then got going on it in earnest the following September.

I wrote a suggested outline, and Chet added some topics to it along the way. After a few weeks, our work fell into a pattern. Chet took the next topic on the outline, hand wrote his thoughts on the topic on a legal pad, and then turned the notes over to me. While he proceeded to the next topic, I took his notes and crafted them into a narrative, sometimes adding background, sometimes rearranging his thoughts, and sometimes taking bits and pieces from notes on other topics and adding them to the chapter being worked on. Those familiar with my writing style will no doubt see my mark on the text that follows, but the thoughts and emotions expressed herewith are very much Chet's.

I have always considered Chet a man of contrasts, and I think the reader, too, will see that in the following pages. He can be right at home eating one of the home-cooked daily specials at the Crystal Cafe in downtown Iola, but I have also seen him put on a suit and tie and order chateaubriand at the Penrose Room restaurant in the five-star Broadmoor hotel in Colorado Springs, Colorado. He once put on a pair of waders and trudged through the drained Iola millpond – maybe more swamp than pond at that point – clearing debris as he went as part of the effort to turn it into Lake Iola. He also once had lunch with the chief justice of the United States. He can speak at length about his world travels and the famous and exotic places he has visited, but he can also tell you how to properly miter the trim around a door.

I still see those contrasts today. Chet will still fly to New York City to bid on a piece of paper money that caught his fancy in an auction catalog, but he will still delight in some accomplishment by the local community or a member of it.

And to those who get a chance to meet him and shake his hand, he will still tell them, "I'm Chet."

Arlyn G. Sieber

J u n e   2 0 0 7

Chapter 1

Family

There is almost nothing in my early life to indicate that some day I would start a publishing venture that would become a worldwide leader in its respective fields. From childhood through my early adult years, I had no knowledge of how to sell advertising, promote subscriptions, and gather editorial content for a magazine. But I knew plenty about picking cucumbers and potatoes, planting corn with a homemade marker pulled by a horse, and laying cement block.

I was born December 16, 1923, in a big house on our family farm in the township of Helvetia, Waupaca County, in east-central Wisconsin. Our farm was about six miles east of the village of Iola. Norwegian dominates the area's cultural heritage, but the name Helvetia is actually of Swiss origin. That's because an early prominent citizen and land owner in the town, Johann Heinrich Leuthold Jr., was Swiss. Helvetia was the Roman name for an ancient region of central Europe between the Alps and Jura Mountains. Switzerland continues to use the name in its Latin form, Helvetica, on stamps and coins.

I, however, have neither Norwegian nor Swiss blood in me. My father, Carl Krause, was the son of Prussian and Austrian immigrants. My mother, the former Cora Neil, was of Scotch-Irish parentage.

My dad was the second of five children – three boys and two girls – and faced a tough go of it from an early age. He was only 11 when his father, a Prussian immigrant named Christian Ludwig Krause, died in 1890 at age 60. Christian married for the second time in 1877 when he took Maria Theresa Pelz, an Austrian immigrant, for his bride. She was pregnant with their fifth child when Christian died. That left my dad as the man in the family with three younger siblings, including a newborn, and an immigrant mother who spoke little English.

Dad's formal education consisted of a grand total of eight days of grade school. But he was one of the smartest men I've ever known when it came to practical knowledge – how to build and fix things, how to live off the land, and just generally how to make the most of what you have. If he had been born in modern times, he would have been a great mechanic. He was even elected to the local school board, town assessor, and town chairman at various points in his adult life. Dad was also active at a local level in Wisconsin's Progressive politics of the 1920s and '30s. I used to ride along with him as he traveled the township roads to get nomination signatures for candidates. He was very proud that one year Helvetia voted 95-percent Progressive. Because of his political activity and service in town offices, Dad was one of the best-known men in Helvetia, and that made me proud, which helped boost my self-esteem when I had an inferiority complex all my early life.

Riding with him on his political rounds was also an educational experience for me. I got to know many of the town's residents, where the school-district boundaries were, how land descriptions fit the land they described, who had good farms, and who were good farmers. In general, I learned there was more to life than the two-mile stretch of State Highway 161, from the cheese factory to the Dow School House, where our farm was located.

But politics didn't put food on the table; Dad's construction business and farming did. Forced to earn money at a young age, Dad was only 13 or 14 years old when he started mixing mortar for a local stone mason. In due course, by watching and doing, he learned how to lay stone himself and started building stone foundations for buildings and stone bridges over the many streams and

My dad, Carl Krause, as a young man.

A wonderful portrait of my mother, the former Cora Neil, as a young woman. I do not know if this was taken for a special occasion, but the dress is certainly beautiful.

rivers in Waupaca County. In July 1926, he was the low bidder at $2,140 for a new bridge at Northland, north of Iola on State Highway 49.

I remember Dad as a stocky but not particularly muscular man – maybe five feet, eight inches tall. His basic demeanor was kind, but he could get terribly mad, and when he did, you knew it. One of the first people I hired in the publishing business was Art Christoph, who was the first advertising manager for *Numismatic News* and who worked for the company for more than 30 years. When we discovered a dishonest advertiser in our pages, Art would put his name in a file he labeled "Once a Crook Always a Crook." That was Dad's philosophy, too. If anyone ever did him wrong, he remembered it to his dying day.

We were poor living on our sand- and gravel-laden farm during the Depression, but like a lot of people at the time, we didn't know it. You didn't buy new stuff; you fixed the old. And Dad was great at fixing lots of things with baling wire or cobbling things together with scraps of wood or metal. He could fix a saw – not only file it but set it and plane the teeth all the same length. My uncle John Edwards used to say that Dad could drive a crooked nail with a rock better than he could with a hammer.

Dad worked hard to support his family and make ends meet. The only time he took off during the week was on Sunday mornings after the cows were milked. That's when he would shave. He shaved only once a week unless he and Mother went somewhere during the week – a school-related function, for example. Then he would shave, wash up, and put on his suit and tie. In those days, everybody dressed up when they went out. One of the few luxuries Dad had in his life was a gold watch that he bought as a young man and carried with him wherever he went. Oftentimes he didn't need it, though. Having worked outside much of his life, he could tell you what time it was just by looking up at the sun.

In many ways, Dad was still a pioneer and knew a lot about the outdoors. He knew how to fell a tree in the desired direction, even accounting for a breeze. If that breeze was strong enough to be called wind, one didn't cut trees. Broken branches were called "widow makers" because if the wind caught them, they would push the tree backward onto the logger.

Dad married my mother on July 2, 1910. My mother was born in 1885 and grew up in Manawa, Wisconsin, a small village east of Helvetia. She was the oldest of Samuel and Susie Neil's five children – all girls. Samuel was a logger, and Susie was a seamstress. After graduating from high school, Mother attended summer school, which qualified her to teach grade school at age 17. She was hired to teach at Blake Brook School in rural Waupaca County. My dad was a member of the school board at the time, and that's how they met. I don't recall my mother and dad showing a lot of outward affection for each other – at least not in the presence of others – but I have no doubt they loved each other and cared for each other. They had to be a great support to each other during some of the hard times they faced during their 44 years of marriage.

If ever there was a perfect lady in this world, it was my mother. Devoid of her husband's sometimes sharp tongue, Mother was patient and soft-spoken, and loved to read books and magazines, and loved to garden. She also compensated for Dad's lack of formal education by tutoring him and helping him with reading and writing in his business and public service. She also wrote a column titled "Dow Corners News" for the local weekly newspaper, the *Iola Herald*. "Dow Corners" was at the intersection of State Highway 161 and County Highway E, just west of our farm. It was one of those interesting local columns that told who visited whom, who got married, who died, or who went to town. And, of course, it was great news if someone was visiting from Chicago or the women's club had met.

I am the youngest of six children. My brother Carlton Neil – or simply "Neil" more commonly – was born in 1911. Then came my sister Mary in 1913, sister Grace in 1915, sister Donna in 1917, and brother Ben in 1920. I have no memory of Donna; she died in September 1925, when I was only 21 months old, after fighting polio most of her life. Our older siblings called Ben and me the "two little boys" because Donna's death left a five-year gap between the three oldest kids and the two youngest.

I, of course, was the youngest of them all, which left me tagging along with my mother most of the day while the others were off to school. Mother was my best friend during this time, and I probably was more of a joy to her than those arriving before me, even though to her I was always under foot. I just recall always being close to Mother physically and mentally, whether we were working around the house or outside.

Mother's garden was one of her great passions in life. Early on, I remember it being near the house, but it wasn't "good ground" there. So we broke ground at a spot about a quarter-mile from the house. It was a long way to haul the harvested product, so some of us "kids," as we were called, would arrange to do that duty. But it seemed Mother, too, usually had a load both coming and going.

*My mother and I pose for a quick snapshot in the earliest known photograph
of me. In those days, all toddlers wore dresses regardless of gender.*

Because Neil was 12 years my senior, I looked up to him second only to my parents. I think he had much the same respect for our mother as I had. But Neil was much like our dad, and that was trouble sometimes. Dad and Neil wouldn't always see eye to eye, and when they didn't, each held his ground. Neil disliked farming – milking cows, harnessing horses, and all the other chores. But he enjoyed the country to no end. Even after we sold the farm and moved into the village of Iola in 1950, you could be out of the inhabited area and in the woods in 10 minutes.

And it seemed like we always had a wild "forty" to go to out in the country – if not ours, one owned by friends.

After serving in the Army in World War II, Neil bought the necessary machines and tools to fix guns. He set up his first shop on the farm and then later had one in the village. He married Mae Wogslund in 1957, and they had one daughter, Patti. Both Mae and Neil passed on, and today Patti is my trusted protector. In my 80s now, I need someone to interface with today's rat race, and Patti does it for me.

Like Neil, Mary was a mentor to me, too, when I was growing up but from the perspective of an older sister rather than an older brother. After Mother and Dad, what she said and did were held in high regard. Mary graduated from high school in 1931. Urged on by our parents and one of her classmates, Hildegard Knutson, she went to Stevens Point Normal, a teacher's college 25 miles west of Iola, for two years. That qualified her to teach grade school. When our cousin Margaret Edwards got married, Mary completed her teaching year in 1933 at Sunny Knoll School, near Loyal, Wisconsin, in Clark County, and then was hired full time the next year.

Mary married Gerald Klug of Loyal in 1938. Jerry worked as a cheesemaker in Granton, Wisconsin, but a year or so after he and Mary were married, they moved to Milwaukee, where Jerry worked in the defense industry. Later they purchased their own cheese factory in Ringle, Wisconsin. It was about 50 miles from the farm, but there was hardly a Sunday that we didn't visit them. While Jerry made cheese, Mary taught at a rural school a few miles from the factory. Often Grace would baby sit for their two children, David and Pat, during the week. Jerry died in 2000, but Mary continues to reside in Iola.

As for Grace, I often said that if you greeted her or called her by her first name, you were her friend for life, and I think that's true. She never had the fear of meeting new people that most of us do. Upon her death on June 11, 2006, at age 91, many well-wishers spoke of her smile, and it was nice to know that others remembered her as we, her family, did because Grace had plenty of sick days that left her depressed. Grace, too, contracted polio at age two – the same time as Donna. She lost her ability to walk and talk until age six, and it left her with a lesser ability to deal with life for the rest of her days.

I don't know how my parents managed with two young children suffering from a debilitating disease, four other kids at home, and a farm and construction work to keep going. Donna's illness was especially a burden. She would spend six months at a time in the hospital in Madison, Wisconsin, which today is about a two-hour drive from Iola. In the 1920s, of course, the trip was made in a touring car with side curtains on narrow two-lane roads. The trip must have taken the best part of a day.

Mother and Grace were great friends, as I recall, but kids being what they are, sometimes we would pick on Grace. I know I did my share of taunting. Neither my mother nor my father did a lot of spanking for discipline, but when they spoke in a certain tone of voice, you knew they meant what they said and the line was drawn. That was the case one day when I went too far in badgering Grace. Mother took me aside and told me to treat Grace better because she wasn't as able to defend herself – either verbally or physically – as well as the rest of her siblings. Grace hated to be called dumb and would react violently if called that. So I learned not to say or imply that after Mother's lecture to me, and I implored my friends to do the same. I still teased Grace and she would pound on me and about beat me to death, but it was all good natured after that.

And Grace was far from dumb. In her adult years, she was a walking encyclopedia of certain information, especially the dates of birth, marriages, and death of relatives, neighbors, schoolmates, and friends. But if for some reason she got mad at me, she would sulk about it. After Mother died in 1980 and Grace and I continued to share a household, Grace always got up at 5 a.m., but I wouldn't get up until 6:30. She would leave notes for me, usually commenting on the weather or a reminder about something I had to do that day. But when she was mad at me, the note would go something like this:

"I'm mad at you and you know why I'm mad, and I'm going to stay mad. So don't do anything to try to make up for it because I'm going to stay mad and don't try to talk to me because I'm mad and won't talk to you."

And she wouldn't talk to me until something broke the ice, such as someone coming to visit or a phone call she had to relate to me. Oftentimes I never knew what had made her mad at me. Maybe I didn't take her shopping for groceries or to a visitation at the funeral home, or maybe I was late for a meal so she couldn't do something she wanted to do. But in time, she would get over it and fall back into the routine of daily living. That would include my taking her out to eat on Friday night or Sunday noon. We tried lots of restaurants, but the Crystal Cafe in downtown Iola was her favorite because she would see friends there who would greet her by her name.

Because there was only three and a half years' difference in our age, Ben was special to me when we were growing up. I suspect Neil had showed Ben around the farm and the woods, and then Ben passed that knowledge on to me. When I was five years old, Ben was eight and was the leader who showed me the barn, machine shed, garage, chicken coop, pig pen, and the sap house, where Dad boiled maple sap into syrup in the spring. Ben also introduced me to Winter Green Island, the Big Rock, how to find lizards under flat rocks, and, most of all, the Juneberry tree at the very top of the high hill. The Juneberries were delicious, and a big rock in the middle of them provided a built-in platform for reaching the higher branches.

Being a bit older, Ben grew into more arduous things before I did, such as helping Dad with the farm chores. That left me at the house to "help" Mother.

Even after we sold the farm and moved into the village, Mother and I remained close. I'd still pick wild blackberries and raspberries with her or help her in the garden. Dad's death in 1954 made me the breadwinner in the household – first as a carpenter and later as a want-to-be publisher. Fortunately, I was a lot older than my dad was when he had to assume that duty.

I remember well how Mother loved to travel in those later years. Sometimes it was just a ride through the local countryside on a Sunday afternoon. I think at one point I had taken her on every road within a 15-mile radius of Iola. But my success in the publishing business allowed us to travel more extensively. I took her to Quebec to visit relatives there. California was also a destination to visit relatives. We also toured Alaska and yet another time traveled to north-central Montana.

For the last ten years of her life, Mother suffered from what today would be called Alzheimer's disease and was unable to talk during that time. Neil, Grace, and I cared for her at home until the final two and a half years, when she resided at the Iola Nursing Home. She probably should have gone to the nursing home earlier, but we wanted to keep her at home for as long as we could. Even at the nursing home in those final years, her smile made her many friends.

Now that I'm in my 80s, I see my parents in a far different light than I did as a youngster and young adult. Neil, Ben, and I all served in the Army in World War II, and our mother kept every letter each of us sent her. Recently I had occasion to sort them and re-read mine. They were factual but not very loving, which didn't reflect the special bond we had throughout our lives together.

My dad was always looking for a way to accomplish a job easier and faster to get maximum results. Somehow he relayed that to me without a written formula. I didn't always learn it without a tongue-lashing, but there was no grudge over how something was to be done. Left-handed or right-handed was fine with him. At the time, I took this knowledge for granted; it was just daily living then. But as I look back on it, I realize how special it was and how valuable it was to me later in life in the business world.

Family Album

Maria Theresa Pelz was my dad's mother. The original of this portrait is a pencil sketch that I believe was drawn by an artist in the village of Iola, maybe during a fair or festival of some sort.

My sister Grace lived with me until her death in 2006 at age 91. When I was in grade school, my mother had to take me aside one day when my badgering of Grace went too far.

My niece Patti Krause keeps close tabs on me today.

One of the last pictures of Grace (center), taken with my sister Mary and me.

My brothers and sisters and I gather with our mother for her 90th birthday in 1975. To my left are Neil, Mary, Ben, and Grace.

Chapter 2

Life on the Farm

Life on the Krause farm began early in the morning, especially for Dad. If it was cold, he would get up and start a wood fire in the kitchen stove. Sometimes there would be coals left over from the night before if the last one to bed had put a large piece of wood in the firebox late and then shut off all the dampers or if Dad had gotten up during the night and fired it up. He would also go into the basement and fill the furnace with wood. Then he would grab a lantern and the milk pails and head to the barn to do chores.

Mother and Neil got up about the same time. Mother would start fixing breakfast, while Neil would head to the barn to help Dad. Ben and I, when we were still too little to help with the chores, would be up in time to greet the men as they came back to the house from milking cows. Then it was time for a hearty farm breakfast. The staple was fried potatoes, which were made from boiled potatoes left over from the

day before. There would also be eggs and either bacon, sausage, or ham. We raised hogs, so bacon was often on the menu. I never lost my taste for it. I always washed down breakfast with hot cocoa that came from a rectangular Hershey can with a pry-off lid.

Dad would finish eating in time to listen to the news on a battery-powered radio. It ran off three C batteries and one six-volt car battery, but when one of them got low on power, you couldn't hear the radio very well. We didn't turn it on just to have background music or talk in the house during the day. We turned it on only when there was something specific we wanted to listen to. Usually that was the news on WLS out of Chicago or WTMJ out of Milwaukee, but we'd also listen to WLS' National Barn Dance on Saturday night. It was quite a luxury when we got electricity in 1938, thanks to the Rural Electrification Administration, and could get a plug-in radio.

At some point in the morning, we all had to make a trip to the outhouse. And yes, it was

Days on our farm began early in the morning. Winter provided a respite from the growing-season tasks of planting, cultivating, and harvesting.

equipped with either a Sears, Roebuck and Co. or Montgomery Ward catalog. Most of the pages were newsprint-quality paper; we avoided using the glossy pages. It was a bit of a game to use the pages that pictured knives, scissors, or other sharp instruments.

After breakfast and the news, Dad and Neil would head back outside for more farm work if it wasn't bitter cold or raining. Mother would then start her chores. Twice a week that meant baking "batches" of bread – about six to eight loaves altogether. Mary graduated from high school in 1931, when I was only seven years old. She then spent the next two years at teacher's college in Stevens Point. Sometimes she would return home on the weekends, making the hour-and-a-half to two-hour drive in a Ford Model T.

Ben and I would hurry to get dressed for school. We lived a little over a half-mile east of the one-room Dow School, built by my dad in 1918. Ben was the leader as he, Grace, and I walked to school. Oftentimes I wanted to inspect some new

piece of paper or junk I found in the ditch on the way, but Ben would keep us on track and direct us off the road when cars passed by. We would head down our driveway and turn west, and then walk half a forty to the bottom of a slight hill. In the winter, by the time you got to the top of the hill, oftentimes there would be a cold west or northwest wind that took advantage of about a half-mile of flat country to pick up speed. That made that last quarter-mile a real bugger. But we were lucky; some of our classmates had to walk a lot farther.

Snowsuits had yet to be invented, so we depended on wool coats, and mufflers and mittens knitted by our Grandma Neil, to stay warm in the winter. Leather shoes and overshoes were our foot protection. All of that went over a layer of cotton socks and long underwear with a one-piece trap door. When we made it to school, the outer layer was removed and hung in the hallway, and we would crowd around a big stove at the rear of the room to warm up. It was part of the teacher's job to start the fire each morning and keep it going all day. Later on, the stove was replaced by a furnace, and we would crowd around its registers to warm up. We thought our school was warm, and it certainly was a lot warmer than walking face first into a Wisconsin winter wind, but as I think back on it, the school's main doors faced north into that same wind and had to be drafty by today's standards. As we warmed ourselves, the first order of business was to discuss with our classmates what we had seen or didn't see on the way to school or on the way home the previous night. That lasted until lessons started at about 8:30 or 9.

I started first grade in 1929, the same year the Great Depression hit the country, so you can see what I caused. If I had known that was going to happen, I never would have gone to school. But I stuck it out through all eight grades at Dow School. Many times I've been known to express some unknown or useless information I learned there. But in retrospect, I had wonderful teachers who each had their own wonderful way of teaching me what I would have to know in the years to follow. I had a chance to tell one of them, Albertina Bensen of Wittenberg, Wisconsin, that when she visited Krause Publications at its new location in 1976. I was proud to have her see what one of her students had accomplished. Miss Bensen was my teacher for fifth and sixth grades. I had Lillian Gable for first grade; Ella Wandtke of Manawa for second, third, and fourth; and Amy Johnson of Iola for seventh and eighth.

Lessons consisted of the usual reading, writing, arithmetic, geography, and history, among other subjects. At recess time, we would get to go outside, but sand burs were abundant in the school yard and would get hopelessly entangled in your shoestrings and work their way up your pants legs. A nice crop of poison ivy grew in the shade. I got it so often I think I became immune to it in later years, but it took a lot of scratching to get to that point. One time we heard a terrible car crash on the highway, and the teacher wouldn't let us outside at recess. We learned later that a car and a milk truck had collided and one person died. We also had Christmas programs, where each of us had to recite some long-forgotten poem and take part in a skit. And would you believe I would sing a solo?

School dismissed at 4 p.m., and in the depth of winter, it would be dark by about 4:30. So we would just make it home in the daylight. Ben and I would have to hurry home so we could carry wood into our house. Before electricity, we used kerosene lamps for light. The kerosene was stored in a 50-gallon drum, and it was part of the daily routine for Mother and Grace to clean the lamp chimneys. The chimney was the glass that surrounded the flame of a lantern or lamp. After washing it, they would leave a little bit of water in the bottom and take it to the kitchen stove. They would turn it upside down over the warm stove, and the heat from the stove would steam up the chimney. The steam would remove the carbon, and the chimney could be wiped clean.

As Ben and I got older, we were required to help out more with the chores after school and during the summer. One of our tasks was to get the cows from the pasture and bring them to the barn for the evening milking. Sometimes they were in a pasture with some trees; other times they would be in the swamp. I had never seen the swamp before I started going with Ben to get the cows, so I learned that part of the farm well from him. Summer was barefoot time, so when the cows were in the swamp, Ben and I would roll up our pants legs and walk in the mud in the swamp. After reaching high ground again, we'd walk the rest of the way with our pants rolled up so the mud would dry off. Once the cows were in the barn, we would walk a short distance to our gravel pit, where rainwater would collect. There we would wash the mud off our legs so Mother would be none the wiser as to what we had been doing.

Eventually I learned how to milk a cow, too, but I resisted for a long time and was never very good at it. But given enough time, I got the job done. I also learned how to treat a cow that liked to kick the milk pail out from between my legs.

Ben and I were also charged with fixing fences. We never had any good fence and were graced with a couple of miles of it. So when a cow would "get out," Ben and I were sent out with a fencing tool, a combination hammer, tongs, and pliers. I didn't enjoy it, but Ben, who probably learned the skill from Dad and Neil, did it with a sense of duty.

In the summer, we helped load and unload hay. It seemed that we never made hay on a cool day; it was always 80 to 90 degrees. We never had a hay loader, and Dad always wanted to haul big loads of hay. So the hay would be loaded onto the wagon with three-tine pitchforks, and we'd get to stomp down on the loose hay. We also alternated driving the horses that pulled the loaded hay

wagon to the barn, but I hated it when we got to the barn and it was time to unload the hay. Neil would set the hay fork into the load, and Dad would drive the horses to haul the fork to the top. The hay fork traveled on a track in the center of the loft, and as it unloaded the hay into the center of the loft, Ben and I had to mow it to the side. If it was hot outside, it was hotter than hades inside that loft, and Ben and I would come out of there wringing wet after unloading the hay. But it made throwing the hay down for the cows in the winter much more pleasant because you would remember how hot it was up there the previous summer when you unloaded the hay from the wagon.

Our methods for planting and harvesting corn were about 10 years behind the rest of the neighborhood, but with three boys, Dad had ample labor around. Corn could be planted in "hills" with a horse-drawn planter, but we never owned such a piece of equipment. Instead, we relied on two homemade wooden "markers." One marked rows 36 inches apart, another 42 inches. The 36-inch version was a cedar log, perhaps five inches in diameter, with legs about 36 inches long and about 36 inches apart. They were affixed to the bottom of the log through holes drilled in it. The legs were also made of cedar, about three inches in diameter. There were six legs, so the whole machine was 18 feet wide. A set of "fils" was affixed to the front along a single tree to attach the harness on the horses' tug. The marker stood upright with a slight list to the back, so when it was pulled through the field by a horse, it would leave six "marks" where the rows should go.

Dad would guide the marker, and I would steer the horse. (In due course, I learned how to harness horses, hook them up as a team, and then hook up a wagon, disc, plow, mower, hay wagon, grain binder, or cultivator.) We usually started on a straight side of the field (most fields had one straight side; the rest were rather meandering). When we got to the end of the field, Dad would pick up the marker as I changed the horse's direction to reverse our tracks and add another set of marks alongside those we had just made. One leg of the marker would be set in the outside track of the row we had just made, so we would net only 11 rows per "round," or one trip back and forth across the field. But 33 feet at a crack soon got you across even a large field.

Next came the trick of establishing marks that went crosswise at exactly a 90-degree angle. If there wasn't a straight side to start with, we would go to the center of the field and mark crosswise. Once the cross marks were made, Ben and Neil would follow and do the actual planting with a hand-held planter. The planter had steel jaws on it that would make a hole in the ground as it was pressed down. Then three or four kernels of seed corn would drop in the hole made by the jaws. As the person walked down the marked rows, he would drag his foot over the dirt to the cover the hill of seeds he had just planted. The planting process was called "checking."

Setting up the rows by marking allowed the field to be cultivated both ways to control the weeds. We didn't use any chemicals. A field of corn had to be cultivated at least twice each way during the growing season. The corn was harvested in the same direction as the last cultivating so the wagon wouldn't have to go across the cultivator tracks. Harvesting also required a lot of manual labor. We stored our corn in a silo, so we harvested it the old way, without a corn binder. (A corn binder was another contraption, similar to a grain binder, which cut and spit bundles out the back of the machine. The bundles were then tied with twine made from hemp.)

A hill of corn had three or four stalks in it, and we would cut the stalks near the ground with a corn knife. What a beast that knife was! It made a terrible job worse. It had a large blade, maybe 10 to 12 inches long, attached to a handle maybe 20 inches long. The sharp edge faced up, toward you. You had to grab the stalks with one hand and try to cut them off with a single swing. It didn't take long for you to tire out, and then it would take two swings to cut off the stalks. Then your hand would get sore from stretching it to get it around all the stalks. Then your other hand would start to blister from wielding the knife.

Once we had the stalks cut, we would lay them down forward of where we were cutting to form a loose bundle of stalks from six or eight hills on the ground. If I was lucky, I'd be part of the crew loading the stalks onto a wagon rather than cutting stalks. Loading entailed grabbing the bunch of stalks that lay on the ground and placing them on the wagon crosswise. When the wagon was loaded, the horses pulled it to the silo filler. This contraption cut the stalks into pieces about an inch long. The pieces fell into a blower that would send them up a pipe that went through a hole at the very top of the silo, and the pieces would fall into the silo, giving you silage.

That led to another nasty job that oftentimes fell to me. First, someone had to make sure the silo doors that were removed and hung in the chute last season were put in place so the silage didn't come out the chute. If all went well, the silage pieces would fall into a heap in the middle of the silo. But someone – usually me, with my shirt buttoned tight at the collar and a hat on – had to be in the silo with a scoop fork to keep the silage level. If not, the leaves tended to fall next to the wall, which would form air pockets. Air pockets led to moldy silage.

I didn't like any of the farm work, but it did teach me that a little hard work never hurt anyone.

Unloading hay in a hot mow and keeping the silage level as it blew into the silo were nasty jobs, but there are three jobs in my lifetime that I remember as pains in the back: picking cucumbers, picking potatoes, and laying cement block. The last was the worst. Picking cucumbers and potatoes were almost equal. Both required bending over and picking something off the ground for hours at a time. Carrying wood was a soft job compared to picking potatoes, which was worse than picking cucumbers because it was day after day. At best, cucumbers were every other day. And you could break the monotony by throwing a cull at somebody or just seeing how far you could throw it.

The most efficient way to pick cucumbers was with two people – one on either side of the row and a common pail in which to put your harvest. When the pail was full, it was dumped into a gunnysack, which was loaded onto a wagon or pickup truck and hauled to the market, which was in Iola. The village had what was commonly called a "pickle factory," but in reality it was a huge storage unit consisting of a series of round vats perhaps eight feet across and about as high.

When we arrived at the pickle factory with our cucumbers, we waited in line to unload. When it was our turn, we dumped our cucumbers into a huge machine that poked needle-sized holes into the cukes' skins and sorted them by "grades," or size. "No. 1s" were the little ones, about three inches long. The price was much higher for these, but we never had many of them. After sorting, the cukes were dumped into one of the vats. The holes poked into them by the sorter allowed the cucumbers to absorb the saltwater in the vat, which displaced the cukes' natural water. The workers at the pickle factory constantly added salt to the brine. If I remember correctly, the brine was 90-percent salt. The resulting pickles were loaded into tanks on railroad cars and shipped to Milwaukee, where they were processed, packaged, and sent to stores.

Years ago the pickle factory was shut down, the vats were hauled away, and the accompanying buildings were razed. Today the site is a piece of level ground, home to the River Road Community Garden. Some in the village were sad to see the old pickle factory go, but every time I drove by it, it just gave me a backache.

Planting and picking potatoes were even worse jobs, but I loved to eat them from a very early age. During the Depression, we depended on potatoes much more than any other homegrown staple. It was pretty much a regimen to peel and boil potatoes for "dinner," which for us was the noon meal. Then we'd fry the leftovers for that

Threshing season was always a busy time on the farm. Here the threshing machine is depositing the straw onto a pile, while the grain is loaded into sacks and then carried to the grain bin.

night's supper and the next day's breakfast. To slice up the potatoes for frying, Mother used a baking-powder can with the top cut off, so it would have a sharp edge, and a few holes poked in the bottom. Then she would grab it by the sides and use it to chop up the whole potato in the frying pan.

Dad always planted early potatoes – he called them "tramps" – so we would have new potatoes for the Fourth of July and the rest of the summer. The early potatoes were carefully harvested one at a time by unearthing a hill and selecting the largest one. Eventually we'd fill a 12-quart pail. The rest of the patch of early red potatoes lasted well into the fall, but we'd leave them in the ground until then because they kept better there. The bad side of potatoes was that we tried to grow them as a cash crop, too. Mother Nature had a lot to do with whether we had a good crop.

Potatoes usually followed hay when we rotated crops in a field, so that meant the hay field had to be plowed in the fall with a "walking plow." Horses pulled the plow, and you walked behind it. Earlier walking plows had a wood beam on which the plow, coulter, and depth wheel were attached. Later ones had a nice curved-steel beam and were much lighter and easier to handle. A walking plow required a stout team of horses and a set of reins that were adjusted to fit over one shoulder and rest atop the other. That freed up both hands to steer the plow and make sure it stayed in the ground.

When you completed a furrow and had to turn around, you would push down on the right side of the plow and lift up on the left to lay the plow on its side. This allowed you to grab the reins and turn the horses around. You would position the horses so one would walk in the furrow and the other would walk on the unplowed ground. Then you would lift the plow upright again so the beam's point would plow into the ground. This turnaround was done in one smooth motion, and after a round or two, the horses knew what to do with almost no verbal commands or use of the reins. The most miserable part of the job was having to walk between the plow's handles. If you hit a stone or root, the handles would let you know with a not-so-gentle nudge in the hip and lower ribs.

I thought I would escape ever having to use one, but this time being the youngest didn't play in my favor. This must have been in the fall of 1939, because Neil and Ben were still living at home. Dad had taken a job some 12 miles from home jacking up an outbuilding of some sort and putting a foundation under it – the type of work he excelled at. So it fell my lot to plow a field of perhaps five to six acres about three-quarters of a mile from the farm buildings.

The whole time I was in the field I looked forward to making the trek back to the house at noon and night. First, though, I had to stop at the creek that ran through our farm to water the horses. Then, when I got back to the barn, I had to feed the horses before I could feed myself. At night, I had to unharness the horses. That wasn't a hard job, but the smell from the horses' sweat wasn't very pleasant and the harnesses had to be hung in a certain fashion so it wasn't complete confusion when you put them back on the horses the next day. But when I finally got back to the house, Mother had prepared a great meal for me.

After all, I was now doing a man's work.

Generally a potato field was plowed in the fall and harrowed, or worked up, the following spring. Time was the biggest factor. Plowing was slow, but you had more time in the fall. When planting in the spring, you had to work around rainy days and were under a time crunch to get the seeds in by a certain time. The first step in the spring to prepare a plowed field for planting was to disc it. Then you would go over it with a spring-tooth drag, which picked up pieces of sod. The final step was to go over it with a smoothing drag, and then it was ready for marking.

Plowing wasn't any fun, but planting potatoes was even worse. Again, we used a hand-held planter made of steel with two large jaws that came to a common point and had to be stomped into the ground. A broomstick-sized handle was fastened to the steel planter with a socket and rivet. Whoever was doing the planting carried a supply of seed potatoes in a bag that held perhaps half a bushel – 30 pounds. He would grab four or five seed potatoes in one hand and hold the planter with the other. He would hold up the planter, drop in a seed potato, lower it to the "check mark," and push the handle forward. That opened the jaws and deposited the potato in the ground. Again, he would do this while walking along the marked rows and then dragging his foot over the dirt to cover the seed potato.

It seemed to take forever for the potatoes to sprout and start to "come up" out of the ground, but some nice rain, warm days, and cool nights brought them along. Once they started to come up, they had to be cultivated. If they didn't come up fast enough, you had to "blind cultivate" them, or cultivate between the marked rows without seeing exactly where the plants were. Not long after the potatoes started coming up, Dad would announce that the potato bugs needed to be picked. That was another back-breaking job. We would take a quart oil can with a little waste oil and kerosene in it and handpick the potato bugs off the plants. To this day, I think it was an exercise in futility, but with Mary, Grace, Ben, and I lined up picking four rows at a time, it seemed to go fast even if it was time consuming. And we got paid for it, too – 15 cents for a quart of bugs, which was about a season's worth of picking for one of us. That gave us money to buy firecrackers for the Fourth of July, and we could forget about potatoes until September or October.

Dad also used to concoct a spray, which was much more effective than picking at getting rid of pests but couldn't have been environmentally safe by today's standards. I can still hear him telling Ben and me to stand back as he mixed arsenic with Paris green poison. Then he would go out in the field and spray the potion early in the morning – maybe 3 or 4 o'clock.

Come fall, those potatoes would still be waiting for us and ready for harvest. A "digger" would go back down between two rows with a six-tine pitchfork. He would place the fork next to a hill, being careful not to stab any potatoes with a tine. He would dig up two hills with the pitchfork, shake the dirt from the potatoes, and carefully arrange them into a row. Then a "picker" – that was usually my job – would come along and put the potatoes in a crate. We oftentimes didn't pick

them until hours after they had been dug so the dirt would dry and fall off as they were picked. The picker didn't carry the crate along with him; the crate stayed in one spot and the picker would throw the potatoes into it going as far as he could while still being able to hit the crate. One picker could easily keep up with two diggers.

When the picking was done, the diggers would hitch a team of horses to a wagon and haul the filled crates to the house, where the potatoes were stored in the basement. A filled potato crate weighed about 60 pounds, so you had to learn how to carry it down the stairs and not miss a step or catch your heel on the entrance tread. The potatoes were dumped in the basement, and the empty crates were placed on the wagon so they would be ready for the next day's picking. Sometimes the filled crates in the field were loaded onto a one-ton Ford Model T truck and hauled to a buyer in Iola.

Later in the fall – before the ground froze in November – that same truck might be used to haul potatoes from the "potato pits" in the field. We always thought potatoes needed to be out of the ground by October 11. I'm sure we never accomplished that, and if I recall correctly, that's one of the reasons why we made pits. Despite what the term may imply, potato pits were above ground. Crates of potatoes would be dumped in the middle of a field and then covered with dried potato vines and dirt. Later the dirt and vines were removed, and the potatoes were scooped from the pit with a scoop fork, always keeping the tines just below the potatoes, and dumped into bags or boxes.

Potatoes could be dug faster than they could be hauled to market, and they couldn't be hauled to market in freezing weather. So some of them were stored all winter in the basement and then sold in the spring, when you could get a higher price for them.

One spring evening when I was in seventh or eighth grade, I came home from school and went to the barn to throw down silage only to discover that our scoop fork had been used by Dad and Neil to sort potatoes in the basement of the house. I hurried to the basement to get the fork and tripped going down the stairs. I hit my chin on the potato sorter and bit my tongue about half way off. It bled, of course, but we had no health insurance – nor did anyone else – so it fell upon my mother to take care of me. I never went to a doctor. To try to stop the bleeding, Mother put baking soda in my mouth and told me to shut it. My mouth swelled so much I couldn't talk or eat for several days. Then it began to heal and I could drink liquids and eventually eat things like apple sauce. I stayed home from school for several days but went back before I could talk. Speaking came back slowly. For years I had a buttonlike rise on the side of my tongue, but eventually it healed and I went back to talking 90 miles an hour.

Unlike my good (eating them) and bad (planting and harvesting them) memories of potatoes, I have nothing but good memories of the homegrown tomatoes Mother raised in the garden she loved so much. They're another favorite food of mine – canned, cooked, or otherwise. We lived on tomatoes from the time they got ripe in the late summer until the last

quart Mason jar of them was consumed in the spring.

In addition to the crops and produce it provided, our farm was beautiful and offered a great diversity of nature – woods, the swamp, the high ground, and, of course, the big hill. We didn't realize it at the time, but Dad was a great teacher of natural history. Thanks to him, Ben and I could tell the species of a tree from 50 feet away and knew its characteristics as well.

Our farm consisted of six 40-acre parcels. Two of the forties were covered with timber; half of two others consisted of a timber swamp. The timber provided us with cooking fuel, heat in the winter, and some additional cash.

Saturday was wood-sawing day. We'd saw up a week's or two-week's supply of wood for the kitchen stove and basement furnace. We would haul the logs from the woods and pile them into tree lengths or half lengths so two or three of us could lift them. Then we would cut them into pieces 12 to 14 inches long so they would fit in the stove or furnace. When I was little, it was my job to throw the small pieces into our woodshed. Neil and Ben hauled the bigger ones around to the north side of the house about a hundred feet and threw them into the basement. In later years, they hauled the wood to the house on a bobsled Ben had built, probably for me.

Because the men could always use a board or 2-by-4 now and then and there was a market for the extra lumber, we even set up our own sawmill. To saw lumber you had to have a "husk," which transferred power from a source – either a steam engine, stationary gas engine, or a tractor

– to a shaft. In our case, we used a tractor. At the opposite end of the shaft that received the power was a large saw, 48 to 60 inches long depending on how much power we had and whether we were cutting softwoods or hardwoods. This contraption also had a friction device consisting of pulleys and belts that powered a carriage. A log was loaded onto the carriage, and the head sawer engaged a clutch that allowed the carriage to move the log toward the saw.

One year we used the sawmill to make new potato crates. The first potato crates I remember us having were an odd lot; none was a standard size, and they always seemed to be in a sad state of repair. So we decided one season to discard almost everything and start over. We kept one of the better ones, whose cubic-inch capacity was just right to hold 60 pounds, or one bushel, and used its measurements as a pattern for the new crates.

Not every log we put through the sawmill was straight, so sometimes we had to saw heavy slabs off either end of the log and the belly of the opposite side to get straight lumber. Thus, the sawmill would cut a few three-eighths-inch thick boards that had no common edge (these were called "live cuts"). A much smaller saw cut these boards to about two and three-eighths inches wide, as I remember. Whatever the actual measurement was, it was just right so that three of them – one on top another on the bottom and yet another in the center – cut to the proper length and joined by one-inch by one-inch corners made a perfect crate.

It was the first time I had ever heard of a "jig," which was a form that was used to make sure the crates were square. I also learned the importance of using nails that were the right length so they would protrude through every slat far enough so they could be bent. This would prevent the nail from being knocked loose by rough handling.

I think we made about 40 to 50 crates. We used them to carry the harvest from Mother's garden, carry cob corn into the crib, and to make a low staging by placing a plank between them. You couldn't operate a small, ill-equipped farm such as ours without them. That fall after potato picking, Dad gave me the job of gathering up the new crates. I kept close tabs on them and never let them get scattered around the yard and buildings too much.

We also owned a shingle mill and made wooden shingles from the cedar trees that grew in the swamp, in addition to cedar fence posts and telephone poles. The shingle mill was basically a saw, too, but it ran horizontally rather than vertically, as most saws do. There was a carriage about 20 inches wide and a foot deep close to the saw. It had a trip device on it, so as you were sawing a block (a piece of cedar about 16 inches long), you would lower one side and raise the other to keep the block even. The shingles were tapered from about a half-inch thick at the bottom to almost nothing at the top so they would lie flat on the roof.

The cut shingle would fall off the bottom of the saw to a table below. Then a "knot sawer" would edge the shingles and eliminate big knots in the middle. The wood off the edge of shingles was called "splints," and they made good kindling. The knot sawer would then throw the shingles over his

shoulder into one of three different bins.

Being about 10 to 12 years old at the time, I was forbidden to be near a saw, but I had lots of other things to do, such as keeping water in the cooling tank of the big one-cylinder engine, forking the shingle tow (sawdust) that came off the main saw, carrying away the splints with a large four-tine fork, and, when I wasn't doing anything else, packing shingles. A bundle of shingles was 20 inches wide and about 26 to 28 inches deep, and contained 25 courses – deep enough to cover 25 square feet lying four inches to the weather. Later there were only 20 courses in a bundle because they were figured to lie five inches to the weather.

I'm quite sure our shingle mill was the last one around in the area because wooden shingles were the cause of many roof fires in those days.

Of all the species of trees that grew on the farm, we thought the white ash were particularly special because we could make handles from them – ax handles, hammer handles, maul handles, and cant hook handles. A cant hook was used for rolling logs. It consisted of a handle about two inches thick and three feet long. At the end of the handle was a hinged arm about another 10 inches long with a sharp hook at the end.

Perhaps the best use for the white ash was the pitmans of a hay mower. I learned why later in life: You would change direction hundreds of times when mowing a hay field, and it was the best wood for absorbing shock.

A draw shave and a spoke shave were our basic tools for making handles. Of course, a rasp and a bit of sandpaper gave it a nice, smooth finish.

The trees on our farm also provided a more unusual treat – fresh honey. Although it's a lost art today, finding a bee tree and stealing its contents were a great hobby when I was growing up.

The secret to finding a bee tree was to set up near a good crop of goldenrod, where there would be bees. Dad would put a saucer on top of a potato crate and put some store-bought honeycomb in the saucer and a bit of anise oil on the crate. Then he would go into a patch of goldenrod with a baking-

I was about 16 years old when somebody's camera captured me in a fashionable fedora and crewneck sweater.

powder can with holes punched in the bottom. When he'd find a bee on the goldenrod, he'd hold the can near the bee with one hand and push it into the can with the other. Then he would hold the can upright, and the bee would go to the top.

He'd take the bee back to the honey on the potato crate and let it go. Soon the bee, attracted by the anise oil on the crate, would be full of honey, fly one circle, and make a "bee line" for home. We'd watch the bee fly and mark a spot on the tree line where it went. Then we'd catch another bee or two and repeat the process. Soon we'd have several bees to watch. They weren't always from the same hive, but after a while, their flights would establish a pattern.

Then we'd move our crate a few hundred yards away and repeat the process. If we were lucky, we'd find bees going toward the same spot in the tree line and maybe even be able to establish a third bee line to get an idea of how far into the woods the bee tree might be.

This gave you an idea of where to start looking. A tree had to be hollow for the bees to produce comb. Usually the entrance would be in an old hollow limb or the crotch between the trunk and a limb. It could be near the bottom or several feet up.

Once we located a bee tree, we had to wait until a dark night in November to cut it. After cutting the tree down, we would plug the entrance to the tree, which would drive the bees crazy. Then we'd take a crosscut saw and cut above the entrance maybe a third of the way into the trunk. Then we'd make another similar cut about a foot above the first one. Then we'd take an ax and chop into the base of the cuts and pry the resulting block of wood up. We'd shine a light into the tree to see if we had reached the comb or bees. If necessary, we'd make several more cuts until we reached the top of the comb.

Once we found honey, it was a great treat to eat a bit of it on the spot. A bee tree might yield only a lunch bucket full of honey or several washtubs of it, but either way, it was bee hunting at its best.

Although today Waupaca County is known for its abundant wildlife, especially whitetail deer, it wasn't always that way. Dad used to tell how he and Severn Bestul would hunt deer with dogs. The dogs would chase the deer, as Dad put it, "half way to Big Falls" and eventually out of hearing range. But deer tend to run in circles, so if the hunters were patient and the dogs didn't get tired, they knew that eventually the deer could come back to their starting point or close to it. As the dogs worked their way back, Dad and Severn would calculate where they should be, and each took a "stand," or a place to wait for the deer to come by.

Many in the area used this method to hunt deer because it was effective. Unfortunately, it was too effective. Deer became extinct in the area, and hunting was stopped. I didn't see my first deer in the wild until about 1937. We were going to the free show in Big Falls and saw one cross the road in the woods north of the farm. Sometime later, Neil saw a buck near a gate that went into our fields. It was a great thing just to see tracks,

which started to turn up more frequently. But it wasn't until the early 1950s when deer hunting resumed in Waupaca County.

I've bagged a few deer in my time but never anything to write home about. Wild turkeys were reintroduced in the area around 1990 and are now abundant enough to be hunted. I did get a nice one a few years ago – two ounces shy of 24 pounds. It hadn't started fighting other toms, so it had all of its breast feathers. My nephew Carl Krause had it mounted for me, and it has been guarding my office ever since.

The outdoors were a wonderful part of growing up on our farm. The work was drudgery, but at least it taught me that I didn't want to be a farmer. As I look back on them, those prewar days growing up with Dad, Neil, and Ben as my leaders are a great part of what I was to become later in life.

Chapter 3

Cars, Trucks, Stamps, & Coins

I learned more about the Great Depression studying it in my adult years than I did living through it as a child, when I didn't have the power of observation or know what to read, record, or remember. I learned about the bank holiday of March 1933, one of the first acts in President Franklin D. Roosevelt's New Deal. Many banks were failing, and none was strong. So Roosevelt shut all of them down for four days. During that time, examiners looked at each bank to determine what condition they were in. Gradually, the stronger ones were allowed to reopen, but the weaker ones stayed closed until it was determined whether they should be allowed to reopen or be liquidated. If the latter was the case, that task was generally assigned to a neighboring bank. In some cases, the mother bank chose to merge with the closing bank.

At the time, Iola had two banks – the First State Bank of Iola and the Bank of Iola. The state bank was the stronger one; the Bank of Iola was liquidated. My siblings and I had meager savings of less than $5 in the weaker bank. In due course, savings of $2.41 would get a total settlement of $1.61 spread out over perhaps four payments. All depositors suffered the same percentage of loss.

FDR also knew he had to get people back to work, so he devised the Works Progress Administration, or WPA. It was funded by the sale of savings bonds and gave men jobs doing things for the public good. It was great for the country, and the result was noticeable in the overall economy within two or three years. Dad never worked for the WPA, but we were able to generate some extra income during the time by raising cash crops, cutting fence posts, logging, and cutting and selling Christmas trees right from the farm, thus saving transportation costs.

Compounding the economic conditions of the 1930s was a great drought that affected Waupaca County and much of the rest of the country. Dust storms would begin in the Dakotas and come across Minnesota and half of Wisconsin before arriving at our house. At their worst, visibility would be but a quarter of a mile. Sand came through every crack and crevice of the house. Our eyes were always red, and food had sand in every mouthful. Growing crops during this time was another challenge. Sometimes seed wouldn't even sprout. We were forced to farm a few acres of lowland. How Dad, Mother, Neil, and Mary got us younger kids through that damnable time I'll never quite appreciate.

We kept old machinery going by repairing and patching. From a mechanical standpoint, a basic workhorse on our farm and many others at the time was the Ford Model T. We owned a small fleet of them in various states of condition. I remember one time Dad came home from an auction with a Model T he bought for $3.25. Another time he sold our best one for $25 to a family that was receiving "township aid."

The Model T cars and a truck provided transportation and hauled crops to market. It was quite a production to keep them running in the winter. If you had visitors in the evening in the winter, they would drain the radiator in their Model T upon arrival and throw an old blanket over it. When they were ready to leave, you had to give them hot water so they could refill the radiator.

On cold mornings, Mother would have a bucket of water heating on the back burner of the wood stove so Dad could pour hot water over the block of a Model T sitting outside or in a shed.

That would warm up the oil so the motor was easier to turn over. Then he'd jack up the back wheel and put the lever in gear so it would get the wheel going when he tried to start it. "Chug, chug" it would go if it started. If it didn't, sometimes Dad would build a fire under the crankcase. He'd wrap a rag around a pole, soak it in oil, gasoline, or kerosene, start it on fire, and stick it under the car. That really heated it up.

Gradually, though, the Model T's wore out. So imagine our jubilation one day in 1935 when Dad purchased a 1934 Ford demonstrator for $400. I'm at a loss to say where the money came from; at the time, we were all too proud and too young to ask. Just two years later, he traded that same car and $312 cash for a brand new 1937 Ford four-door sedan. Eventually, it became my first car, and I drove it until 1951, when I bought a new Chevrolet two-door fastback.

Cars, trucks, gasoline engines, and machinery were big parts of our farm life, and I remember them well. I was only five or six years old when they upgraded the road in front of our farm from a county highway to State Highway 161. We had two gravel pits on our farm – one just southeast of the barn and another about a half mile south, on the east edge of our fields. I'm told the one near the barn was there when Mother and Dad bought the farm in 1920. The one in our field was opened when the road was upgraded.

That brought lots of men, trucks, and machinery to our area. The crew had two sleeping shanties and a cookhouse, which was staffed by two female cooks who slept in the rear of the combination kitchen and dining room. Most of the crew went home on the weekends. They didn't finish the job in the fall, so the equipment was left on site over the winter.

I remember there was a gravel crusher, a drag line, and a fleet of trucks to haul gravel to build the road bed from Iola to the Symco four corners – a stretch of about 14 miles. The drag line dragged gravel from the pit to the crusher, which was powered by an Avery tractor. From the crusher, the gravel was loaded into trucks. There were two four-wheel-drive trucks – one made in nearby Clintonville and another in Oshkosh, Wisconsin – and a half-dozen Menomonie trucks. The large trucks could haul three to three and a half yards of gravel; the smaller ones could manage only one yard, but they "went like sixty," to use an old expression for a fast car or truck.

I didn't know it at the time, but the cars and trucks of my youth planted the seeds for a lifelong automotive interest that later allowed a business and a hobby to grow.

I didn't know it at the time, but the cars and trucks of my youth planted the seeds for a lifelong automotive interest that later allowed a business and a hobby to grow. In fact, in the 1990s, that very Avery tractor that powered the gravel crusher turned up at the Symco Thresheree. I tried to buy it but was unsuccessful. The seeds of my coin and stamp collecting also were sown during my youth, but they took on a much more formal structure than my automotive interests at the time.

When I was growing up, Hank Fritz was my close friend and neighbor. He lived just a quarter mile east of our house. He was a great influence on my life and I on his, I suspect. Both of us were mechanically inclined, and one of the things we did to satisfy that inclination was fix old clocks. At first, that consisted of just a quick cleaning in a couple of inches of gasoline (you could buy six gallons for a dollar then) and a bit of 3-in-1 oil. That was a marvelous discovery that provided us with hours of entertainment.

Hank, however, took the idea much further than I did. He begged old clocks from all the neighbors and eventually obtained catalogs for ordering clock and watch parts. By the time we entered high school, he could fix jeweled watches and was a custom clock and watch fixer-upper.

I consider Hank's dad, Godfrey, my mentor as a collector. He was a Spanish-American War veteran and a first lieutenant in a reserve unit based in Oshkosh. He went to Cuba but did not charge up San Juan Hill. He did, however, contract malaria and suffered from the effects the rest of his life.

Godfrey had a bag full of coins he had collected as a boy. They included half cents, large cents, Flying Eagle cents, two-cent pieces, silver three-cent pieces, nickels, half dimes, dimes, quarters, and half dollars. They had images on them that I had never seen before. It would be years before I would learn about all those nice coins Godfrey had. Then one day he gave me a large cent, and if ever a collecting seed got planted, it was right then and there.

Indian cents were still plentiful in pocket change at the time, and, of course, one could assemble a set of Lincoln cents out of circulation, which I did with the aid of all my relatives. Especially helpful were two of my mother's sisters – Aunt Margaret and Aunt Leafa. They purchased Whitman "penny boards" for me. The boards had

holes into which you could insert an example of each date and mint mark of Lincoln cents. In due course, I filled them all and still have most of them, although not all the coins in them were acquired from circulation.

Many of the one-cent coins that filled my penny board came from Dad's pocket change. Whenever I thought of it, which was often, I'd ask him, "Dad, got any pennies in your pocket?" One time he pulled out the lone one-cent coin in his pocket – a 1931-S, one of the key dates in the series.

At about the same time – the early to mid-1930s – I also got the bug to collect stamps. In those days, it was used stamps that came free on envelopes and postcards sent to us. All you had to do was steam them off the paper. I assembled a collection going back to about 1920 and acquired a low-end album and some stamp hinges. I was grateful to have both. I soon found ads for stamps in *Popular Mechanics* and supply catalogs, so I learned how to use the mail to get things that weren't offered in our country stores.

Though my collecting means and resulting collections were modest, my collecting interest was strong and was the one portend from my early life of what the future held for me.

Chapter 4

Off to High School

It was a moonless night, and I had been on one of my frequent visits to Hank Fritz's house. I left Hank's house and started heading down his driveway to walk home. I didn't realize just how dark it was – pitch dark, in fact – until I got out of range of their yard light. I walked along the road toward home with one foot on the blacktop and the other on the gravel shoulder. About half way home, I saw the lights of a car coming toward me. So I began running as fast as I could. By the time I met the car, I was within a hundred yards of our driveway. Then things really got dark, and I was out of breath. So I stopped to count my blessings for having gotten so close to home and recovered my breath and wits.

Proceeding very carefully, I reached out with my arm to feel for our mailbox. Upon touching it, I knew I had to make a 90-degree turn to enter our driveway. This was accomplished without incident, as I felt the gravel of our driveway under my feet.

That gravel soon turned into grass between two tracks, so I followed the driveway to our house by walking with one foot on the gravel and the other on the grass. From the back of the house, a dim light left on as a nightlight guided me to my room and a deep sleep.

Our house and farm – however humble they may have been – were home for me when I was growing up – safe, familiar places where I was surrounded by family. A typical day seldom took me far from them – whether it was venturing out into the fields, making the relatively short walk to Dow School, or visiting Hank Fritz. Soon, however, the quickly advancing years and world events forced me to venture farther and farther from the small world of our farm and the countryside immediately surrounding it.

One of the highlights of my later grade-school years was a new steel-runnered sled. I was in seventh or eighth grade when I got it. I kept it over the years and passed it on to some of my nieces and nephews.

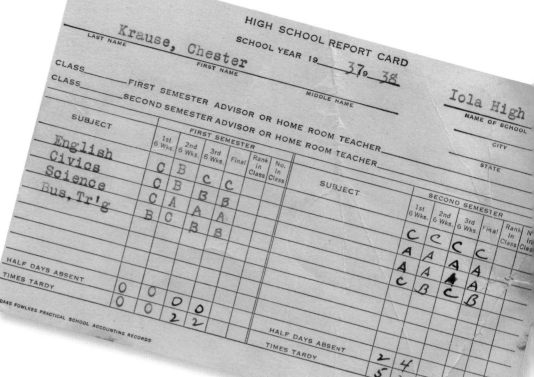

My final report card from my freshman year at Iola High School gives a good summary of my academic strengths and weaknesses – A's in civics and science but only a C in English.

HIGH SCHOOL REPORT CARD

Krause, Chester

LAST NAME   FIRST NAME

SCHOOL YEAR 19__37__9__38__

MIDDLE NAME

Iola High
NAME OF SCHOOL

CLASS

CITY

CLASS   FIRST SEMESTER ADVISOR OR HOME ROOM TEACHER

STATE

SECOND SEMESTER ADVISOR OR HOME ROOM TEACHER

SUBJECT	1st 6 Wks.	2nd 6 Wks.	3rd 6 Wks.	Final	Rank in Class	No. In Class
English	C	B	C	C		
Civics	C	B	B	B		
Science	C	A	A	A		
Bus. Tr'g	B	C	A	A		
			B	B		

SUBJECT	1st 6 Wks.	2nd 6 Wks.	3rd 6 Wks.	Final	Rank in Class	No. In Class
	C		C	C		
	A	A	A	A		
	A	A	4	A		
	C	B	4	B		

HALF DAYS ABSENT

TIMES TARDY

First semester: 0 0 0 0 / 0 0 2 2

CA45 FOWLKES PRACTICAL SCHOOL ACCOUNTING RECORDS

HALF DAYS ABSENT

TIMES TARDY

Second semester: 2 4 / 5 2

COPYRIGHT 1930, E. M. HALE & CO., MILWAUKEE

By this time, I was also well on my way to indoctrination into the construction business. My first exposure was when Ben and I pumped water for mixing concrete for one of Dad's masonry jobs. I remember one job in particular, when Dad jacked up the Blake Brook School House and poured a new foundation under it. I don't remember exactly how old I was, but I was young enough that Ben got the worse of the deal. The pump was outside and needed some repair; it just wasn't very productive. You really had to pump fast to get enough water out of it. When we did get enough to fill a bucket, we had to carry it a few feet and dump the water into a barrel. That was pretty much a common practice for mixing cement in those days.

Our family started to change as everybody got older. Mary started her first teaching job, and the time Ben and I spent together started to decrease as Ben spent more time with his older friends. No longer did we climb the "big hill" just for the sake of climbing it. Wading in the mud to get the cows in the late afternoon was no longer on our agenda. Nor did we eat Juneberries together unless we were close to them while on some other task or if one of us made the hike by ourselves.

In the fall of 1937, it was time for me to start high school in the village of Iola. There were no school buses then, but Clarence Thom, a senior who lived a mile and a half or two miles east of our house, had a Ford Model A. He would pick me up at the end of our driveway and give others along the way a ride to school for a fee of $1.25 a week. That included Joyce Bonikowske, a sophomore, so at least I knew one other student out of the hundred or so attending Iola High School.

It seemed most of the others knew each other because they attended the Lutheran church in the village, so I felt like an outsider – a lost sheep – on those first days of high school. But in due course, I got to know them all. A hundred people aren't that many.

The school day would start with an "assembly," or all of us together in one room. During the first few days, we sat wherever we wanted to in the assembly, but after a few days, the principal, Mr. Roels, assigned us seats. When classes started, we would march down a long hallway to our classrooms. We had assigned seats in each classroom, too. It was considered quite unlucky to get assigned a front-row seat, where the teacher could keep a better eye on you. Also, everyone else was behind you, so you couldn't have any fun.

It was my lot to be seated in the front row in Miss Fish's class. That made me think that she thought I was a tough cookie and needed to be watched. But as it turned out, it wasn't that bad because I got off on the right foot with her and got into but a few things that even came close to violating her discipline rules.

At the one-room Dow School, we had just one teacher for all eight grades. Now in high school, I had a different teacher for each subject. Miss Fish taught science, as I recall, which was one of the few subjects I excelled in. I liked math, too. I didn't particularly like spelling in grade school, and English and reading in high school fell into that same category. I still read slowly but methodically, and I guess that's part of the reason why I like math and science. I did all right in geography, too.

When it came to extracurricular stuff, I was much better in attendance than performance. Music and singing, despite my experience in the Christmas programs in grade school, were all sour notes to me. And not being very athletic, I

didn't make a great showing as a jock. Combine all that with an inferiority complex and you had a rather simple country boy who never quite spread his wings. By the time I was a junior, however, I started to leave that complex behind. In my sophomore year, Mr. Roels' assembly seating assignments put me in the middle of four older girls who were all good looking, popular, and bright. I sometimes think he did that just to help divest me of some of my inwardness.

As I progressed through high school, I grew more comfortable with my surroundings, my classes, and my classmates. But the late winter of my junior year – March 11, 1940, to be exact – brought one of the saddest days of my life. I was called out of class to Mr. Roels' office and was told my mother had called the school, which she had never done before. Mr. Roels then told me our house burned. He said my mother wanted me to finish the day in school because there was nothing I could do at home, so I went back to class. I remember that it had snowed four inches the night before, so Mother figured I was better off at school than sloshing around a fire that was still smoldering. When school dismissed for the day, our entire car pool rode to our farm to see the remains. It was level to the foundation but still smoldering.

As I stood there looking at what was once my home, all I had left were the clothes on my back. Even today that sounds terrible, and it was. But we had great neighbors who pitched in, and it was already determined that I would stay with a schoolmate, Dave LaStofka. With the LaStofkas' help and a trip to J.C. Penney in Stevens Point, I

The original house on our farm. On March 11, 1940, the principal called me out of class at Iola High School to tell me the house had burned.

was back in business again after a few days. And Dave's mother, Bertina, was an excellent cook.

The rest of the family stayed with other neighbors and relatives, except for Dad, who set up in what we called a hunting trailer, which was located near our garage. Dad, Neil, and Ben then created some rather crude living quarters in the garage for the family. Later we moved an outbuilding near the site of the former house and remodeled it to create rooms. As small as they were, they were still a far cry better than the garage.

That summer and fall were occupied with everyone staying close to home and helping to build a new house on the old foundation. We took full advantage of having our own source of timber and our own sawmill. With the help of a neighbor, Dad, Neil, and Ben cut trees into logs and produced enough lumber to build the new house. Of course, with Dad's construction skills

and help from Neil, Ben, and I, we did much of the work ourselves. The house we built still stands today on the property, which is now owned by John Starcheske.

I've often heard of people who move and then can't find things they packed when they get into the new house. Try going through things salvaged from a fire; there's no order at all. Somehow, an old four-legged bathtub got saved from the old house and carried out into the yard. It became a repository for all the small objects that were saved from the fire. The bathtub and all its contents were carried the day of the fire into the granary. So when somebody questioned whether something got saved, we went to the granary and dug through the stuff dumped in the bathtub. One day I was digging in the bathtub and I found my coin collection. My stamp collection, however, was lost to the fire.

My high-school graduation picture.
The country was on the brink of war
when the class of '41 left school.

Finally settled in our new house, I completed my senior year at Iola High School with grades that made both Mother and Dad happy, and I graduated in the spring of 1941. That year I also took a mechanical course offered free by the government one night a week. At the time, it appeared so many young men would be heading off to war, and the course was designed to give those of us who were mechanically inclined some hands-on experience. The course was held in a garage and was taught by an auto mechanic. Later, I took a similar course that was held in a machine shop.

Meanwhile, in a faraway land called Europe, Adolph Hitler was sword rattling across the continent and the Battle of Britain had been fought in the summer of 1940. In retrospect, it seems we all knew our country was headed for war. The only question was, "When?" The answer came on a Sunday afternoon – December 7, 1941. Dad was listening to the radio when the news came across that Pearl Harbor had been attacked. He called out to the rest of us, and we all gathered around the radio.

I was just days away from my 18th birthday. For all of my young life, I had known little more than our farm and home – a safe and comforting destination on a dark night's walk – and the countryside around it. Just going to high school in Iola six miles to the west made me feel out of place at first.

Now, I was about to be taken a whole lot farther away and sent to a place that was anything but safe and comforting.

Chapter 5

Off to War

World War II involved more people and countries than any other event in modern history. It involved more than 16.3 million members of the U.S. armed forces – 11.2 million in the Army alone. Neil, Ben, and I contributed to that total.

The war affected my family months before the United States entered it. In 1939, when the war in Europe began, Neil was 28 years old, Ben was 19, and I was 16. In 1940, the Selective Service Act was passed, which required all men ages 21 through 35 to register for the draft. Neil was the only one who had to register in the first wave, but Ben and I weren't far behind. Neil had a two-digit lottery number, and as I recall, he was in the second call of draftees in Waupaca County in early 1941. Prior to the United States entering the war, draftees were called for only a year of service. "I'll be Back in a Year, Little Darling" was the title of a popular song in 1941.

Before long, someone discovered that men over 28 years old could not keep up with the younger ones, and they discharged all those over 28 who had already been called. So in about September 1941, Neil came back from Camp Walters, Texas, where he had served only seven months or so. He never left camp during his stay there. But after Pearl Harbor, Neil was called back and was en route to Camp Custer, Michigan, by New Year's Day 1942. Later he was sent to the South Pacific – New Guinea and the Philippines were among his stops – and served in a heavy-ordnance company until 1945. Fortunately for him, there weren't as many tanks in the Pacific theater of operations as there were in Europe, but Neil always said, "We fixed everything nobody else could." After the war, in the early 1950s, he became a senior warrant officer and served in Germany in the Army of Occupation, relieving regular Army and much younger soldiers for the Korean Conflict.

Ben soon followed Neil into the Army in the summer of 1942. He went to aircraft mechanics school and maintained many different types of aircraft in New Mexico and Arizona until his discharge in January 1946.

Uncle Sam asked me to leave just a few months after Ben, on February 11, 1943. Mother, Dad, Mary, and Grace came to see me off the day I left Waupaca for the induction center in Milwaukee. Mary and Gerald were living in Milwaukee, where Gerald worked in a defense plant. But their first son, David, was in the hospital in Iola at the time, and Mary was staying at the farm while David was sick. She left him long enough to see me off.

So the Army claimed all three of Cora and Carl Krause's sons in the span of a little more than a year. I was the last to go, and I suspect it was very hard for Mother to see her third and youngest son go off to war. Among the kids, my departure left only Grace at home. I'm sure my parents missed their boys while they were in the service, but Grace was affected even more severely. I learned later that she was in and out of the hospital several times during the more than three years that we were gone.

The Army sent me to Camp Wallace, Texas, about 20 to 25 miles west of Galveston. Camp Wallace was a training site for anti-aircraft recruits, which were in a big buildup at that time. Nearly 1 million of the 11 million men in the Army were assigned to anti-aircraft, which created a great need for mechanics of all types. I didn't realize it at the time, but that was a great piece of luck for me because it allowed me to get classified as a "014," or auto mechanic, which meant I wasn't assigned to the infantry. The government-sponsored mechanical courses I took after graduation from high school helped me earn that designation. So did the summer between my sophomore and junior years of high school,

when Neil made me repair a Model T engine – tear it down and put it back together again. He supervised my work – the grinding of the valves and fitting of the rings particularly closely. That was a great lesson for me, and it lay the basis for my mechanical work in the Army.

But first I had to get past basic training. That included learning how to live with other men, make my own bed, do my laundry, march in close-order drill, and operate a 90-millimeter anti-aircraft gun. That baby could shoot 12 miles at ground level and six miles straight up. I also got my Army driver's license at Camp Wallace. They should have washed me out, but they knew I needed it so they gave it to me anyway. I had never driven anything but a car before, and I was assigned to a six-ton Mack truck that was about the size of a small 18-wheeler. I scratched the gears up and down the course but steered it back home and left enough gears for the next dozen drivers.

New draftees were assigned to barracks as they arrived at camp. When eight barracks were filled – 1,000 men, which took only a day or two – they were assigned to a particular anti-aircraft battery, or what the rest of the Army called a "company." I was assigned first to D Battery of the 127th Anti-Aircraft and Artillery Recruit Training Center and later B Battery. While still in D Battery, I remember the first time we had to "fall out" (line up outside the barracks) in full uniform. I had never worn leggings before and did not have a clue as to how to lace them up let alone put them on. So the guy who had the bunk above me was assigned to teach me so I could report properly dressed later that day. I made it OK.

I was issued a gun but not a new Garand M1. It was a World War I Springfield that had seen better days. I'm sure it had not been fired in years. It had been cleaned so many times it probably couldn't shoot anymore. But it was used to teach me how to march with a gun, how to salute with a gun, and how to let go of it when an officer reached for it during inspection. That may not sound difficult, but if you held on to it too long, the stock would give you a wallop between the legs that you didn't need or expect. Although that's one of those mistakes you make only once.

Basic training got to be pretty boring for those of us destined to be mechanics, cooks, or truck drivers. Those who were destined for a gun crew received much more training on the guns than we did. Luckily, I was among the first to leave the outfit and be sent to mechanics school. Sometime during the seventh week of the 10-week basic training, I and a couple of truckloads of other troops were transported to the camp rail yard to board a train for Camp Davis, North Carolina, near Wilmington.

Top: My brother Neil served in the South Pacific doing maintenance on heavy ordnance. Center: My brother Ben served stateside in aircraft maintenance. Bottom: My furlough gave me time for a portrait at a photo studio in New London. The AA on my shoulder indicates my assignment to an anti-aircraft training battalion.

This was my first troop train ride, and when we got to Camp Davis seven days later, I hoped it would be my last. We rode in boxcars hooked up to a freight train. We'd stop every night in some freight yard to sleep. Another boxcar was our kitchen, which was manned by Army cooks. There must have been one officer and a couple of sergeants with us, too.

Upon arrival at Camp Davis, we were hauled by trucks again to our barracks and the relative comfort of bunk beds. We were told that we weren't expected for another week and that there were no classes open yet or rations for us. So they fed us several varieties of beans three meals a day for seven days. I think they just wanted somebody to eat up the beans.

Mechanics class lasted four or five weeks, and it was pleasant compared to basic training. A lot of what was taught I had already learned from Neil at an early age, so I breezed through it. At the same time, though, I was introduced to the various types of Army vehicles I would be working on.

Upon completing mechanics school at Camp Davis, I was sent to Camp Stewart, Georgia. Today it still exists as Fort Stewart, but at that time, it was a brand-new camp hewn out of a stand of pine trees, complete with tar-paper barracks. Our train out of Camp Davis was much more comfortable than the one in which we had arrived. This time we had a passenger coach that took us across South Carolina to Savannah, Georgia. A few miles west of Savannah, the train stopped in the middle of a jack-pine forest, and about a dozen of us GIs got off. We waited there for about 30 minutes, and a locomotive with a boxcar attached picked us up and took us to the Camp Stewart rail terminal. We continued to be handled like so much freight until a jeep picked me up and took me to my new assignment with Headquarters Battery of the 565th Anti-Aircraft Battalion.

Camp Stewart became my home for 15 months more or less, except for a three-month stay in Tennessee for maneuvers. I became part of a unit, however small it was, and got to know the others in the 565th, which was a big hurdle for me. I learned later that the unit consisted of contingents of 250 men each from Fort Oglethorpe, Georgia; Camp Custer, Michigan; and an induction center in New York. That by itself created quite a mix of personalities and backgrounds, to say nothing of inserting a farm boy from Wisconsin.

My graduation from mechanics school earned me a T/5 corporal rating (technician, fifth grade). Six months after my arrival at Camp Stewart, I made T/4, a sergeant rating – as a mechanic, not a line sergeant. There were seven T/5s in the motor pool and only three T/4s in the table of organization. Some of those T/5s waiting for advancement were in the unit before I was, and I had just come from mechanics school. I don't think all of them were happy to see me get the higher grade, and that manifested itself in giving me a bit of a hard time, or, as the Southern boys put it, "trying me." But one day it came to a halt.

We always parked the vehicles about six feet apart in a straight line. Everything in the Army was in a straight line, including the radiator caps of parked trucks. When a truck was pulled out of its parking spot, it left a space about 20 feet between vehicles. One afternoon I was the ranking person at the motor pool when one of the drivers took a truck and started driving around the parking area and in between the parked trucks. The other drivers and mechanics didn't like that; if we climbed under a truck to check or fix something, our feet and legs would stick out into that six-foot area between parked trucks. A vehicle driving through there could easily run over our feet and legs.

I finally had enough of Sad Sack's driving, so I halted him and told him he wasn't suppose to be driving around to begin with, and second, we all wanted to go home with our feet that day. My comments weren't taken too lightly. After parking his truck, Sad Sack approached me to say that if I didn't watch what I said, he and his rebel friends would see that I got a permanent spot in a pile of stumps. I replied that if he wasn't careful, he would be the one under the stump pile. Later, several of the friends he thought he had and my immediate superiors thanked me for putting Sad Sack in his place. From that day forward, I had earned my stripes. It felt great to have been defended in words as well as actions. Sad Sack and I never became great friends, but he let me gain the respect of a lot of my cohorts.

Early on the morning of November 13, 1943, we departed for Murfreesboro, Tennessee, for maneuvers. We had loaded all 121 vehicles under our command with our equipment and made overnight stops at Madison, Georgia, and Fort Oglethorpe, near Chattanooga, on the way. We stayed in Tennessee until January 14, 1944, and it was cold and wet for much of our time there. Many

After basic training, I was sent to mechanics school at Camp Davis, North Carolina, where this photo was taken.

men became sick with colds, and two members of the 565th were killed in vehicle accidents.

It was quite a relief to return to Camp Stewart, but our trucks were much worse for the wear. By this time, we were one of the senior units at Camp Stewart, and our equipment and demeanor showed it. On maneuvers, about the only way to wash a truck was to drive it through a creek, and that wasn't recommended in January and February in Tennessee.

After reading about the war years later, I realized why we were sent back to Camp Stewart in early 1944. The D-Day invasion of France took place the following June 6. A lot of anti-aircraft artillery was already in Europe, and along with the air forces, it helped to neutralize the German Luftwaffe after its pounding of London during

I cut a slim and crisp profile in my Army uniform as I stand with neighbor George Nelson. I believe this picture was taken in 1944, when I was home on furlough before shipping out for Europe.

the Battle of Britain. The Allies were shooting down German airplanes faster then they could be replaced, and the Germans had opened two others fronts, in Italy and Russia. Thus, infantry and armored divisions – and the equipment and supplies to support them – became higher priorities than anti-aircraft.

Back at Camp Stewart, we got our equipment cleaned up and were assigned to Tent City, in the northern section of the camp where State Highway 119 is now located. Here we were sheltered in either squad tents, which slept six men, or pup tents, which slept two men. Tent City was away from the main base at Camp Stewart to accommodate

the shooting ranges and more maneuvers, or "field problems." During Tennessee maneuvers, a problem would begin on a weekend and end the following weekend. So we always moved on those days and sometimes once or twice in between. Sometimes we moved only a mile or two; other times it might be 15 to 20 miles.

Upon our return from Tennessee, we were deemed "insufficiently trained," whatever that meant. So our Tent City maneuvers were longer and more complex – not as much play as they had been nine to 10 months before. That took a little cockiness, which was a bad influence on new recruits coming to camp, out of us maneuver veterans.

On the firing range, our batteries practiced shooting at a sleeve pulled by a B-34 Ventura based at the camp airfield. It was the delight of those shooting to hit the cable pulling the sleeve, which was several hundred feet behind the tow plane. This meant a break for the shooters while another plane was sent aloft with a new tow target. Of course, that also meant a reprimand for someone, and not everyone was willing to face the music.

After our stay at Tent City, we were back at the main base at Camp Stewart inspecting swamps. It was said that Camp Stewart was the only place in the country where you could stand in mud up to your knees and have sand blow into your eyes. Between that and the gnats and chiggers, it wasn't a pleasant place to be. Our unit didn't have a good reputation, but I'm sure we were not sent back to Camp Stewart as a disciplinary step or because we were badly trained. There just wasn't room for us in England, and anti-aircraft was not as important to the Army as it had once been.

Spring 1944 also saw a command change for our unit. Major Bayer was relieved of command and sent to Puerto Rico. I believe it was part of his punishment for having chained a soldier to a post inside the barracks. His replacement was Colonel Santilli. I don't think he had a kind bone in his body and dished out living hell for officers and enlisted men alike, but I remember one amusing incident involving him.

The PX was located in a building that stood perhaps 40 feet from another building just like it. The area in between was fenced with a gate to the beer garden and the PX door. The available liquid refreshments were 3.2 beer and seven-ounce bottles of Coca-Cola and 7UP. Building materials for work being done inside the PX were stacked against one end outside the fence. Tables in the beer garden were always at a premium, so sometimes men would sit on the pile of material and 2-by-4s stacked outside the fence.

About a half-dozen of us were sitting on the pile one afternoon when Colonel Santilli came by. All of us stood and rendered the proper salute except a soldier named Sweig. He stood up but had a 3.2 in his right hand. The colonel reached for it, but Sweig drew it away from him, reached into his pocket, and came out with a dime. He held out the dime to the colonel and said, "Here. If you're broke, go get ya one." The rest of us could barely keep from laughing, and it must have had the same effect on the colonel. He turned and walked away from us with the remark, "Take care of that soldier."

To the joy of all of us, Colonel Santilli disappeared into the sunset one afternoon and was replaced by Lieutenant Colonel Kenneth L. Yarnell.

Yarnell was a West Pointer, and it showed. I visited him at his home north of San Diego in the late 1980s, and he and I had a great talk. He told me that he and another battalion commander were on the firing range at Camp Eustis, Virginia, when the camp commanding officer pulled up in a jeep and told them to return to their quarters. They then had 30 minutes to pack their belongings and head for Camp Stewart. He never had a chance to say goodbye to anybody.

Yarnell told me that he would rather have had his Virginia men while in Europe instead of the command of the 565th. We were rejects from Camp Stewart and Tennessee maneuvers, and not as good as his old unit. Yarnell said he would rather have joined us several months before he did instead of when we were on the verge of going overseas. He admitted that he came to the 565th with a chip on his shoulder. He was peeved and took it out on everyone around him. And I've been able to pass on his thoughts to many of the 565th veterans. I'm sure they were glad to hear it.

In August 1944, we packed our small equipment into crates, turned in but a small fleet of vehicles, and went on furlough. These were all signs that we were about to be shipped overseas. We suspected we were headed for Europe but weren't sure.

Chapter 6

A View of the Battle of the Bulge

Much of August 1944 was spent twiddling our fingers. As I recall, half the men in our battalion went on furlough for two weeks and then the other half went. All of our equipment was packed up and headed for Europe, and we were soon to follow.

On October 4, we boarded a train for Camp Kilmer, New Jersey, the port of embarkation. There must have been at least a couple of trains because we totaled 800 men. We all had coach seats, but they got a bit hard after so many miles. I played blackjack most of the way and lost $31.10 – 10 cents at a time.

We rode from the train station in New Jersey to the pier in buses. Upon arrival at the pier on October 6, we all stood in awe at the vastness of the ship – the U.S.S. Christobal – that would take us overseas. In its civilian life, the Christobal hauled fruit from the Caribbean to New York City. As I recall, it hauled 3,000 to 4,000 troops on this trip.

Each of us walked up the gangplank and onto the ship carrying a rifle and a duffle bag, but I got saddled with the battery clerk's fold-up desk, too. The clerk was a guy from Cleveland, Ohio, named Kraus. In the Army, I was known as "Kraus" also, even though back home we have always pronounced it KRAU-zee. With two guys called Kraus in our unit, I was known as "Big Kraus" and the clerk was "Little Kraus."

"Little Kraus" had a hard time getting his feet on the ground let alone toting a rifle, duffle bag, and fold-up desk, too. He was a real nice guy, so I didn't mind helping him by carrying the desk onto the ship.

Once out to sea, we traveled in a convoy of 20 to 30 ships. Our fruiter was pretty speedy, but we could go only as fast as the slowest ship, so it took us 12 days to make the crossing. I always thought we took the northern route toward Newfoundland and Iceland, but in recent years, the D Battery Commander, Captain Nesbitt, told me he saw flying fish on the way, which would have taken us near the Bahamas.

That first ocean crossing was a lulu for a guy from the Midwest who had never seen a harbor, ocean, dock, longshoreman, or ship before. They gave us two meals a day, and I lost the first seven. The latrines were nothing more than a large ceramic sewer tile with the large bell end up. There were 12 of them side by side, and you almost had to have a reservation after each meal because there wasn't room for everybody at the ship's rail.

As we neared our destination at Plymouth, England, our ship left the convoy and sped ahead of the others. We were on deck at the time, and the sensation was like passing a car on a busy highway. Our ship accelerated so fast we soon lost sight of the others, who were probably headed for Le Harve, France.

We arrived at Plymouth on October 18 and boarded a train for Leek in the English midlands, a British army camp called Blackshaw-Moor. We were billeted in Nisson huts (shaped like a half-moon upside down) heated with charcoal, a new fuel for us. The charcoal was piled outside and snow covered. Whoever preceded us at the camp attacked the pile from the top, so it took a lot of digging to get to the charcoal that was half frozen. But it burned well after it dried out.

Upon arrival at Blackshaw-Moor, we learned of a slight SNAFU ("situation normal – all fouled up"): Our crates and guns had been shipped to France. Weeks later, we learned they were on their way to England. In the meantime, we drew our inventory of vehicles – 85 new GMC 2 1/2-ton trucks, 12 three-quarter-ton Dodge weapons carriers, and 24 Ford jeeps. We used these trucks to haul our crates and guns from the pier to camp

In the Army, I was known as "Big Kraus" (center) and our company clerk (right) was "Little Kraus." Pictured with us is another battalion member whose identification escapes me.

once they arrived in England.

Once our equipment caught up with us, we spent several days unpacking and making sure we had everything. Then we loaded it all up again and headed for the harbor at Southhampton. All 121 vehicles and 64 guns were loaded onto liberty ships for the short trip across the English Channel to France.

While on board, we were required to paint a two-inch-wide white circle around the star on the hood of each vehicle. At the time, we didn't have a clue as to why. Later we learned that the Germans had captured a lot of American vehicles, and airmen couldn't tell the German-captured vehicles from those still in American hands while flying over them. So the Army was required to paint these circles around the stars on the hoods to distinguish American-held vehicles from the captured ones. Doing this during our trip across the channel was a surprise to us and the Germans.

Today when you see a vintage Army vehicle as a collector item, that circle is absolutely perfect. The ones we painted freehand with the aid of a flashlight in the hold of a ship were not. We made a circle around the star with a piece of string and then traced the outline with a pencil. A black line on olive drab paint does not show up well in dim light.

Upon arrival at Le Harve, France, we had to lay anchor for a week before we could unload. The little cargo ships used for crossing the channel weren't built to house GI's for the long term, so we were ready to go by the time they finally let us off. We unloaded our ship on December 16. I remember that day for a couple of reasons. First, it was my 21st birthday. And second, the Battle of the Bulge started that day.

Our maintenance section was made available to help the other batteries unload their trucks and guns from the LSTs. They were unloaded into "landing-craft tanks" along side of the ships, which were expected to drive off to shore under their own power. The system worked great most of the time, but if something went awry, we were there to winch, pull, or start them so they could get ashore.

When the last of them got ashore, we followed them to a staging camp near Rouen, about 30 miles up the Seine River from Le Harve. The camp consisted of several tent cities named for cigarettes – Lucky Strike, Old Gold, Chesterfield, and Twenty Grand. Ours was called Red Horse.

Our stay at Red Horse was short. The German army had pushed through the 1st Army's front and was advancing toward Antwerp, Belgium. As I recall, we started heading for 1st Army headquarters at Spa, Belgium, but Colonel Yarnell told me during our 1980s visit that an advance party went to Spa and learned that 1st Army headquarters had moved to the rear. Orders were left for us to join the 3rd Army in Luxembourg City under the command of General George S. Patton.

The advance party had to take a long ride west to avoid the advancing German troops and then south to intercept our convoy coming from Rouen. Just how that was all accomplished remains a mystery to me. But they found us somehow, and the colonel led us to Luxembourg, where Patton had moved his 3rd Army intelligence and operations (G2 and G3) units that very day. It was a long day of travel for us. We started from Rouen well before daylight and didn't bed down in Luxembourg until about 10 p.m.

We stopped about six miles southwest of Luxembourg City at Niederkorn. Headquarters Battery bedded down in a school. We each carried only one round of ammunition, which we had since leaving France in early morning. Those manning our 40-millimeter and 50-caliber guns were short of ammo as well.

Our halt served us well. First, we got some rest. I slept well that night, largely because I didn't know what was going on around me. Second, the next morning our battalion supply passed out ammunition to each of the batteries. We then proceeded to our various headquarters and gun-section locations, and established communications – just as if we knew what we were doing. And we did. The 565th's A and D batteries set up in defense of the city and 3rd Army headquarters in particular.

Our battalion headquarters was in an apartment house. It provided bullet-proof rooms except for the windows, and we weren't exposed to the elements. We had three guard posts – one at the front door, one at the rear, and another across the road at the motor pool. That's where I worked during the day. At night, those of us with "T" ratings became privates and had to take our turn at guard duty.

We also occasionally were assigned to guard duty at group headquarters, which was one step up from battalion headquarters. Group headquarters was commanded by a full colonel, and you'd see generals coming and going there, too. When I was assigned to guard duty at group, I had to be in dress uniform and usually got an inside post because I had some stripes.

For our first several days in Luxembourg, we could see artillery flashes at night to the north and northeast. A bigger concern to us were the missiles being fired at night from Trier, Germany, which was 20 to 25 miles east. I'm told they weren't aimed at any specific target but just the city in general. Luxembourg City was perhaps five miles across, so it covered a big area. I'm told the missiles were launched from a six-inch tube several feet long. The missile had a propellant at its base. As it passed through the tube, other propellants would thrust it at an ever-increasing speed until it left the tube. The missile would be ignited and carried to its destination, where it would all but halt and drop straight to the ground. Then a fragmentary device would explode just off the ground. It was a most unwelcome guest, especially if your guard post was in an unprotected area.

At one point, spent bullets from a dogfight hit our battalion headquarters building. One hit Willie Ford, a cook, as he was washing cooking utensils in the back yard. Others went through some side windows of the bedrooms where I and the fellows I worked with slept. Fortunately, it was during the day and we were all off to our assigned tasks.

We were headquartered on one of the main routes leading into Luxembourg from the south. There was a steady stream of vehicles on the road 24 hours a day, bumper to bumper. I think I must have seen every kind of Army vehicle made at the time pass by. One evening I was standing along the highway near one of our machine guns when another fellow from Iola, Louis Adams Sr., of the 4th Infantry Division, rode by in a truck headed north. I didn't recognize him, but "Puggy," as we called him back home, saw me and told me about it when we met again in Iola after the war.

The 4th and 5th divisions were located north and northeast of Luxembourg City and were our

Top: We used to haul our gasoline in five-gallon cans until we picked up this tanker trailer somewhere in Germany. Center: This parts truck (left) and wrecker were part of our battalion motor pool. This photo was taken at Camp Top Hat in Antwerp, Belgium, after the war. Bottom: This jeep was also part of our motor pool. It was driven by Larry Dougherty, who named it "Sentimental Journey," after the popular song of the time.

protection should the bulge move toward us. The Luxembourg airport was immediately east of the city, and our B Battery was set up around the airport. That would be north of Hamm, the site of a World War II cemetery where Patton is buried.

C Battery set up at Junglinster around the three towers of Radio Luxembourg, which was the most powerful radio station in the world, about six miles northeast of the city. Out of our battalion, C Battery was closest to the front, as close as six to eight miles. Headquarters battery was farthest from the front, south of the city just down the street and across a railroad bridge from the railroad station. The station was operable, but the roof had been blown off it.

Across the street was the Alfa Hotel, which was General Omar Bradley's headquarters. Patton had his headquarters about a half mile away at the Pescatore, which was an old-folks home. A question most every 3rd Army veteran gets is, did you ever see the old boy? Yes, I did.

About once a week, members of Headquarters Battery would take showers in shifts at a facility set up by the quartermaster's corps, near group headquarters. The showers were in a large tent. Upon entering it, we'd take off our dirty clothes and throw them on a pile. We'd set our rifles down and leave our boots outside the showers.

After showering, we'd get a clean towel to dry ourselves off with and then some clean clothes. If something didn't fit, we'd trade it for something that did. Then we'd reclaim our rifles and boots, hop in a truck, and return to our quarters.

One day I was driving back from the showers in a three-quarter-ton weapons carrier with about a half-dozen buddies in the back. The Pescadore was on the way home, and the Old Man (all commanding officers were called the Old Man, no matter what level they were) was walking his dog, Willie, a bull terrier. The fool dog ran into the road between us and the general. If I had hit Willie, I suppose I'd still be in the federal penitentiary at Leavenworth.

That winter was one of Luxembourg's coldest in many years. Coming from Wisconsin, I was somewhat used to the cold, but when I tried to repair a truck that had sat outside for several hours, my flesh would freeze just as fast as the next guy's. But my having dealt with the cold all my life was worth its weight in gold during this time. There are times you just don't try to start an engine. One of them is when it's 0 degrees with a northwest wind off the English Channel. No German army or air force is going out in that kind of weather either.

The 2 1/2-ton GMC trucks had a six-volt ignition system, which could hardly turn the engine over in cold weather. We tried warming the engines in the sun or with a heater, but that never kept pace with the need. Then we found a couple of large 12-volt batteries and brought them back to headquarters in a two-wheel trailer. We had a battery charger adjacent to them and always kept them fully charged. They were great for starting the trucks.

Those six-volt systems were not waterproof either. In rainy and damp weather, World War II Army vehicles could easily short out. If a full fire extinguisher was available, a little carbon tetrachloride in the distributor, coil, wires, and

As the Battle of the Bulge subsided and the Allies pushed the Germans back eastward again, things in Luxembourg City quieted down to the point where you could go downtown and have your picture taken.

spark plugs did the trick. If a cylinder or two didn't want to fire, we'd just let the motor warm up and dry out whatever was damp.

Flat tires were also common among the battalion's vehicles. It was our responsibility at headquarters motor pool to fix them, and that's what we did. Each day we had a tire exchange with each battery's motor pool. We'd load the flats in the back of the wrecker and go to the junkyard,

where the Ordnance Department would have deposited disabled trucks. We'd trade the flat tires for good ones off the disabled trucks and maybe take a few extra, but we would make sure we never left a vehicle without a rim on each wheel, even if the tire on it was flat.

History books say the sun came out on December 22, 1944, in Europe after a week of cloudy weather. The Germans had used the overcast skies as a shield against the superior Allied air power to launch their counterattack. But after the skies cleared, the air forces were able to take off again.

From my vantage point in Luxembourg, I had never before seen so many planes in the air. There was wave after wave of B-17 bombers headed for the "heartland" along with P-51 and C-47 fighters as escorts. The sky all around us was full of shreds of tin foil, dropped by the planes to jam German radar. By noon the ground was covered with it.

The next day, we didn't see as many bombers as we had that first day, but we still saw a lot of them heading east day after day. It was a reinforcing feeling for those of us on the ground who were potentially in the way if the bulge had advanced farther.

At night, it was the Huns, as Patton called them, who filled the skies with bombers headed for England. Our anti-aircraft guns would shoot at them as they flew over. We had no way of knowing if we ever hit anything, and it wasn't our job to know. The 90-millimeter could shoot six miles (30,000 feet) straight up. When the planes were 10,000 to 15,000 feet up, our 40-millimeter guns would shoot at 90-millimeter bursts. This would produce shrapnel, which was as wicked as bullets on its return to earth. We had a sufficient amount of flak to meet them each night.

This kept up for three or four weeks day and night until it started to lessen. It became a common greeting to those standing guard to be asked if they heard any of our guns shooting.

The rounds we took from Trier every night continued until about the end of January. I suspect the missile launchers were soon on the priority list for our planes, which could pick up the flash of a launch and then pinpoint the location. That would be the end of their activity. Also, our ground troops took Trier – from the south and east rather than head-on from the west. We learned later the guns firing at us were mounted on railway cars and were sheltered in tunnels during daylight hours.

Finally the British were able to take Antwerp, which was what they were supposed to do in the fall. The 1st and 3rd armies needed that port badly. If the British had done their job, America's Red Ball Express would never have been needed. This term referred to the extensive truck convoys that supplied Allied troops as they advanced east across Europe in the fall of 1944. A 250-mile ground-supply route was a long haul from La Harve.

On December 31, our B Battery, at the airport, was notified that a B-25 would land on airstrip A97. (Today it is one of the runways at the Luxembourg International Airport. I think I landed on it once or twice on tours back to my old haunts.) It would carry some important cargo. It turned out to be General Dwight D. Eisenhower, the supreme commander for the European Theater of Operations.

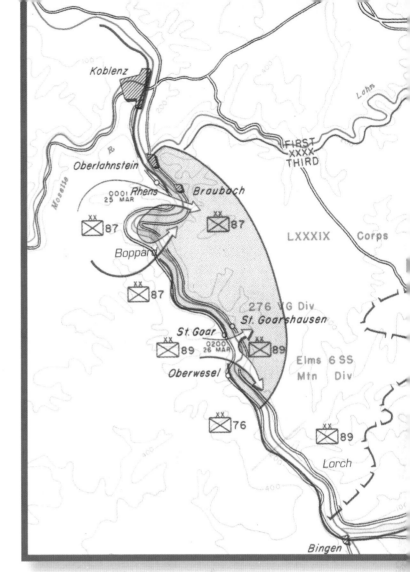

After leaving Luxembourg, the 565th Anti-Aircraft Battalion defended pontoon bridges along the Rhine River, from Boppard to Bingen.

As the bulge shrank and the Germans were pushed back after February 1, 1945, Luxembourg City became a nice place for assignment. We stayed because 3rd Army headquarters stayed. The Old Man and his staff could manage affairs from there without bullets flying around them, receive field reports, and travel to the front easily. Domestic rail service was restored. Freight trains from France started arriving.

The front moved eastward rapidly as Allied forces continued to advance. On March 28, we got word that we would move. The battalion left Luxembourg and was assigned to defend pontoon bridges on the Rhine river. As the name implies, the bridges consisted of a series of pontoons attached to cables that stretched across the river. The cables to the pontoons near the shore were longer than those in the center. That base cable formed a nice arc when observed from above.

Our section of the river extended from Boppard, Germany, to Bingen, but our assignment changed as needed. This area of the river was like a vacation land, and the native people didn't want to spoil its beauty with permanent bridges. So before the war, ferries were used for crossing the river.

There were four pontoon bridges upstream from Cologne – at Boppard, St. Goar, Lorch, and Bingen. The late DeLyle Omholt, who was an attorney from Iola, was the U.S. Army mayor at St. Goar. He was a 1st lieutenant with the 70th Infantry Division, and his assignment was to follow closely behind the front and set up civilian governments in the newly occupied territories. After the war, he told me about the time a French colonel relieved him of his duties at St. Goar with a lot of pomp and circumstance. The French colonel had his whole company of men at the ceremony. DeLyle had four enlisted men with him. I didn't know of his assignment at the time; we never met during our time in the service. It was an after-the-war story.

The area's topography consisted of a giant river gorge with mountains on each side, perhaps a thousand feet high. I'm told 22 castles can be viewed from the river. A main highway and high-speed trains traveled both sides of the Rhine. The 565th's Headquarters Battery was located first at Boppard in a resort hotel and then later at Lorch on the east side of the river at the foot of the bridge.

At Lorch, I got my first good look at a German jeep called a Kübelwagen. It was made by Volkswagen, and you could see the similarity to the postwar Beetle. We salvaged the engine from it to drive a direct-current generator, which we used as a welder. Later, we used a big German direct-current generator for that purpose. I say "we," but I was the only one in our unit who could weld, thanks to one of the courses I took before entering the Army. What an aid to the battalion that was!

Our stay on the Rhine was short-lived. By that time, Patton had things in high gear, and a fully mobile unit such as the 565th was just what he needed. We could and did put all 121 of our vehicles and all 64 guns on the move at one time. We left the Rhine early one morning and headed for Grossenbehringen – about 150 to 175 miles to the northeast as the crow flies but a bit more than that by highway.

The move spread our individual batteries over a larger area, and this was a real headache for the battalion motor pool. It was our job to keep everyone ahead of the battalion wrecker, mechanics, and spare-parts supply. It was dark when we left and dark when we arrived. At one time, we had 17 vehicles ahead of us with our motor officer leading the way.

As was common with convoys, road guards were stationed at critical points along the way to make sure we were on the right route. It was already dark when we encountered a guard who

Berchtesgaden, where Hitler's mountain retreat was located, was largely rubble by the time our battalion got to see it.

told us we could use blackout lights on the lead vehicle to speed our journey because the front was quite a ways forward. He must have been a German in a GI uniform, because a ways down the road, we were strafed by an ME-109 as we were rounding a curve. He missed, but we stopped to take a head count.

We came to a small village and stopped to let several of our trucks catch up. When they did, we learned that the wrecker I had been in most of the day had driven off a sharp shoulder in the road and rolled over several times. We also learned that we had overrun our headquarters by 15 to 20 miles, so we had to reverse our direction.

As we doubled back, we stopped where the wrecker had rolled over. Kelton Herndon and I stayed on to guard the truck and pick up equipment scattered over the landscape. Another mechanic, Adelio Revetti, was taken back to a hospital because he was hurt quite badly in the crash and never did rejoin our outfit. Some of our trucks had found their way to their own batteries, so there were but a half-dozen trucks left with us by this time. We were well into no-man's land.

Once daylight came, Herndon and I picked up the things that had spilled out of the wrecker. As we were working, we heard an FW-190 approaching from the east, so we hid in a large culvert until the plane left. Fortunately it never came back.

We waited for the motor-pool staff to return from headquarters with a winch truck. Once they arrived, we uprighted the crashed wrecker and loaded up the tools, parts, and supplies. After replenishing the truck's fluids, we drove it back.

We wanted to sleep, but the events of the last 24 hours didn't permit that. So we worked on getting things back in order and went to bed nearly 36 hours from the time we last had any sleep.

Our stay at Grossenbehringen was three days at the most. We spent much of that time caring for the vehicle ills that had developed during our convoy from the Rhine. The Ohrdurf concentration camp was nearby, but I didn't go to see it. Those who did saw but little of what had happened there.

The front was moving rapidly now – 25 to 30 miles a day. Our next move was with B and C batteries to the Weimar airport, a few miles southwest of the city itself. The airport was cleared of enemy, but our assignment there consisted

Some of our guys pose by signs left by previous American GI visitors to Berchtesgaden.

of ground as well as air defenses. It wasn't long before DC-3's from Paris began landing there with supplies of all kinds, especially gasoline in five-gallon cans. These were unloaded one can at a time and often into one of our 565th's 2 1/2-ton trucks. They were then hauled to the thirsty Sherman tanks up front.

At Weimar, we were billeted in Luftwaffe barracks. A Luftwaffe pilot's wife threw a raging fit when she was told to move out, but most people there were cooperative. As for us, we were happy to have a roof over our heads. We spread our blankets over the bed clothes that were left behind, and we were told not to touch or take personal items left behind. To a large degree, that code was followed when it came to the belongings of regular civilians, but because the Luftwaffe was not among our friends, I doubt if everyone followed the golden rule for their stuff. But the pickings weren't as good as they were at some of the wine cellars and breweries we encountered during our travels through Europe.

Early on the afternoon of April 15, the motor-pool grapevine provided a couple of bits of information. First, the infantry had cleared the city of Weimar. Second, a couple of days before that, an armored division had found the Buchenwald concentration camp and opened its gates. It was about six miles northwest of the city.

A group of us from the Headquarters motor pool thought this would make an excellent field trip. To be on the safe side, however, somebody went to Captain McCoy, our battalion motor officer, and told him our plan and asked him if he wanted to go along. We knew if we didn't and got caught being gone without permission, there would be hell to pay. Plus, the captain was a real fine leader – in fact, one of the best. Even if he was an officer, we never held it against him.

This time, I went along on the excursion. The things I saw and smelled there have stayed with me for the past 60 years.

Chapter 7

A Tour of Buchenwald

When we asked Captain McCoy if he wanted to go to Buchenwald with us, his response was, "When are we leaving? How about 5 o'clock if you aren't hungry?" The anticipation of such a visit superseded being hungry. Plus, we always kept a private stash of food in the wrecker.

We drove about four miles north of Weimar and crested a hill. On the ridge was a road that ran east and west. We had just made our turn to the west, toward Buchenwald, when we began seeing bodies along the road. They were in the ditches and a wooded area beyond the ditch line. We didn't know at the time how they came to be there, but later we were told a large contingent of prisoners had left the camp for a march to Czechoslovakia several days before. Those that couldn't keep up were disposed of by means of an S.S. bullet. The closer we got to the gate, the more bodies we saw, although there was none around the gate area proper.

We were met at the front gate by a 17-year-old boy who must have been a prisoner but maybe was the camp's interpreter because he spoke perfect British English. I wish I could remember his name; that's the least I owe him. He took us to the camp hospital, which consisted of 17 beds, and introduced us to the camp doctor. I don't know what function this hospital had in the active camp because everyone there suffered from various stages of malnutrition and every complication it manifests – that plus all the normal maladies of man.

The doctor explained many of the camp's functions to us. We met a Belgian supreme court justice, another prisoner who had once played second base for the Philadelphia Phillies. These people and many more at the camp thanked us for liberating them as if each of us had done the job single-handedly. It almost made me cry. It's the only time I've ever been required to accept such gratitude. But from their perspective, I can see why they felt as they did. We were the first American

Headquarters Battery of the 565th Anti-Aircraft Battalion gathers in formation after the war. "Little Kraus" carries the flag for our unit.

soldiers they had seen; we even beat Patton and Eisenhower to the camp. And I think we were great ambassadors.

The doctor asked us if we had any K rations (chocolate bars). We had some that we usually carried as emergency food. We gave them what we had on us at the time and then got more from the truck. The doctor said such rich food would probably kill a malnourished prisoner, but he could use them for medicinal purposes.

The camp consisted of two barracks. The upper barracks were a non-Jewish residence and housed bunk beds two or three high. I don't recall seeing a kitchen in this barracks, but the residents

there must have had something to eat because they were up and active but thin. In a way, they were the lucky ones.

The lower barracks were reserved for Jews. There was no kitchen, and apparently the prisoners there had not seen food for a long time because they were mere skin drawn over their every bone. They couldn't or wouldn't speak to us and probably didn't know who we were. Their bunks were made from boards and 2-by-4s, six feet high under about a nine-foot ceiling. The bunks were continuous with a post about every six feet.

The smell we encountered in this barracks – a combination of clothes that had never been washed and dead flesh – became permanently etched in our brains.

As prisoners died, their bodies were taken to an eight-foot by eight-foot shed at the end of the barracks. There were 40 to 50 bodies in the shed when we toured the camp. There were probably just as many bodies still in the bunks, left there when the Germans abandoned the camp ahead of the Americans' arrival.

There were hundreds of more bodies piled on wagons parked outside the camp's crematory. The crematory itself consisted of three ovens side by side. Three bodies would be placed in a single oven at once – two across and one on top. Off to the right of the ovens was a room I'll call an assassin's chamber. A long flight of steps led from the ground level to this basement room, which was maybe 20 to 25 feet square. On three of the walls were two rows of hooks at different levels. The hooks were specially shaped and sharpened so they would insert into the base of the skull when bodies were placed on them.

As prisoners were forced down the steps, and as they turned to the right and entered the room, an S.S. trooper would crush their foreheads with a club. I can best describe the club as a baseball bat with the striking area about eight inches in diameter and about a foot wide. It was leaning against the wall when I was there, and I remember picking it up and looking at it. I soon put it down because its end was frayed to the point of being concave. I'm sure it had never been washed or cleaned. It was the only thing that smelled worse than the lower barracks.

As we left the camp, we drove by a sign that said "Buchenwald Botanical Garden." That's what the place was before it was converted to a concentration camp. It's hard to believe such a horrible place once had such a serene and peaceful function. As we drove back to our quarters in the wrecker, Captain McCoy remarked, "My God. We were Buchenwald's first tourists." I'll never figure out just what kind of honor that is, but I often tell anyone who wants to hear the story that I was among the first tourists to Buchenwald. Unless someone offers evidence to the contrary, I'll continue to do so.

The day after our visit to Buchenwald, we spoke of nothing else. Many more from our unit made the trip, too, but probably didn't get to meet the young English-speaking man or the doctor. The citizens of Weimar were forced to visit the camp, too, and Eisenhower and Patton finally saw it on April 17. It was reported that Ike became physically sick during the visit. Upon our return from our visit, we "forgot" to eat.

Back on duty, life at the Weimar airport was dull. Hitler was defeated, but we had a bad feeling that he wouldn't say, "I give up." Eventually he had to determine whether to live or die. He chose death, on April 30, 1945.

We thought our next move would be to Leipzig. Major Fry and Sergeant Gravenstein went to check it out but got only two or three blocks into town when they discovered the infantry had yet to clear the city of German soldiers. We then got orders to pack up and make a right-angle turn south toward Nürnberg, Regensburg, and finally Straubing, southeast of Regensburg. We stopped a day or two at each place beginning on April 18.

The 87 members of our Headquarters Battery found quarters at an old hotel that had shops, an old horse stable, and ample parking at the curb. We set up our motor pool in Straubing's main street, which must have been 200 feet wide. While there, some Limey (English) soldiers with thick accents who had been captured at Dunkirk enlisted our help. They had commandeered a couple of cars to take them back to Dunkirk, from there, back across the English Channel to home, but the cars needed some work. So we hauled them to our work area with our wrecker and checked the cars' fluids, brakes, and wheel bearings, and gave each of them a new battery. We were concerned about the old tires on the cars, but there wasn't anything we could do about that.

The Germans recaptured Dunkirk, in northern France, in 1940. Many British and French soldiers were able to escape back across the English Channel before the city fell, but apparently the soldiers we helped were left behind. I felt a bit guilty about helping appropriate those two cars, but I felt somewhat justified in helping the Brits after they were prisoners of war for so many years.

When the cars were ready, the Brits invited us back to a nice two-story home where they had taken up residence. They toasted each of us with a glass of white lightning. We were lined up against a wall in the house, and one by one they raised their glasses to thank us and we raised our glasses to bid them bon voyage. I noticed the fellas ahead of me were having trouble downing the nearly pure alcohol. Fortunately, I was standing by an open window. So when it came my turn to offer a toast, I kept my lips closed as I held my glass up to my mouth. Then I put it behind me and dumped it out the open window. For the sake of anybody who may have been standing below, I am sure it vaporized before it hit the ground. That was awful stuff.

I avoided that white lightning, but I wasn't able to avoid a flash burn during our stay at Straubing. A flash burn occurs when unprotected eyes are exposed to an arc welder. It leaves little blisters, and you feel like you have sand in your eyes. Fortunately, eye tissue heals quickly, and with a little ointment from the medics, it was over in 24 hours.

The 3rd Army as a whole continued to drive southeast toward Austria. It was rumored that the Germans had sent a whole army to Austria to try to regroup and launch another counterattack similar to the Battle of the Bulge. But nothing came of it. American units continued into Austria unchallenged. Our battalion went as far as the Isar River before we were given orders to report to a rear assignment. There were so many 3rd Army troops in such a small area that it was hard to maneuver.

We left for Schwarzenberg Castle, northwest of Nürnberg, on May 4. That's where we were on May 8 – V-E Day (Victory in Europe). V-E Day to us was not a time of a big celebration as we knew the war was over; it was a matter of announcing the date. We were already in the rear echelon.

Upon exploring Schwarzenberg Castle, we discovered a broad stairway, maybe 10 feet wide, that led straight down about 40 feet to a basement. In the basement, our flashlight picked up the image of several beer vats. Unfortunately, some previous Army visitors must have made the same discovery

At Schwarzenberg Castle, Kelton Herndon and I fixed the clock in the tower, while other soldiers stationed there tried to drink up a basement full of good German beer.

because the vats were full of machine-gun holes and there was about six inches of beer on the basement floor. As a result, most of the vats were empty, but there was still some beer left in a few of them below the bullet holes.

We got some bricks and planks and improvised a walkway to the vats. We then drained some nice cool beer – it was about 50 degrees in the basement – into water cans. Some sampled the beer right there in the basement. Those who did couldn't walk straight when they came up out of

that basement and hit the 80-degree temperature outside. We had set up our motor pool nearby and could tell when someone had been down in the basement drinking beer too long. Despite the previous machine-gun raid, there was still plenty of beer in the vats for the whole battalion. We stayed there two weeks, and the 600 to 700 troops in our unit couldn't drink it dry.

Kelton Herndon and I took on a more productive project during our stay. The castle had a four-faced clock on a tower, but it wasn't running.

So we found our way up into the tower and discovered the clock's workings were ancient and rusted. Others got interested in the project, too, and with the help of some penetrating oil, wire brushes, and files, we got it cleaned up and running again.

We eventually got the striking mechanism to work, too. The mechanism was made of hand-forged gears with square teeth. It was powered by weights that were not original. They were made from a couple of cylinder heads from old cars.

When the villagers heard that clock toll the hour again, they visited us and told us they hadn't heard the clock in years. They were very happy it was running again. To them, it proclaimed the war was over and we Yanks had touched their hearts by fixing the clock.

I got to see Schwarzenberg Castle again in 1992 when four other veterans from our unit, their wives, and I retraced our trek across France, Luxembourg, and Germany. The clock had stopped again, and the castle was now an orphanage. Other than that, however, it looked pretty much as it did in 1945.

Our official duties in the Schwarzenberg area ranged from guarding bridges to picking up displaced persons – or DPs, as they were called – which became a big part of our assignment. They were transferred to temporary collecting points, where they were sorted by country of origin and then awaited transportation home by train. There may not have been regular schedules, but rail service in Germany was up and running again by this time and was important in returning the DPs to their homes.

We left Schwarzenberg Castle on May

18 and traveled east a few miles to Forchheim. Here we saw trainload after trainload of DPs pass through. Our troops were assigned to guard a prison camp of the Wehrmacht – the regular German army. The good and the bad were sorted out here, and those allowed to go home were put on trucks.

At Forchheim, our motor pool languished for lack of things to do. We played a lot of softball during this time. Each battery fielded a team. Headquarters Battery wasn't the best, as evidenced by the fact that I made the team. Our battalion started losing members, too. A point system was in place for determining who could go home first. The commissioned and non-commissioned officers who had accumulated a lot of points through years of service and overseas duty left us. Some had been in the Army for a while before joining our unit.

And then one day the battalion was asked to turn in its guns at a receiving point about 60 to 70 miles away. That was a memorable day for the batteries, because by this time, the guns were just dead weight. We didn't use them anymore, but yet they had to be kept clean if only for lack of anything else to do.

On July 3, we received orders to return to Rouen, France, the assembly area from which we had left on December 21, 1944, for the Battle of the Bulge. That was good news, because the port of La Harve was just down the road, and we thought we were going home. It turned out that way for those who had enough points to go home, but for the rest of us, it was a way of marking time. The move to Rouen was about 400 to 500 miles, which took us three days, but we were able to rest and

The house in Forchheim where we were billeted. The beds were made up for us, but we were told not to touch or take any personal items in the house.

Thomas Allen, a fellow motor-pool mechanic from Camden, Tennessee, and I take a break during our stay in Forchheim, Germany.

eat at facilities prepared for troops moving out of Germany. We were getting out of the way of the occupation army.

Our stay at Rouen was rather short. We left August 15 for Antwerp, Belgium, another port from which troop ships were leaving daily and into which supplies were coming. Our battalion's assignment was to guard the docks, but I personally didn't draw that duty because we still had 121 vehicles to maintain and our long trip from Germany took its toll on them. As I recall, if a truck required a major repair, we would just take it to an ordnance depot and exchange it for a good one because there were a lot of surplus vehicles left from units that had left the port.

In Antwerp, we were billeted in an old Belgian military barracks perhaps six miles from the prep station where our personnel clerks and others with the necessary skills helped with the paperwork required to load soldiers headed home. Every soldier had a file that contained a history of everything that had happened to him from the day he entered the service. A soldier's file traveled with him on the ship as he headed back to the States and on to the separation center.

Once we got the trucks back in shape, there wasn't much for our section to do except mark time. I commuted back and forth to the barracks once or twice a day or maybe drove a shuttle for others. Meals steadily improved because now we were able to get fresh foods instead of just C rations. We also lost more of our high-point men. At full strength, we had 37 officers in our battalion, but by this time, each battery had only a couple and there were only three or four in the

headquarters battery. Thus, in Antwerp, our table of organization looked much different from the wartime gang.

Then one afternoon, I and about a dozen others were loaded onto a 2 1/2-ton GMC truck and were transferred to the 563rd Anti-Aircraft Battalion at Namur, Belgium, perhaps 60 miles away. I ended up in B Battery of the 563rd as motor sergeant. I suspect I got transferred because the 563rd needed a motor sergeant, the 565th Headquarters Battery had an excess of mechanics, and I was the only T/4 (sergeant) left in the battery. Plus, the 565th Headquarters Battery had no assignment at the time.

The 563rd's lettered batteries were also assigned as military police in the Namur area. My new battery still had trucks, but we didn't use them much. Although our unit served as military police, fortunately I didn't pull any of that duty.

One Sunday afternoon, however, someone looked me up and asked if we could help pull a small British flatbed semi off an embankment on the Meuse River, a short distance from Namur. Four of us took a couple of winch trucks and headed to the scene. We found the British truck had moved to the side on a narrow road and hit a stone railing of sorts. One of the stones – about 18 inches square and six feet tall – got caught under the truck's front axle. We determined it wasn't safe to just pull the stone out from under the front of the truck with one of our winches because we might all end up off the embankment. So we decided to back one of the winch trucks into the ditch on the opposite side of the road and anchor the truck's trailer to it.

On the opposite side of the road, we looked for a tree big enough to attach an anchor and small snatch block, which we could then attach to the stone. But all we could find were smaller, brush-type trees. So we chained three of them together and attached the snatch block to the lowest one. We then ran our cable through the snatch block and hooked it onto the stone. We attached the cable from the second winch truck to the British truck's fifth wheel to hold it back. We were then able to pull the stone out without sending the truck over the embankment.

But we still had to get the truck off the embankment. So we reconfigured our cables and inched it back onto the road again. It took a lot longer to pull out the truck than it did the stone, but once we made it, the result was one happy British truck driver. I don't think he was supposed to be in our territory, but I never asked. We sent him on his way so the road would be clear. By this time, a lot of local traffic had backed up. After he left, it took us a long time to gather up our chains and rewind our winch cables. Once we did, fortunately somebody remembered how to get back to the barracks.

Another Sunday afternoon a couple of Red Cross women stopped by with a staff car that didn't steer well. A quick check indicated the front tires were badly worn on the inside. This told me the toe-in was out of adjustment. I drove the car onto one of our grease pits and discovered the tie-rod – the part of the steering mechanism that controls the toe-in – had not been tightened. So I adjusted the toe-in, got a big kiss from each of them, and sent them on their way.

In late September 1945, I was transferred to Charleroi and assigned to B Battery of the 769th Military Police Battalion. I don't remember much about that assignment, but I do recall meeting a few former 565th members there. My stay at Charleroi was short. One day all of us began boarding trucks that took us to a liberty ship that would take us back to the good ol' USA. We boarded the ship after checking in with a boarding officer, who made sure we and our personnel files matched.

Liberty ships were the smallest ships the Coast Guard used to transport troops. They were converted freighters and about the worst accommodations available, but somebody had to ride them, and I and the 249 others who joined me were just happy to be headed home.

My trip back across the North Atlantic in January 1946 wasn't much better than the one over in October 1944. We bobbed around in that little ship like a top on a lake blown by a strong wind. The North Sea and North Atlantic did their best to make our ride long and arduous. There were times when the ship's bow would dive into a wave and the stern and propellers would race as they came out of the water. Power to the propellers was cut, and we'd be dead in the water for a few moments. Then the propellers would start up again and repeat the cycle every 10 to 15 minutes. We spent a lot of time in our bunks when the seas were this rough because it was impossible to stand up.

The tables in the galley were anchored with steel posts and were about 40 inches high, so you stood up when you ate. It was a struggle to get your food, walk to the table, and hold on to your plate and cup as you tried to eat. At times, the sea would roll us from side to side. Then all the plates would slide off the end of the table and onto the floor.

One time, about a four-inch-deep mixture of milk, water, pancakes, cereal, eggs, and bacon accumulated on the floor and sloshed back and forth with the rocking of the ship. But no one could stand up long enough to clean it up. When the seas finally calmed, several seamen put on rubber boots and cleaned it up.

Like the trip over, I lost my first seven meals on the way back, too. It got so we would bet one another as to who could hold on to their food the longest. It was common to go right from the galley to the deck and relieve yourself over the rail. But my hunger must have finally overtaken the sea sickness; by the fourth day, I was able to keep down two meals a day.

It was a great day when we could finally go on deck as we approached Halifax, Nova Scotia. What a relief that was after being closed up like bees in a hive for several days! We lay anchor outside the harbor for a few hours as we waited for our turn to refuel and resupply. The longshoremen accidentally dropped a supply of fresh milk on board – enough for each man to have an entire quart. They were all heroes, and we let them know it.

The final leg of our voyage, to New York, was smooth sailing. All we had to carry off the ship was one duffle bag; we had turned in our rifles shortly after V-E Day. After an informal inspection of our bag, we were on our way to Fort Dix, New Jersey.

From that point on, we were treated like special guests. After depositing our duffle bags on our bunks, we had time to take a shower and put on some clean dress uniforms. We then walked a short distance – and at a leisurely pace; no formation marching – to a dining room. We were seated by a hostess at a table with a linen tablecloth and linen napkins. Steaks were the main bill of fare, and they were cooked to order. We were formally served at a table fit for a king – a most unanticipated welcome.

At Ford Dix, we were quickly prepared for our individual trips to a discharge center. In my case, that would be Fort Sheridan, north of Chicago. There were dozens of us on the train from New York to Chicago. I believe we had to change trains in Chicago, but a host at the station guided us to our final destination. At Fort Sheridan, we were assigned to a barracks but could again walk at our leisure to the discharge center. As I recall, I arrived at Fort Sheridan late in the afternoon and was on the Northshore train to Milwaukee in less than 48 hours.

At Milwaukee, I boarded a Soo Line train scheduled for arrival in Waupaca at midnight. In a few hours, I would see my family and home again for the first time in 18 months.

Chapter 8

Tears of Joy

Wisconsin winters did not get any warmer while I was away in the Army. It was bitterly cold – probably 0 degrees or below – when I stepped off the train at midnight in Waupaca. Dad, Neil, and Ben were there to greet me. Neil had returned home the previous August; he was a high-pointer. Ben had returned home about a week before. We men were not much for hugging, but there was not a dry eye among us when we were all together again at the little depot in Waupaca.

We loaded my gear into the '37 Ford, which Dad had driven throughout the duration. It needed some care and parts, but none was to be had during the war and the immediate time following it. Neil probably "tinkered it up" as best he could. Our trip to the farm was only a 15-mile drive, but it took us more than an hour because the old Ford's fuel pump would not cooperate in the cold weather.

When we finally arrived home, the tears flowed again. Mother and Grace were more of the hugging type, so that turned on the waterworks for the whole family. Mother had all three of her boys home from war again with nary a scratch on them. That made our reunion even that much more important to her. It was almost 2 a.m., but Mother had a big supper waiting for me. We all sat down and had a great meal as only she could make. There were more hugs when we finally all went to bed and again at breakfast.

As I look back today on my Army service, I think of all the things my father taught me when I was growing up. Dad was a great teacher, and he passed on his mechanical aptitude to all three of his sons. That served the Army well during the war. Dad never knew what he had done for us nor did we ever get to thank him per se because it is not until you become old and look back on your life that you realize exactly where your talent took you and how you received it.

Nor did I realize at the time how much this knowledge affected where I ended up in the service and how much it contributed to my safe return

After the war, our family sold our farm and moved into this house at 290
East Iola Street in the village of Iola. We renovated it in the 1990s, changing
the cupola and restoring the porch to its original, open design.

home. My job as an auto mechanic in the Army kept me in the rear echelon of the war zone and carried far less risk than many others.

The rejoicing continued for several days after my return. It was the dead of winter, so there were no crops to be planted or harvested. There were, however, a lot of visits to be made with relatives and friends, and catching up to do. Those of us who served bonded with others who had served in the various theaters of operations. Dad had been chronically sick since I left for the Army, and Grace, of course, was not in the best of health most of the time either.

Eventually we all started to settle in to postwar life. For Ben, that meant working with our brother-in-law, Jerry Klug, at the cheese factory. Neil began assembling a machine shop, which led to a full-time gunsmith trade he pursued until his death in 1980.

The late 1940s were almost as bad a depression as the 1930s. Unlike the Great Depression, people had money after the war, but there was nothing to buy. New cars were few. Rehashed 1942 models did not show up until 1947, and newly designed models did not show up until 1949.

As for me, I inherited a number of carpenter jobs that Dad had started or promised. I especially remember being the only roofer in the family, probably because heights did not bother me. There were dozens of roofing jobs waiting for me but no shingles for them. Cement was still rationed at the merchant level and could be hard to get. Lumber was a local product, so with a little ingenuity, that problem was soon solved.

While all his boys were in the service, Dad made plans to build a house to sell but had no clear-cut idea of when that might happen. He did, however, manage to accumulate some logs for making lumber. Our sawmill was still intact when I returned home from the Army. We built a house on South Grove Street in the village of Iola and sold it to Lee Johnson, a local insurance agent with whom I would later share an office in my early years in the publishing business.

In the late 1940s, Dad purchased a house at 290 East Iola Street and with it came three lots, including two more on Grove Street. We built another house on Grove Street, immediately north of the first one, and sold it to Julia and Morton Tackman. In 1950, we sold the farm and moved into the house on Iola Street.

As Dad's health continued to deteriorate, I set out on my own in the construction business. Somewhere along the line I acquired a table saw and jointer, and built stands for them. They accompanied me to all of my house-building projects as well as my other repair projects. To haul them, I purchased a 1937 Ford that had been in a wreck and was only partially restored to its former self. Its back seat was missing, so that gave

me more room to haul tools and other equipment. Later I acquired a red 1941 Dodge pickup truck, which was a great improvement over the old Ford.

I also acquired a tract of land in the northwest corner of the village. Today the parcel is bordered by North and Frogner streets on the east and an alley on the south, and is filled with homes. When I owned it, it was commonly known as Morton Lovdahl's sand pit. Morton used to make cement blocks there, and the blocks for the old Gray Stone Building in Iola were made there. The Gray Stone Building stood on Main Street for many years but was one of several old buildings destroyed by the big fire in Iola on Father's Day, June 21, 2001.

I used the sand-pit site to store lots of odds and ends that didn't need to be inside, and if somebody stole something, I would never miss it. I also hauled many pickup-truck loads of sand out of the pit. I screened the sand and used it for mixing mortar when laying concrete blocks and bricks. A bag of mortar and 14 shovels of screened sand was just right for my mortar box to handle. Around 1950, it became more common to use bags of ready-mix concrete. It was still hard work to lay blocks, but the ready-mix made a hard job go faster.

The building of a house started with roughly staking out the corners of the building. The exact corners were then established by lining up with a road or sidewalk or another adjacent building, and the hole for the basement was dug. I will always remember walking down into a newly dug hole for the first time and re-establishing the corners using the previous reference points. This was done with lines stretched on the surface of the hole with string, a straight board, and a vertical level. Once the exact corners were re-established, a footing along the lines was formed up and filled with concrete.

The next big event was the arrival of the concrete blocks for the basement, which had to be unloaded by hand. When I started in the construction business, the blocks we used measured 7 1/2 inches by 7 1/2 inches by 15 1/2 inches and weighed 40 pounds each. Later the size was increased to 11 1/2 inches by 8 1/2 inches by 15 1/2 inches, and the blocks weighed 80 pounds each.

Building the basement with concrete blocks on top of the concrete footing was heavy work and could not be done in the cold of winter or early spring. I always looked forward to having a building framed and enclosed by fall so we could do the inside finishing work in the winter.

Whether laying concrete blocks or building the wood frame, three elements were required: that the structure be level, plumb, and square. It did not matter if the building was 10 feet square or 100,000 feet square. That's still the rule today, although today builders use a fancy transit with a laser beam for leveling. I used a spirit level and a straight edge, which in my case was a 16-foot-long piece of 1 1/4-inch clear pine. It was perfectly straight – one edge parallel to the other. The top ends of the board were tapered, leaving a five-foot section in the middle on which the level could be placed. Plumb was established with a straight 2-by-4 and a vertical level, and square was established by measuring diagonally from opposite corners and

making sure the measurements matched.

My time in the construction business saw several advances in the trade. Power hand saws and other power tools were great inventions. A six-inch Maul power hand saw was the first of three or four that I have owned. I still have the last one I bought, but it has been years since I plugged it in. I also purchased a pull saw – forerunner of today's chop saw. Both beat the old hand saw by leaps and bounds. I still sharpened the new saws myself by hand on evenings and weekends, but even that was much easier.

I also welcomed the opportunity to buy ready-mix concrete by the truckload from Faulks Brothers in Waupaca when it became available. Back then it cost $13 a yard. When drywall started to replace plaster, I even did that with no instruction book to follow – only a four-inch knife, a plasterer's trowel, and a cement that dried as hard as iron. What I used sure was primitive compared with today's materials and methods.

Although I did much of the work myself on a project, I had the pleasure of working with some true artisans. Ray Twetan installed furnaces and was a character of the first order. He had a way of expressing things unlike anybody else I have ever known. Leo Haroldson was an electrician par excellence. When Leo did a job, it was done right. Al Langland did business as Iola Plumbing and Heating, and he did both well. He was also like an older brother and confidant to me. When I built a spec home, Al did not require that I pay him for his work on the place until it was sold.

One year I built a house in Manawa for Melda and Henry Mortenson. It took nine weeks

Neighbor George Nelson got in the picture when I (from left), Ben, and Neil assembled for a postwar snapshot.

from the time we poured the footing until the key was turned over to them. I made $1,800 on the job and bought a new one-ton Ford pickup with a four-speed transmission. That was a wonderful truck compared to the old Dodge, although the Dodge served me well in its time, too.

In all, I built 23 houses during my time in the construction business and charged a dollar an hour for my labor, but I worked on some more unusual projects, too. Soon after the war, when Dad was still able to work with me, we completed a project that continues working every day – the main dam and overflow dam at the old Wipf's mill on Main Street in Iola. Dad got the job because of his experience in building bridges, where you have to work below the water level.

First, the water in the mill pond had to be drawn down. Then a coffer dam had to be built in front of the normal dam. This was accomplished by placing some large, strong beams in front of the normal dam and driving staves into the solid

bottom below. Dad had Frederick Wipf get some 1 1/2-inch by 5-foot oak staves sawed specially for the project. They were sharpened on both sides and one edge to keep them tight against each other when a new stave was driven next to an existing one.

Once in place, the water flowed through the overflow dam while we worked on the permanent dam. This required pouring lots of concrete prepared by small mixers. Steel forms were not available yet, so we used wooden ones.

Another time I was hired to replace the shingles on the Methodist church in Iola and paint the steeple. I was also told that a lighted cross for the top of the steeple had arrived and I should install it. So I did, but it nearly led to disaster.

The base of the steeple was a bell tower that had four gabled ends. My helper, Rinhard Krause (Dad's cousin), and I placed a plank between each gable and nailed each of the planks so they would not slip. We then placed the legs of a 16-foot ladder as far out on the planks as possible and secured the top of the ladder to the steeple with a rope. This allowed us to reach the top of the steeple at eye level, and we could lift the cross up on top of it.

I do not remember how we attached the cross to the steeple, but I recall there were two wires on the cross for connecting the electricity. So I ran a normal 2-12 Romex wire from the cross and down the steeple, and then connected the wire to a timer.

Some months later, we had an electrical storm, and the wire that led to the cross burned off. Fortunately, it did not set the church on fire; maybe the Lord intervened on my behalf. By this time, I was no longer the person to call when the cross did not light up. Whoever was called knew more about electrical work than I did. I was later told that the wire connected to the cross should have been high tension, like a spark-plug wire in a car. I was lucky the whole church did not burn down.

The cross still sits atop the steeple today, but now when it needs repair, bucket trucks are available to reach it – a much safer method than leaning a ladder against the steeple and raising the cross above one's head.

I suppose any small town produces many a pro-bono project. One that fell my duty was to build the rear tower of a ski-jump scaffold for the Iola Winter Sports Club in the late 1950s. When I arrived at the job, four concrete footings had already been poured for each corner of the tower. From there, I started to build the framing, which was a simple structure 10 feet square. We worked upward from the ground in 10-foot sections, installing a single 2-by-6 every five feet to use as a scaffold for working on the next section up. The 2-by-6s were installed horizontally every 10 feet and were braced to the section below them with four-20-foot-long 2-by-6s, which were used to form each corner

I had lots of help up to 50 feet, but after that only Leonard Haroldson stayed with me for another 20 feet. At that point, a crew on the ground hoisted materials up to me with a rope and a pulley. I worked alone to 90 feet, but then the project became stagnant for a while until we got a crew together one Sunday morning. The crew included Al Langland, who spent seven years as a sailor and was not afraid of heights. We raised the last sections in short order, and that afternoon,

work was completed with decking all the way to the top floor – 110 feet high.

It was a job unlike anything I had ever tackled before. It stood for many years until some loggers felled a tree on a guy wire. It saw only limited use after that, and it was soon determined that it should be replaced. I did not work on the new tower; I just paid for it. It still stands today and is an important part of club events.

I was just hitting my stride as a carpenter when another profession that was consuming a big part of my time beckoned to me full time. But many things I learned as a builder served me well in the years to come in my new business. A good work ethic was probably the most important, which included not being afraid to pick up a broom, mop bucket, or snow shovel.

Building and selling houses provided good lessons in business and people skills. They included hiring help, buying materials, and finally selling the project to a customer and taking care of him after the sale. I also had to keep track of payroll and vendor payments, and learned how to report my financial business to Uncle Sam.

I also became head of our household – which consisted of Mother, Grace, and me – after Dad died in 1954. It was not a big transition, but it was true in fact as well as assumption. Another transition was in the making that would lead me down a career path I never imagined in my early life.

Chapter 9

The Quest for Coins

While I was hammering nails for a living in the 1950s, the coin-collecting seed that had been planted in me as a child came into full bloom. I was not able to add to my collection significantly during the war, although I did save some specimens of the Allied Currency that we used in the European Theater of Operations. Neil also saved some examples of Allied Currency used by him and others who served in the Pacific. In more recent years, I have assembled quite a general collection of World War II War Bonds and World War I Liberty Bonds but sold all the military currency.

I also started collecting stamps again after the war, the collection of my youth having been destroyed in the house fire. I started buying uncirculated singles of new stamps as they were issued. I remember the first ones I purchased were the Great Americans Series, and I still have them. I tried to stay current with new stamps and also started building backward to obtain older issues.

Coin collecting, however, was at a peak of its popularity in the 1950s, and I pursued it with a passion. The coin collection of my youth survived the house fire and provided the foundation for my postwar collecting. Local merchants allowed me to go through their cash registers and take collectible coins for face value. In the early 1950s, one could still find quite a few Liberty Head nickels and occasionally Indian cents in circulation. You could still find some Liberty (also called Barber) dimes, quarters, and half dollars in circulation, too. I also purchased collectible coins advertised in *The Numismatic Scrapbook Magazine*, published in Chicago by Hewitt Brothers.

The Whitman Publishing Company in Racine, Wisconsin, which produced the penny board that started my coin collecting in the 1930s, was still producing holders for collectible coins but now in a more convenient three-paneled folder format instead of the old large boards. In 1946, the company published its first edition of *A Guide Book of United States Coins* by R.S. Yeoman. New editions are still published annually today, and the book is still commonly referred to in the hobby as the "Red Book" because of its distinctive, brightly colored cover. The Red Book lists every date and mint mark of every U.S. coin and values each in several "grades," or conditions of preservation. In the 1950s, the hobby anxiously awaited the release of the year's new edition of the Red Book to see how values compared to the previous edition.

With the availability of the inexpensive Whitman folders and new annual editions of the Red Book, more and more people in the 1950s began collecting coins. They searched their pocket change and even rolls and bags of coins to complete their sets.

Sharing my interest in coin collecting locally was a friend named Jim Dimmock. Jim owned a farm at the intersection of county highways G and GG, just north of Iola. Today, the remains of a red brick silo still stands at the site. That old silo is a landmark to me because my father laid the bricks for it around 1900-1910.

Jim, Neil, and I used to hang out in Wimpy's basement. "Wimpy" was the nickname of Sherman Cleaves, and he was the proprietor of Cleaves Sport Shop on Main Street in Iola. As the name implies, Cleaves Sport Shop sold sporting goods, but you could also buy things such as pencils and paper there and newsstand copies of the *Milwaukee Journal*, *Iola Herald*, and *Popular Mechanics*.

Right after the war, when I was still trying to find my way in life, Neil invited me to join him and Jim in Wimpy's basement to shoot targets with pistols. Jim was the best shot with any firearm you put in his hand; Neil was not far behind. I was quite a ways behind both of them, in part because I did not practice as much as they did. Afterward,

we would adjourn to a neighboring restaurant and shake dice to see who would pay for an early evening treat – usually a chocolate malt or a sundae.

During these sessions, Jim and I would also talk about our mutual interest in coin collecting. Like me, Jim pulled coins from circulation; Wimpy's till was among his sources. At that time, there was a new periodical called *Shotgun News* that had recently appeared on the market. It was published monthly and offered subscribers a free 20-word classified ad in every issue in addition to the larger display ads purchased by gun retailers. The publication provided enthusiasts across the country an inexpensive medium for buying and selling guns among themselves. Jim and I asked ourselves if that same idea could be applied to a periodical for coin collectors.

The question went unanswered for months, as neither Jim nor I took the initiative to turn our idea into action. Months turned into years until one day I asked him directly if he was or was not willing to pursue the idea. Jim told me that if I wanted to pursue it, I should go ahead on my own. Jim said he had three kids in high school who wanted to go to college, and he did not think he should invest in a venture if a profit was not guaranteed.

So in May 1952, I set out on my own and began planning and investigating how to launch a numismatic equivalent to *Shotgun News*. I had gathered some names and addresses of coin collectors through clubs and the pages of the *Numismatic Scrapbook*, and I sent them the following letter:

Before renting office space, all of the work for Numismatic News was done out of our home with help from my family. I worked as a carpenter by day and a publisher by night.

Fellow Coin Collectors:

"I have for some time felt the need of a numismatic publication that would provide the individual collector with low cost advertising to buy, sell, or exchange coins of their particular needs. But before I would undertake such a project I felt I should first write you as well as others for opinions.

"What I have in mind is a small size newspaper carrying classified ads. Each subscriber would receive 20 free words of advertising each month with an additional charge for extra words. He could, however, have as many as desired. Dealers too, I believe, could use the columns to good advantage. News of interest, submitted by subscribers, could be passed on also.

"Realizing the first few issues may be small and as promotion too, the first few issues will be published free with all advertising free.

"However, that is for further discussion. What I would like to know now is, would such a publication be desirable?

"Sincerely, Chester L. Krause."

As I look back on that letter today, I do not think I was asking for opinions as much as I was asking for blessings to go ahead with the project. But nevertheless, the letter garnered some positive responses. So the following Labor Day weekend, I went ahead with composing the first issue of what I was to call *Numismatic News*. I wrote several articles including "A Short Biography of Your Publisher," "Publisher is Not an Ad Jumper," "To Work Out Coin Grading Schedule," and "A Suggested Way of Making a Trade."

I took my copy to Firman Cooper, publisher of the *Iola Herald*, the local weekly newspaper. At the time, I did not know a point from a pica, but Firman set the type for me, printed the copies, and taught me about newspaper graphics. I learned the weight of lead (type metal) and how to melt it and put it into a form ready for the press. We moved at a turtle's pace by today's standards, but that first issue consisted of only one page with "Introductory Issue" in big bold type at the top beneath "Numismatic News." Besides the copy I wrote, we added a form for ordering advertising in one bottom corner and a form for ordering a subscription – $2 for one year – in the opposite corner. We printed 600 copies and mailed 500 of them to the various names and addresses I had gathered. The issue was dated October 13, 1952, the day it was mailed.

The two issues that followed – November and December 1952 – were four pages each, and all the ads in them were published free and there were no subscription charges. The first two issues of 1953 were six pages each, and all advertising and subscriptions were now paid. By the December 1953 issue, *Numismatic News* had grown to 10 pages.

I don't have those early records anymore, but I recall completing a simple profit and loss statement monthly on a cash basis. At some point – I believe in early 1954 – I broke even after having invested $1,342. Of course, I did not draw a salary from the project nor did I pay Mother for her help, which was invaluable to me. She was my secretary and proofreader. She hand addressed those first few issues and checked my copy and correspondence for spelling and grammar. She also tolerated paper stacked on her dining-room table and my long hours as I continued to work full time in the construction business while publishing turned into another full-time job. Through it all, she was her usual calm, patient self.

Dad, on the other hand, was a worrier. "You're going to go broke," he told me on more than one occasion. He would go down to the post office and pick up the mail for me every day. He would then come out to wherever I was working on a construction project and tell me how many pieces

were in the day's mail. If the day's mail volume was low, he would tell me, "You better watch this." But on those days when there was more, he would proudly announce the total to me.

The January 1954 *Numismatic News* grew to 12 pages, and it was time to get the business out of the house. Lee Johnson was just starting out in the insurance business, and we agreed to share a Main Street office and a secretary. We hired Lila Aanstad at $35 a week. I paid Lila's wages; Lee paid the office rent. Later that same year, I hired another office worker, Alice Wolberg.

The issues kept getting bigger, and Firman Cooper's press could not handle them anymore. So I contracted with the Waupaca Publishing Company for printing. By the end of 1955, we were publishing 40 pages a month, and paid subscribers totaled 4,100. One of the things that boosted ad sales at this time was the release of the 1955-P half dollar. It was minted in 1955 but was not released until July 1956. Many collectors needed one to keep their sets complete, and the demand resulted in lots of ads in *Numismatic News*. As a result, dealers began to realize the paper was a valuable medium for increasing their sales.

We also outgrew the little back room that we occupied in the office we shared with Lee. So in late 1956, we moved across the street to another Main Street building. I knew, however, that this move would be only temporary, and I knew that I was going to have to give up one of my two full-time jobs. On a typical day during this time, I would be at my construction job by 7 a.m. If I was working nearby, I would check in with Lila and Alice over the lunch hour. It was back to

The Numismatic News building at the corner of Washington and Water streets in Iola, under construction and shortly after its completion in the fall of 1957.

As our products and staff expanded, our building grew, too, with a couple of additions in the early 1960s.

construction in the afternoon. After a full day of construction work, I would become a publisher in the evening, working either at home, in the office, or in the composing room of the *Iola Herald*.

By this time, I was traveling a lot, too, to coin-club meetings in the area and throughout Wisconsin and to coin shows in the Upper Midwest. In 1955, I boarded an airplane for the first time and flew to Detroit for a show. Later that year, I flew to San Diego, and after that, flying became a common mode of transportation for me. In August 1956, I attended my first American Numismatic Association convention, in Chicago.

About the time we moved the office, I started winding down the construction business. People would approach me with new jobs, but I would have to explain to them that I was phasing myself out of construction. One of my last construction jobs was to build a new office for *Numismatic News* at the corner of Washington and Water streets in Iola. I started in spring 1957, as soon as the frost was out of the ground. I did not lay the brick for the building, but I did all the other work.

The 1,600-square-foot building was completed the following September. It had a parking lot and a ramp for loading and unloading papers. It also had a scale for weighing papers to be mailed. I bought an Addressograph for addressing papers to individual subscribers and a keyboard Graphotype that embossed a plate with the names and addresses for use in the Addressograph. I also bought new filing cabinets for keeping subscriber records by state and city. (There were no ZIP codes yet.)

We thought we were in hog heaven.

After completing the Water Street building, I laid down the hammer and became a publisher full time.

In 1956, I built the classroom wing at the Methodist church in Iola, and in 1957, I built two more houses – one for Fred Gross on East Ellefson Street in Iola and one for Carl Nygaard on County Highway G. I am quite sure I built one last house in 1958 – the projects blur in my memory over time – but when I completed the new office, I essentially laid down the hammer and became a publisher full time. I had to choose between the two professions, and I made a good choice. But I have always wondered if I would have been just as good as a contractor.

Joining us in the new office in 1957 was Art Christoph, the first advertising manager and first numismatist I hired. Art lived in Milwaukee. I met him on the coin-show circuit, and we became friends. Art loved to drive, and I loved to ride. We traveled to shows together even before he joined the staff. Numismatic organizations started offering *Numismatic News* free tables at their shows, and Art and I would drive to events in Milwaukee, Chicago, Minneapolis, and various other destinations.

Although Lila Aanstad and Alice Wolberg left the paper to raise their families, my clerical staff now numbered five employees in the new building. We had to move the printing of *Numismatic News* again, this time to Worzalla Publishing Company in Stevens Point. There was yet another change in printer in 1961, to the presses of the *Shawano Evening Leader* newspaper in Shawano, Wisconsin, where *Numismatic News* is still printed today.

Several other key hires followed Art in the late 1950s and early '60s. In 1959, I hired Tom Fruit as the first editor of *Numismatic News*. Tom had been curator of the numismatic collection at the Neuville Public Museum in Green Bay. In late 1960, Ed Rochette was added to the editorial staff, and he was later promoted to editor when Tom resigned. Ed was a native of Worcester, Massachusetts, but had been editing a trade magazine published in St. Louis. Starting in 1954, I regularly published a cartoon written and drawn by Ed called "The Numismapest" and paid him $5 a cartoon for the effort. He was "guest editor" for a special section of our August 1960 issue for the American Numismatic Association convention in Boston that year.

On the business side, Bob Strand joined us as an accountant in June 1961. Bob was a former Iola High School business teacher and a fellow coin collector. Harry Becker, then the current business teacher at the high school, followed in 1963 as circulation manager.

Also in 1963, Ed hired Cliff Mishler for the editorial staff of *Numismatic News*. Little did I know at the time how important this young coin, token, and medal collector from Vandalia, Michigan, would become to the organization.

The growth in staff – Harry's hiring brought us to 20 employees – prompted an addition to the office building and reflected the growth in the business. In 1959, we had acquired the *Flying Eaglet*, a numismatic magazine published by Frank Spadone of East Orange, New Jersey. With the January 1960 issue, we changed its name to *Coins* and made it a newsstand publication.

That is when "Krause Publications" came into being. Now that we had two publications, I started to use the Krause Publications name and initials KP to identify our overall operations. We used the individual magazine names for matters pertaining directly to them. The Krause Publications name was incorporated in 1964.

Everything seemed to be going fine until somebody else noticed what was happening. J. Oliver Amos, publisher of the *Sidney Daily News* in Sidney, Ohio, wanted to enter the numismatic publishing field, too. He visited me in Iola one day in 1960 and offered me $50,000 for *Numismatic News* and a job in Sidney. That was a fair offer,

but I had no intention of leaving Iola. So the answer was no. Amos Press went on to launch *Coin World*, a weekly tabloid publication similar in style to *Numismatic News*, and the two have been competitors ever since.

Krause Publications, however, went on to break new ground in other numismatic publishing niches and other hobby fields in general. But not before we survived the roughest times I ever experienced in the business world.

Chapter 10

Survival

Through the columns of a periodical or a letter to a subscriber, I never blamed the U.S. Postal Service for slow or non-delivery of a product. The postal service had a delivery system that worked; it was its customers that caused the problems. I learned early on in the publishing business that if we delivered our product and mailing labels to the printer on time, we got the best possible delivery to subscribers.

Into the 1990s, that meant delivering actual-size photographic negatives of finished pages to the printer, who then made printing plates from the negatives. The plate went on the press and transferred the images and text on the pages to the paper. Today, an electronic file of the finished pages is sent to the printer over a dedicated communications line.

To produce a product at the lowest possible cost, a printer has to have enough business to keep its presses running. That results in some tight scheduling. If our product was scheduled to go on the press at 3 a.m. but we did not deliver our negatives on time, the printer had to fill in with something else and our job might get delayed until, say, 10:45 a.m. the next day. That would mean our product would not make the 5:30 p.m. mailing time on the day it was supposed to be printed. It might not go out until 3:30 p.m. the next day. That would mean the mail truck traveled half-empty to the bulk-mail center in Chicago on the day our product was supposed to be mailed but was overloaded on the day it actually did mail. Once in Chicago, the product missed its scheduled sorting time and outbound truck on the previous day, so now it must wait for a time to be sorted and shipped. The result of all this is that a subscriber in Macon, Georgia, might get his copy of *Numismatic News* on Monday afternoon instead of Saturday morning.

At Krause Publications, we adopted the motto "On Time All the Time," which served us well for many years. In the 1960s, we even started our own graphics shop as a subsidiary of Krause

Publications. It was called Iola Graphics and was located at 315 Depot Street in Iola.

We tried to control the things we could control – meeting our internal deadlines and delivering our product to the printer on time so the printing and mailing schedules would be met. One of the challenges in business, however, is dealing with the things you can not control.

The mid-1960s saw the coin hobby decline greatly. There were a number of reasons for it. In the late 1950s and early '60s, there was a great emphasis in the coin market on buying rolls and proof sets as investments. Some knew how to do that; others did not. Thus, the market produced a lot of accumulators who never turned into true collectors.

Also, 1964 was the last year silver coins were struck for circulation in the United States. Until 1961, the government controlled the price of silver. After that, it allowed the free market to set the price, and it rose to the point where it cost the government more than 25 cents to produce a quarter. The Coinage Act of 1965 eliminated the 90-percent silver composition of circulating coins in favor of base metals for dimes and quarters, and 40-percent silver in half dollars.

The government as well as profiteers started hoarding the old coins and selling them for their silver content. The result was a coin shortage as the old coins were withdrawn from circulation faster than the U.S. Mint could replace them with new coins. The Mint blamed coin collectors for the shortage, but the relative small holdings of true collectors contributed little to the coin shortage.

All of a sudden, there was a steep drop

This photo must have been taken for some type of promotional item in the 1960s. I normally did not wear a tie to the office or have coins spread out on my desk.

in the number of ads and subscribers coming in to *Numismatic News*. We had expanded our staff in the early 1960s and had invested in new production equipment at Iola Graphics and new business machines. Now the revenue coming in could not support it all.

I got more bad news in summer 1966 when Ed Rochette came to me and said he was leaving to become editor of *The Numismatist*, the official publication of the American Numismatic

One of my first collectible-vehicle purchases was this 1924 Ford Model T truck, which Neil and I restored. It's shown here ready for parade duty in the early 1960s. Lyle Kjer (in front of truck), Ed Rochette (behind the wheel), and Bob Strand (behind the truck) were Krause Publications employees at the time.

Graphic designer Doug Watson and I check some photos for an upcoming issue.

Association. With Ed's departure, I promoted Cliff Mishler to editor of *Numismatic News*, thus beginning Cliff's eventual rise to the No. 2 position in the company – executive vice president – and eventually president. Cliff became my right arm and confidant in managing the company through some critical times. The use of "Cliff and I" rather than "I" in company matters became the norm.

We then took a number of steps to try to survive as a company. Much of the equipment for Iola Graphics had been purchased on a monthly payment schedule, and the payments brought this subsidiary company to its knees. I established Iola Graphics with six senior employees, including me, as stockholders. I bought all the stock at face value, assumed all the debt, and merged the employees and equipment into Krause Publications. I then drove to Chicago, where the equipment note was held, and negotiated a four-month hiatus on the payments.

Numismatic News ad revenues got an important boost when the federal government passed legislation stating it would no longer redeem silver certificates for silver bullion after June 24, 1968. The certificates would continue to be legal tender like other U.S. paper money.

This looks like another set-up for some promotional literature. Seated and facing the camera from left are editorial staffers Cliff Mishler, Bob Poeschl, and Clem Bailey.

Redeeming a $1 silver certificate for a silver dollar or in volume for bags of silver bullion got you a little more than three-quarters of an ounce of silver. Silver was trading on the open market for more than $2 an ounce. Coin dealers, through ads in *Numismatic News*, offered a premium over face value for silver certificates. They would then redeem the paper for silver and sell the silver at a profit.

Starting in 1970, the fad of collecting silver art bars produced some more important ad revenue for *Numismatic News*. The bars were privately produced and contained an ounce of silver. They had some artistic rendition on them, whether it was just a simple greeting like "Happy Birthday" or the image of a person, place, or thing. My image even appeared on one issue. I don't think too many of them were made, but I still have one.

A secondary market developed for the bars, so *Numismatic News* got ads for new issues and old ones. We sold extra space just by suggesting that a picture of the bar accompany an ad. I spent quite a bit of time working in our advertising department during this period, so I and others in the company became quite knowledgeable about the various issues and could speak intelligently with advertisers about them.

I purchased one example of every bar issued and also bought some produced well before 1965. I believe I owned more than 450 examples at one point. The fad was nothing more than that. I eventually sold all of my bars, and I suspect they and a lot of others ended up in the melting pot. But the ad revenue they produced helped *Numismatic*

News and Krause Publications tremendously during some tough times.

Managing a publishing company through a depression caused by outside sources is a real challenge. It was one of the greatest learning experiences of my life. To keep a staff of employees, you have to pay them or they will look for other work, which is a terrible public image problem for a company. I was on the payroll, but there were times when I received only a bookkeeping entry as an IOU. I personally lived off my meager savings for a while. To acquire some cash, I sold my large-size paper-money collection for $15,000, which was a pretty good chunk of money in the 1960s. I loaned some of the proceeds to the company.

The late 1960s were not about expansion and growth at Krause Publications. They were about survival. But eventually we did survive, thanks to the events mentioned here, some belt tightening, and some loyal employees who stuck with me during the hard times. We hoped better times were ahead, and in the years that followed, we found out they were. In fact, they were some of the most exciting times in Krause Publications' history.

Chapter 11

Diversification

Despite the hardships of the 1960s, we did not think all was lost, and we were determined to survive somehow as a company. I say "we" because by this time Cliff Mishler and I were a team in managing the company. We came to two conclusions during the numismatic business depression of the '60s: First, the company had to diversify to survive. We could no longer rely on just one publishing field. Second, we had to get more deeply involved in world coins.

By the early '70s, business conditions had improved enough that we could pursue the first goal. We looked at a number of possibilities for diversification but finally settled on old cars. At the time, I was not as active in the car hobby as I had been in the coin hobby. But I had purchased a couple of collectible vehicles by then – a 1923 Ford Model T roadster and a 1924 Model T truck – and I had grown up with cars of the 1920s, '30s, and '40s, which were collectible by then.

Our decision to enter the automotive publishing field, however, was based on business considerations rather than my personal involvement. We thought the field offered an opening for another publisher, and we thought we could adapt the business and publishing systems we had set up in numismatics to an automotive publication. So in early 1971, we set forth to launch Krause Publications' first non-numismatic publication.

One of our first steps was to hire automotive hobbyist David Brownell, who was working for an advertising agency in Rhode Island, in spring 1971. We put Dave to work developing a pilot issue of what was to be called *Old Cars* in the same newsprint, tabloid format as *Numismatic News*. The following fall, we printed 93,000 copies of that pilot issue and took about 25,000 of them to the fall car show in Hershey, Pennsylvania. We stuffed the copies in shopping bags, and I stood at a busy crossroads for spectator traffic at the show and put a shopping bag with a pilot issue of *Old Cars* in the hands of everybody who did not refuse.

We started monthly publication of *Old Cars* in October 1971, and a year later, we returned to Hershey with a 104-page first-anniversary issue. *Old Cars* is still going strong today as a weekly. Although it was our first venture into a non-numismatic field, we knew what it took to launch a successful publication – a large base of subscribers. We knew the rudiments of getting such a base.

At the same time we were launching *Old Cars*, we were laying the groundwork for our expansion into world coins. We covered world coins to some extent in *Numismatic News* and *Coins*, but Cliff and I felt there was a need for a standard reference for world-coin collectors – something comparable to the Whitman Publishing Company's *A Guide Book of United States Coins* ("Red Book"). Through Cliff's efforts, we started publishing values for coins of selected countries in *Coin Prices*, a newsstand publication that we launched in the 1960s. *Coin Prices* was developed by simply reworking the U.S. coin-value section in *Numismatic News*. It was a relatively inexpensive product that proved successful and helped us survive the business challenges of the '60s.

The concept was that we would publish one or two countries at a time in *Coin Prices* and eventually we would have enough material to start our Red Book of world coins. But Cliff came to me one day and advised me that the pace and the time he could devote to it were not going to cut it. So I took over the project and commandeered the help of my secretary, Marian Moe.

Our goal was to cover coins issued from 1801 to date. I first took the copy Cliff had gathered so far and dummied it into working galleys. I then went down the list of coin-issuing countries that Cliff had compiled and tried to fill in the gaps in our coverage. I enlisted the help of other references covering those countries and the help of many collectors, who responded to my inquiries with listings and values. There were also field trips with a photographer to take pictures of coins for the book. One time Fred Baerwald and I went to California and spent 14 hours a day photographing 200 coins an hour.

It took the better part of two years to complete. In fact, we had to go back and reset some of the first countries we worked on because the values were out of date. But finally in March 1972, we introduced the first edition of the *Standard Catalog of World Coins*. It listed more than 30,000 coins from 261 countries and contained more than 15,000 original photographs.

From the time it was conceived until the time it hit the market, the *Standard Catalog of World Coins* was meant to solve Krause Publications' financial crises, and it worked. We quickly went through our first printing of 10,000 and then a second printing of another 10,000 and then a third printing of a like amount. As sales started to slow down, we knew we had to produce a new edition.

The first *Standard Catalog* included a self-mailing form that collectors could use to submit additions, corrections, or other revisions. We knew the *Standard Catalog*'s first edition would have its share of errors and omissions. The number of responses, however, was unbelievable – more than 20,000 from the approximately 30,000 copies printed. Each response probably presented

20 listings of additions and changes, and some included notes on additional sheets of paper.

Cliff and Marian took on the monumental task of organizing all of this feedback for inclusion in a second edition. First, they sorted the responses alphabetically. For example, if a response had information on Belgium, France, and Switzerland, it went in the "B" file first. Once the revisions for Belgium were complete, the response then went into the "F" file and so on.

We had galleys of type for the first edition in big green-covered four-ring binders. Cliff made the revisions by hand on the galleys, which were then sent to various country specialists for review. When returned to us, the revised galleys were then sent to the typesetting department. It took us until November 1973 to release a second edition of the *Standard Catalog of World Coins*. The number of pages grew to 864, and the number of countries listed grew to 273.

By the fourth edition, we contracted with R.R. Donnelley & Sons Company, based in Chicago, for printing of the *Standard Catalog*. Donnelley is a major printer of big-city phone books and the *Official Airline Guide*, which are similar in physical format to the *Standard Catalog*. Thus, some in the coin hobby nicknamed the *Standard Catalog* the "Phone Book." That moniker is not quite as flattering as the "Red Book," but as long as dealers and collectors kept buying the book, we did not care what they called it.

Also with that fourth edition, Colin R. Bruce II joined us in Iola as the book's full-time editor. Colin contributed to the book's first three editions. His knowledge of how world coins are produced and distributed and how different languages are used on coins and paper money is second to none. Hand him any coin – from medieval to modern – and he can decipher its country or province of origin and denomination. He worked all hours of the night and weekends – just a fabulous guy. We paid him for his efforts, but I think he would have done it for room and board.

In addition to its positive impact on Krause Publications' bottom line, the *Standard Catalog* opened the doors to the hobby book publishing world for us. In 1973, I traveled to Europe to meet Ernst Battenberg and Albert Pick. Albert was the author of the book *World Paper Money*, and Ernst was its publisher. I wanted to get the *Standard Catalog* distributed in Europe, and Ernst wanted to make a name for himself as a publisher in America. He called me the "locomotive" to help him accomplish that goal.

Ernst became the European distributor of the *Standard Catalog*, and Krause Publications reached an agreement with Ernst to publish an English-language version of *World Paper Money*. Eventually I acquired the rights to publish Pick's *Standard Catalog of World Paper Money*, as it is known today. Ernst did not want to give up rights to the book covering general issues of paper money, but he did not object to our publishing a Standard Catalog of specialized paper money. So we proceeded with a book on the specialized issues. In due course, I was able to acquire the rights to the general-issue German catalog and used that as the basis for creating a *Standard Catalog of World Paper Money*, General Issues.

Although I am no longer associated with Krause Publications, I am proud of the *Standard Catalog*'s legacy. It not only brought the company back from the brink of bankruptcy, it created a whole new department that in 2002 accounted for 40 percent of the company's revenue. The *Standard Catalog of World Coins* has evolved into a multivolume series covering coins as far back as the 17th century. The Standard Catalog concept has also been extended to other hobbies, such as comic books, baseball cards, and records. Another offshoot of the *Standard Catalog of World Coins* was the launch of *World Coin News*, a monthly periodical focusing on non-U.S. issues.

By 1980, Krause Publications was back on firm financial ground, thanks to a better business environment, the perseverance of those on our staff, and the success of our new ventures. The following decade brought even more expansion and diversification, which led us to claim the title "World's Largest Hobby Publisher." But the decade also brought some important decisions on my future and the company's future.

Chapter 12

More Diversification

It seemed that we never had enough space to operate despite a couple of additions to the original 1,600-square-foot Krause Publications office built in 1957. We added another 2,400 square feet to the building in 1960 and then another 1,700 square feet in 1964. That space served us until the mid-1970s, when we emerged from the setback of 1965 with an expanded product line and staff.

Much thought went into how to relieve our space crunch. Some property adjacent to our building was available, but it was not large enough. We looked at a number of other options and finally decided to purchase 47 acres on the eastern edge of the village on State Highway 161, or State Street. We purchased it from a farmer named Howard Jenson, who had it planted in corn. Ground was broken in June 1975, and the new 20,000-square-foot building was completed in December. In the dead of winter, the staff loaded our equipment into pickup trucks and moved our operations to the new building.

A dedication celebration followed in the summer of 1976. My mother helped me cut the ribbon, officially opening our new office.

While we were waiting for the new building to be completed, the staff had to work in the cramped quarters of the old building. When they would complain about it, Cliff and I would tell them, "It'll be better when we get into the new building." That became a running joke that went on for years.

The 1980s and '90s saw Krause Publications expand into many other fields on our way to becoming the world's largest hobby publisher. Each time we expanded our product line and staff, the existing building became cramped. We added on to the State Street building five times during this period. Each time, while waiting for the addition to be completed, somebody would comment, "It'll be better when we get into the new building."

Fortunately, though, the acreage we purchased gave us plenty of room for expansion.

I address the crowd at the dedication of Krause Publications'
new State Street building in the summer of 1976.

The move to a spot where we could expand was a giant step forward and a great bit of foresight. We had plenty of parking at the new building, nicely landscaped grounds, a nice breakroom, and a building that was adaptable to modern publishing equipment, such as computers, which started to play an increasing role in our operations in the 1980s.

The last half of the '70s saw the company grow through acquisitions and start-ups, along with the addition of many new book titles. We launched a periodical covering the world-coin field, *World Coin News*, as an offshoot of the success of the *Standard Catalog of World Coins*. We also acquired *Bank Note Reporter*, a periodical for paper-money collectors.

In the 1980s, Krause Publications expanded into many hobby fields I never would have imagined when I launched *Numismatic News* in 1952. Among them were comic books, records, toys, firearms, and baseball cards. That last one turned out to be the biggest of them all and generated great profits for the company, but it would not have happened if Cliff and I had not relented to the persistence of two employees – Bob Lemke and Doug Watson.

Bob joined the company in 1974 as an editorial staffer for *Numismatic News*. With a brief stop on the *Old Cars* staff, he worked his way up the ranks in the numismatic division to assist Cliff in managing that department while Cliff was executive vice president of the company but still publisher of the division. Doug originally joined us in 1964 as a graphic designer. He left for a while several years later but then returned in the mid-70s as production manager.

Doug and Bob had collected baseball cards as youths – Doug in the late 1940s and Bob in the late '50s. Their respective interests in baseball cards and other sports memorabilia were rekindled in their adult years. There were some periodicals serving the field, but they were largely mom-and-pop operations that were extensions of individual hobby interests rather than the work of professional publishing companies. The products reflected this; publishing frequencies and deadlines, for example, were oftentimes adhered to loosely.

Doug and Bob thought the field presented a great opportunity for a professionally produced magazine. They proposed an initial one-shot newsstand product to be called *Baseball Cards*. Cliff and I were not convinced. We just did not think baseball-card collecting offered enough depth to support the type of magazine we needed to produce to be profitable. Cliff thought it was similar to the beer-can collecting hobby.

Doug and Bob kept asking, and Cliff and I kept saying no. But they kept asking, so finally we relented. I told Cliff one day that I did not think the project would be successful, but it would not cost that much and might be a good lesson for Doug and Bob on launching a new product.

As for our impressions of the baseball-card collecting field and our reluctance to approve the project, I am not too proud to admit today that Cliff was wrong. And I guess I was, too. A total of 100,000 copies of a 100-page issue of *Baseball Cards* magazine, including 38 pages of display advertising, hit the newsstands in spring 1981. They sold so fast that some retailers reordered, so we went back to the press and printed another 25,000 copies. Advertisers enjoyed large sales from the large distribution. We increased the frequency of *Baseball Cards* each year following until it became a monthly magazine and was retitled *Sports Cards* to reflect its coverage of football and other sports. The title was discontinued some years ago, but the monthly sports-collecting magazine concept lives on at Krause Publications in the form of *Tuff Stuff*, part of a larger 1999 acquisition.

The success of *Baseball Cards* led to the acquisition of *Sports Collectors Digest* in the fall of 1981. SCD was one of those mom-and-pop operations in the sports publishing field of the day. John Stommen, a collector in Milan, Michigan, launched the periodical in 1973 as a family project. It came to Krause Publications with a biweekly frequency and a circulation of about 8,500. Circulation and page counts increased rapidly in the ensuing years, and frequency eventually was increased to weekly.

Krause Publications entered sports collecting just as the field was beginning a boom period, and the company benefited handsomely from it. It established another division in our company – sports, in addition to numismatics and automotive – and a number of new products, including a wide-ranging line of books. Among them was the

Standard Catalog of Baseball Cards, one of many extensions of the Standard Catalog concept into a non-numismatic field.

It also opened the door to acquisitions in other fields that previously we may have ignored. Pursuing those acquisitions allowed me to meet some interesting people and make some interesting deals along the way. In December 1982, we acquired *Comics Buyer's Guide* and hired Maggie and Don Thompson – a husband-and-wife team – to be editors. They were from Pennsylvania originally, but Don was working in the newspaper business in Cleveland at the time. I have met many avid and knowledgeable collectors in many different fields in my time, but none surpassed Maggie and Don. It seemed like they knew everybody in the field and everybody knew them. Unfortunately, we lost Don to a massive heart attack in 1994. Maggie, however, continued as a CBG editor until retiring in the fall of 2007.

In 1987, just as *Sports Collectors Digest* was creating great cash flow through subscription and advertising sales, I was contacted by Sue Golden and Michael Tenny of Columbia, Missouri, about acquiring a trader publication called *Gun List*. They had started the publication in March 1984 while they were still students at the University of Missouri, and it turned out they had a good idea that was successful. I purchased it for cash, with 51 percent going to pay off the investor who loaned them the money to start the publication and the rest going to Sue and Michael. I also had to include a prairie-dog hunt in Montana.

The deal required, too, that Sue and Michael come to Iola for six months and help with the transition. I had never structured a deal quite like that – prairie-dog hunt and all – but it was a sweetheart deal for both parties. *Gun List* went on to become another profit-maker for us in the field of antique and other collectible firearms.

In a way, the *Gun List* acquisition was a throwback to the company's roots. It was similar in format to *Shotgun News*, which was my inspiration for the founding of *Numismatic News*. Krause Publications also had the opportunity to acquire *Shotgun News* when its founding owner died and his surviving family looked for a buyer. We offered $8 million for it but could not get the deal done. As I recall, there were several strong strings tied to it that we did not like.

Another significant move of the late 1980s occurred behind the scenes when we upgraded our IBM System 3 business computer to a more current AS/400. It was not easy to move all of the data from one to the other; it was like trying to learn a foreign language overnight. Then a hired expert pushed the wrong button one day and 75 percent of our data went down the well with no way to recover it. At one time, we had eight outside programmers working on it but never did recover some data, such as the performance of past direct-mail marketing programs.

I celebrated my 62nd birthday in December 1985. The company was going great, but I had determined that I wanted to be clear of the president's role by the time I was 68. So now it was time to get to work on that goal.

Chapter 13

My Four Retirements

To address the future of Krause Publications after Chet Krause, I had to look at two areas – management of the company and ownership of the company. As for the first, I and many others always thought Cliff Mishler would fill those shoes. As mentioned previously, I had considered Cliff and I a team in managing the company since the late 1960s. He was certainly capable and was certainly qualified to be president.

But I asked Cliff three times to become president, and each time he declined. He simply did not want the responsibility of being the No. 1 person in the company. After the third "no" from Cliff, my only alternative was to go "head hunting," as an executive search is commonly called. So I called a man I knew who was in the head-hunting business and engaged him to find a new president for Krause Publications. A head hunter also knows the other side of the business

– that is, who is looking for a position or might be persuaded to do so. The process is more involved than simply finding a couple of candidates to interview, but in the end, that is the result.

Our choice was Don Nicolay, who was living in suburban Chicago and was ad manager of Farm Progress Companies Inc., which published farm periodicals and books and sponsored an agricultural trade show. Don became president on January 1, 1987. Cliff remained as executive vice president. I took the title of chief executive officer and shadowed Don during his first year at the company.

With Don in place, I could turn my attention to the second aspect of Krause Publications' future – ownership of the company. Previously I had approached Cliff about becoming majority owner, and again Cliff declined. Upon his hiring, Don was awarded equity in the company, and he had an option for future majority ownership, too. Another option, of course, was to simply sell to another company. I had received a number of offers over the years, including a viable one from a publisher in Virginia late in 1986. But I was fearful that selling out to a company in another locale would eventually be the end of Krause Publications in Iola. At the time, we employed about 200 people. That was the biggest the company had ever been, but it was still small enough to be absorbed by another company in another location.

Finally, I discovered an Employee Stock Ownership Plan. An ESOP, as it is commonly known, would allow me to sell my stock to a trust created by the company. Each employee of Krause Publications would have an account in the trust, and each year a certain amount of company stock would be allocated to each of these individual accounts. The per-share value of the stock would be determined annually by an independent appraisal company. When an employee left the company, he or she would be given the cash value of their individual account based on the current appraisal.

The advantage to employees was that it gave each of them a financial stake in the company's performance. If the company did well, the value of their ESOP accounts reflected that. It had the potential to pay off far greater than the conventional pension plan that it replaced. The advantage to me was that it allowed me to liquidate my equity in the company but also keep ownership and management of the company local. There were also tax advantages to an ESOP for the company and me personally.

We announced the establishment of an ESOP to Krause Publications employees on October 3, 1988. At first, I sold 30 percent of my stock to the ESOP. But over the next 10 years, Krause Publications became 100-percent ESOP owned.

With Don's hiring and the ESOP in place, I thought I had provided for Krause Publications' future. I kept a desk in the building but coasted from 1988 into 1990. One of the highlights of my day was sharing conversation with the staff over a cup of coffee in the breakroom.

But my coasting ended one Saturday morning in June 1990 when Don came to me and told me he was leaving. The company continued to expand during the three and a half years Don was with us. Notable among the acquisitions of that time were a couple of hunting magazines. They were added to in 1991 and 1992, thus creating an outdoors division at Krause Publications. The value of the company's stock rose markedly during this time, as did the value of the stock Don owned. His resignation allowed him to cash out his stock. Also, Don had wanted very much to buy Krause Publications and remarket it, but the ESOP built a hurdle to such a move.

So I was back to looking for a president again. As soon as Don told me his intentions, I contacted Cliff to let him know so we could mull it over the rest of the weekend and talk about it the following Monday. After the weekend, I again asked Cliff if he would take the job. He again said no, but it was not as emphatic as the previous "no" answers. We decided to pursue another executive search, but this time Cliff was in charge of it. Cliff further agreed that if we could not find the right person, he would take the job. I was satisfied with that plan, except that I had to become president of the company again for the final six months of 1990.

Our head hunter again produced two candidates. As it turned out, I knew one and Cliff knew the other. Both were good candidates, but Cliff and I agreed that both needed a few more years of experience for the job. So Cliff made good on his promise to take the job if we could not find another qualified candidate.

The 1990s were heady times for Krause Publications. Under the leadership of Cliff, Roger, and Giles, the company continued to grow rapidly.

By this time, it was already early November, and Cliff was to officially become president on January 1, 1991. So I decided to wait until our annual company Christmas party on the second Saturday in December at the Stevens Point Holiday Inn to make the announcement. When I went to the microphone to give my annual remarks, I told the approximately 350 employees and spouses in attendance that Krause Publications would have a new president on January 1 and that he was with us that night. Of course, in a crowd that size, it was possible that a stranger had slipped in undetected.

When Cliff's name was announced, a standing ovation for him followed and lasted more than the usual moment or two. In fact, I had trouble regaining the crowd's attention. When I finally did, I turned to Sally Mishler, Cliff's wife, and added, "At no increase in salary." That got a big laugh.

With Cliff's promotion to president, we promoted Roger Case to vice president-publishing and, three years later, executive vice president. Roger joined us in March 1988 as publisher of the numismatic division after 15 years in the daily newspaper business in his home state of Montana. We also had the benefit of an excellent financial person on staff in the form of Giles Heuer. Giles, who had previously worked with Don Nicolay, joined Krause Publications in February 1988 as vice president-finance.

The 1990s were heady times for Krause Publications. Under the leadership of Cliff, Roger, and Giles, the company continued to grow rapidly. The book division alone doubled in size in 1996 with three major acquisitions, including DBI Books of suburban Chicago. In April 1999, we acquired Landmark Specialty Publications, which included the venerable *Antique Trader* magazine, a line of regional antiques publications, *Tuff Stuff* magazine for sports collectors, and a line of antiques books. At $19.5 million, it was the largest acquisition the company ever completed.

As the company grew, ESOP participants saw their account values grow proportionately.

Although Cliff finally agreed to take the job of president in late 1990, he always considered it a transitional role. Part of that role was to groom his successor, who turned out to be Roger Case. On January 1, 2000, Roger became president of Krause Publications and Cliff took the title of chairman of the board. Throughout the 1990s and into 2002, I continued in an emeritus role with the company and continued to enjoy daily conversation and coffee with the staff.

In 2002, the Krause Publications board of directors, and ESOP trustees, decided to sell the company to F+W Publications – another specialty publisher, based in Cincinnati – and dissolve the ESOP. The announcement was made in June of that year. My association with

the company ended completely the following October as it moved on to new ownership and new management.

As I look back on it, I retired of sorts four times. The first was when Don Nicolay joined Krause Publications on January 1, 1987. The second was when Cliff was named president on January 1, 1991. The third time occurred in 1998 when I received the last check in payment for my company stock. That occasion was marked with an official retirement luncheon attended by all of our employees plus U.S. Representative Tom Petri and a representative from U.S. Senator Russ Feingold's office. My fourth "retirement," of course, occurred in October 2002 as Krause Publications celebrated its 50th anniversary.

Although it took me longer than I had planned, I eventually was able to retire from the business that had been my life since 1952.

Chapter 14

The Holy Land

One of the perks I enjoyed from Krause Publications' success was the ability to travel – not only our nation but the world. When I say that, I disregard my tour of Europe on Uncle Sam's tab during World War II. My postwar travels as a private citizen were much more enjoyable. I got to see some of the most famous sites in the world, the food and lodging were much better, and I did not have to fix Army trucks in the bitter cold.

My travels included three trips to the Holy Land – in 1966, 1969, and 1973. To document how the initial one came about, I first have to explain who Cale Jarvis was.

Cale was Canadian, born in British Columbia and schooled as an electrical engineer. I do not know, however, if he ever pursued that profession as a civilian. I first met him at a Florida United Numismatists convention. I believe it was around 1963, when we launched *Canada Coin News*.

Cale was an interesting character with a colorful background. He was a captain in the Canadian army during World War II. The Canadians served under the British and General Bernard Montgomery in northern Europe. After the war, Cale was transferred to an inspector general's department and was assigned to gather excess petroleum products in North Africa that had been left behind after the early war action there. The assignment went smoothly until he ran afoul of an Arab who had claimed the abandoned oil as his own and took Cale to task for interfering with his supply source. Cale was alone in defending himself, and a fighter plane had to be sent to fly him back to safety.

His post-service life found him in charge of two or three drilling rigs for oil in northern Canada. One day his Toronto financiers offered him stock in these wildcat oil ventures and enough money to supply food for his crew and gasoline for the engines that drove the rigs. Eventually, Cale sold his stock and moved to Toronto, where he became a gentleman about town and dabbled in the futures market. He also wrote a numismatic column for *The Globe and Mail* newspaper in Toronto. I do not know how he originally became interested in coin collecting.

When Krause Publications launched *Canada Coin News*, we envisioned it as a counterpart to *Numismatic News* north of the border. I hired Cale as editor, but we ran into delivery and other logistical problems trying to publish a Canadian periodical in the United States. After just a few issues, we had to abandon the idea, but I did not want to just stop publishing it. So one day I flew to Toronto and met Cale at his small office at 62 Richmond Street West and offered *Canada Coin News* to him. He was reluctant at first to become a publisher, but eventually he took the periodical and did a great job with it. Years later he sold it to another publisher, and *Canadian Coin News*, as it is known today, is still being published.

Indicative of his colorful background, Cale was a resourceful fellow, and that resourcefulness led to a business relationship with Robert Weber. Bob came to the United States in the 1960s to head sales of Israeli coins for the Israel Government Coins & Medals Corporation. Bob did a great job founding the American Israel Numismatic Association, which subsequently formed branch clubs in many major U.S. cities. I attended some AINA meetings, and it was a great club.

Bob also set up sales outlets through American banks but was unable to get into any of the 13 chartered banks of Canada. Resourceful

Cale Jarvis and I on one of our many tours together.

Cale went to work and called Bob one day to tell him that he had broken the ice for him. As Cale related, Bob was jubilant on the phone but then all of a sudden the conversation fell silent. "What is this going to cost me?" Bob finally asked. The two apparently just had a verbal agreement and had never talked about compensation. Cale responded, "A free tour of Israel for six people."

We had to walk a short distance on my first visit to the Western Wall because our Arab cab driver was not allowed to approach the site.

Cale and I on the first of my three visits to the Masada.

Bob was able to arrange the tour through the Israel Tourist Bureau, and it was a wonderful one at that. Besides Cale and me, there were Dick Yeoman of the Whitman Publishing Company; Lee Hewitt, publisher of *The Numismatic Scrapbook Magazine*; J. Oliver Amos, publisher of *Coin World*; and Russ Rulau, *World Coins* editor.

Today, many people get all excited about the added security measures at airports. But they are nothing compared to the Israeli airports as far back as the 1960s. A baggage search was mandatory, and instead of a pat-down or a scan with a metal detector, passengers were subjected to a body search. That meant you undressed. On one of our trips, a friend of mine did not like that very much and was quite embarrassed.

Bob could not arrange for all six to travel at the same time, so we were broken up into three separate tours of two. Cale and I were paired off. We traveled by limo with a tourist emblem – two men carrying a bunch of grapes on a pole laid across their shoulders – painted on the door. The driver's girlfriend accompanied us part of the time and showed up at breakfast one morning. Cale was very unhappy about that. He thought it was quite improper for the driver to bring his night's partner to breakfast, and he told the driver so.

My first trip to Israel produced several revelations for me. "Kibbutz," which refers to the country's collective farms, was a new word for me. They raised some good crops on these farms, but the farmers in the occupied territories had to be guards and soldiers, too.

For others, being in the army was like an 8-to-5 job. Many soldiers were billeted with their families, and many rode buses to work, which were a common form of transportation. It was not unusual to see male or female soldiers riding a bus to work and carrying a gun – not a long gun or a pistol but a submachine gun. I never asked if the guns were loaded, but I think the response would have been "yes."

I was surprised when I saw olive trees for the first time. These trees are soldiers of time, too, fighting for every drop of moisture against dust storms and soil that is 75-percent rock and 25-percent earth. When an old tree is harvested, its roots are stacked up to dry. Every cut is carefully calculated to get the most from every branch and root.

I have often heard the saying "When the good Lord built this world, he threw one handful of rocks on Israel and the other on the rest of the world." That may not be true, but the few cobblestones I used to help pick off our farm fields as a youth were a song compared to what I saw in Israel. In central Wisconsin, we bury rocks to get them out of our way. If you tried that in Israel, you would not be able to find enough soil to cover the hole.

There was a big tourist market for olive wood statues in Israel. I bought a Nativity set with 10-inch-high figures for my mother. I believe it cost nearly a thousand dollars. I still have it.

In Nazareth, we saw the Church of the Nativity, which is built over a cave that tradition says was Christ's birthplace. In Jerusalem, Cale and I passed through the Mandelbaum Gate into the Jordanian side of the city. To do so, we each had to have a certificate of religion. That meant finding a Catholic church for Cale and, because I am Methodist, a Protestant church for me.

I believe we were in Tel Aviv at the time, and Cale quickly found a Catholic school. The priest in charge was a monsignor, and his chief assistant was a brother from Washington, D.C. As visitors, we were offered wine. Cale fought alcoholism during his life and was not drinking at the time, so he declined. The brother had only one glass, but the monsignor and I imbibed a bit heavier.

We explained to them why we were there, and at one point, the good brother left the room and came back with certificates of religion for Cale and me. As the monsignor signed Cale's, he looked at me and said, "What about you?" I told him I was Methodist, to which he replied, "If you don't care, I don't." He then proceeded to sign a certificate for me and make a Catholic out of me. Cale told that story until the day he died, and I repeated it during a eulogy at Cale's funeral.

After crossing into the Jordanian side of Jerusalem through the Mandelbaum Gate, we asked a cab driver to take us to the Western Wall. He said he could not do that because it was forbidden for an Arab to go to the wall, but he said he could take us a short distance from the wall and we could walk from there. At the time, what is now open ground in front of the wall was filled with what looked like low-income housing but was probably the home of some respectable Jordanians.

Upon dropping us off, our cab driver told us to walk straight ahead and then turn right, and we would be at the wall. Cale and I were the only two tourists there. We each had our picture taken with our backs to the wall, which would indicate that we were not Jewish. On my later trips to the site, the housing in front of the wall was gone, and Jews and other tourists alike could approach the wall with fewer restrictions.

In Jerusalem, we also saw the Dome of the Rock, Al Aksa mosque, the Stations of the Cross, the site of the Last Supper, and the garden of Gethsemane. As our limo driver left Jerusalem for the Jordan River and finally Amman, Jordan, we passed the home of Mary Magdalene.

We also passed some internment camps where Arabs who had fled Israel were housed. Today, more than 40 years later, I often think about those camps. Probably few of the people who lived there in 1966 are alive

I scan the Negev Desert in Israel while standing next to a British-made vehicle with some type of official status.

today. Thus, the current generations still housed there today have never known a home as their forefathers knew it. Is it a wonder, then, that today's generation can't negotiate a peace?

In Amman, we visited the Bank of Jordan and acquired sets of Jordanian coins and paper money. We then flew to Beirut, Lebanon. At that time, Beirut was the financial capital of the Arab world. While there, we visited a friend of Cale's from the Bank of Nova Scotia.

Cale and I split up in Beirut, with Cale flying to Cairo, Egypt, and me flying to Athens, Greece, and then on to Turkey. From there, I flew to Austria, via Athens, and met up again with Cale in Vienna. Before our departure, Cale had arranged with Air France to exchange our return tickets so we could travel to several Mideast and European countries via that airline before heading back to the United States from Paris.

We had a great tour of the mint in Vienna.

They had every press ever used to strike coins there, and all of them were in working condition, although the older ones were no longer in service.

Our next stop was Karlsruhe, Germany, with a side trip to Zurich, Switzerland. We split up again; Cale headed for northern Germany to visit some of his old haunts from his army service, and I headed for Paris and then London. Cale joined me again in London, and we made the usual tourist stops along with visiting several coin shops. We stayed at a hotel and dined where Winston Churchill used to take afternoon tea. I dined there a day before Cale joined me, and at least five people were involved in service to my dinner. That was rather nice for an old farm boy from Iola. But I also caught hell at another place for putting my feet up on a chair. There was no tip for that guy.

After our stay in London, we doubled back to Paris via Brussels, Belgium. As I recall, we took a train from Brussels to Paris. While in

The Israeli mint was another stop on tour.

Paris, we stayed at the Hotel George V, a rather nice place. I lost a bet with Cale on how many tips it would take to get from the room to a cab. There were five – the maid, bellman, lobby greeter, a 6-foot, 6-inch guy who opened the revolving door, and the guy who hailed a cab that was already waiting for me. We took different flights back to New York City, but met again at a hotel there so Cale could claim some mementos I was carrying for him.

It was a long trip covering 12 countries and 13 mints in five weeks, all made possible by Cale's swap of return tickets with Air France. But what a fantastic trip it was!

After that 1966 trip, I returned in 1969 with my sister Mary Klug as my traveling companion and again in 1973 with my brother Ben.

On the 1969 trip, Mary and I were two of only eight Christians on the tour. The rest of our entourage consisted of more than 100 Jews, and they all made us feel welcome. But it seems like in every group, no matter its background, there is a matriarch with her henpecked husband in tow. This group was no exception.

Whenever we boarded a tour bus, Mrs. Matriarch positioned her and her husband in the first seats. She was always up front so she could direct traffic. One of the other women in our group, who had a heart condition, moved too slowly for Mrs. Matriarch, who referred to her as "one of those damn goys." I had never heard the term before, so I asked one of the other Jewish members of our group what "goy" meant. I learned it was an old Yiddish slur for a non-Jewish person.

Cale and I chat with Yitzhak Avni, director of coins and medals operations for the Israeli mint. Avni was a former secretary to David Ben Gurion, the first prime minister of Israel.

It was an embarrassment to the other Jewish members of our group, but the Christians just laughed about it.

On the 1973 journey, Ben and I took a side trip on a Sunday to the Monastery of St. Catherine at the foot of Mount Sinai. A tourist could stay overnight there and start climbing Mount Sinai at midnight so he could see the sunrise in the morning, but we did not make the climb.

Ben and I also visited the Israeli National Maritime Museum in Haifa, one of the best museums of its type in the world. I brought with me about 40 U.S. Mint naval medals to present to the curator. Upon entering the country, I thought Israeli customs might seize them. Each were wrapped and sealed, and I had to unwrap each one for the agent. He did not know what they were,

and I was not sure he would let me pass. Tourists generally take home gifts, not bring them with them.

My three trips to Israel allowed me to see the country from Elat on the Gulf of Aqaba and King Solomon's Mines in the south to Haifa and Akko in the north. I also visited the Golan Heights, taken by Israel in the Six-Day War in 1967, and the Mount of Beatitudes on the northwestern shore of the Sea of Galilee (Lake Tiberias). I walked the Stations of the Cross three times.

I also saw the Masada, on the southwestern shore of the Dead Sea, three times. In A.D. 71, Roman soldiers laid siege to about 1,200 Jews at this mountaintop fortress. The Jews held out for two years, fighting starvation, before the last of them committed suicide. Before they did, they are quoted as saying, "We shall die, but we shall die free men."

On my first two visits to the Masada, I walked up a ramp built one bucket of sand at a time by Roman slaves. Originally, it must have risen 200 to 300 feet. Over the years, wind and rain erosion decreased it to 20 to 25 feet from the top. Cale, our guide, and I walked up the ramp on my first visit.

On my second visit, a woman in our group named Ruth Moskowitz, from Detroit, wanted very much to go to the top but had to walk slowly. I had been there once before, so as the others went on ahead, Ruth and I walked up at her pace. After a brief tour at the top, we started our descent ahead of the others so we would not hold them up. Ruth was so grateful for my accompanying her that I was her friend for life after that. Whenever I saw her again, I got a big hug and was thanked all over again.

On my third visit to the Masada, we ascended on a cable car from the Dead Sea side. A lovely woman whose name has long departed my memory wanted very much to see the royal palace on the north end, which was several stories below the top surface. The stairway there was just a series of iron pipes – perfectly safe but scary looking. I had never been there before, but she followed my lead with a few rest stops along the way. When we got there, I took her picture against a blue wall that was part of the original castle. We then made the climb back up with a few rest stops along the way again. She, too, was very thankful.

It does not rain very often in Israel, but of course it had to rain the day we went to the Masada on this trip. On our return home, our bus could not make it all the way, so we were transported part way in Israeli army GMC 2 1/2-ton trucks, like the ones I worked on in World War II. When we got back to the bus, I used a stick to clean the stones and dirt off my shoes. I put the stones and dirt in a plastic bag and brought it all the way home with me.

That following Christmas and Hanukkah season, I added a little bit of water to the hard clay, removed the small stones, and put a little bit of the clay in some 2-by-2 plastic envelopes. I then sent an envelope to each of the tour members as a memento of our rainy trip to the Masada. I received many cards and letters of thanks afterward. Recently, I reread them, and they were just as meaningful as they were when I first received them.

We flew back to JFK International Airport in New York on El Al Airlines. Our plane parked at the end of a taxiway, and we and our baggage were bused to the terminal. I do not recall seeing them, but I suspect armed guards protected the plane all the time it was parked, serviced, and reloaded.

Collectively, Israelis are perhaps the most educated people in the world and, I believe, the most industrious. On my three trips to the country, the guides provided by the Israel Government Coins & Medals Corporation were Jews with what I would compare to a bachelor's degree in history. They knew more about Christianity than most Christians. Given a choice between a tour in the country offered by a Christian or Jewish guide, I would chose the latter.

Cale and I view the reputed birthplace of Jesus at the Church of the Nativity in Bethlehem.

The three trips to the Holy Land were great, with wonderful memories. If age were not against it, I would love to go again.

Chapter 15

— Australia, via Hong Kong —

My travels have twice taken me to Australia, thanks in part to a prominent coin dealer, friend, and good Krause Publications advertiser and distributor there named Bob Roberts. I first met Bob, who lives in Sydney, on one of his frequent trips to the United States for coin conventions and other related business. He even included Iola among his destinations a few times. From the United States, he would go to Great Britain – or the "U.K.," as he called it. He would then complete his trek around the globe and return to Sydney.

My first trip to Australia, in 1980, was at Bob's invitation. He was a great host. I stayed at his apartment in the tallest building in Sydney, overlooking the harbor, which, by the way, is the best in the world. He had us taxied about town in a chauffeur-driven Rolls-Royce.

We also went to Rotorua, the capital of New Zealand. Rotorua is in an area of many geysers and warm springs, which gave off a distinct odor. That did not bother me, though, once I got used to it.

We also went to Auckland, where I visited automotive friend Bob Madgwick. He was the head mechanic in New Zealand for International Harvester Company. Unlike the United States, where there is a repair shop in just about every city, IHC had to provide its own central facility for maintaining the products it sold in the country. Bob owned a 1918 FWD Model B truck, which was made in Clintonville, Wisconsin, about 30 miles from Iola.

Bob also made it to Iola once. He was part of a tour group that went to Detroit. While there, he was able to break away long enough to come to Iola. He entered the United States at one of the major West Coast cities and had a layover there. At the hotel swimming pool, he struck up a conversation with some other guests who were American. He mentioned that he was going to visit a small town in Wisconsin called Iola. One of the others said, "To see Chet Krause?"

The Jumbo restaurant in the Hong Kong harbor seats 3,000 people. Water taxis shuttle diners between shore and the restaurant.

Bob Roberts greeted me at the airport upon my arrival in Australia and also saw me off for my return trip. I crossed the international date line in the air, so I gained a day on my inbound flight but lost it again on the return trip.

My second trip to Australia came in 1982, with my niece Patti Krause as my traveling companion. We took a rather circuitous but most interesting route through Hong Kong so we could attend the first coin convention hosted by Richard Nelson and The Money Company.

Our airplane landed at a most unusual airport. The entire runway, which was more than a mile long, was built on pilings driven into a bay.

From the airport, we proceeded to the Regent Hotel, located on the southern tip of Kowloon Peninsula, via a hotel limousine. It must have been the Monday of America, or wash day, in Kowloon. Every veranda on the multistory apartment buildings we passed by had a wash line on it filled with drying clothes.

We arrived at the Regent early – about 8 or 9 a.m. – and were told our rooms would not be ready until about 1 or 2 p.m. Patti and I had been up some 30 hours – except for a catnap or two on the planes – so we were not in the mood for sightseeing or much walking. So we killed the time in the Regent lobby watching people.

The Regent was noted for its cleanliness. I watched a worker with a dust mop repeat a circular route about 15 feet across from the front door to the registration desk, affording every courtesy along the way to guests who were registering. Another worker did the balance of the rather spacious lobby with the usual tools of the trade, save for a toothbrush, which she used to clean between the marble floor and a pillar.

Eventually, a bellhop came and graciously told us our rooms were ready. An army of attendants accompanied him to help. By this time, Patti and I had gone 37 hours with no sleep to speak of, so we crashed in our rooms until dinner.

The exceptional service continued after we were in our rooms. We noticed there were always

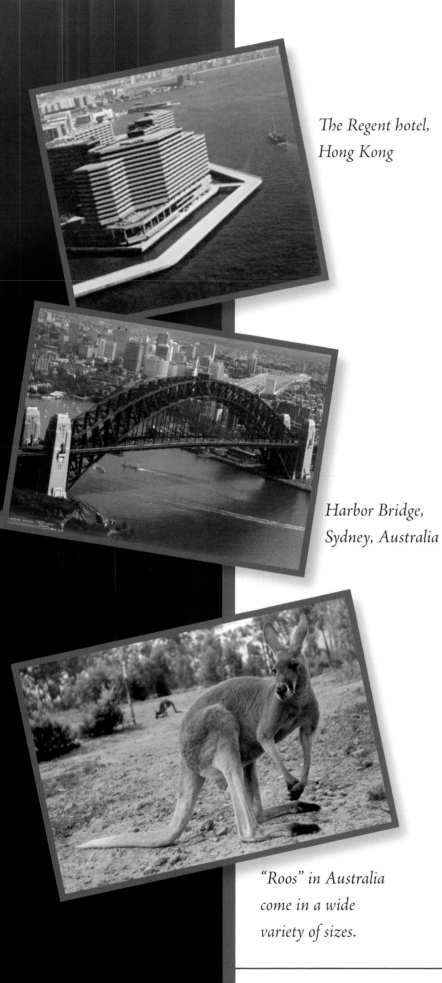

The Regent hotel, Hong Kong

Harbor Bridge, Sydney, Australia

"Roos" in Australia come in a wide variety of sizes.

two young men – maybe in their late teens – on hand to watch for whenever we left our rooms. Upon our return, the rooms were touched up as if freshly made up by a housekeeper, including clean towels.

We requested and received harbor-view rooms, so we spent a lot of time just watching the water traffic. We saw coastal and ocean-going ships aplenty from all nations. We also occasionally saw a junk or two and numerous sampans. The latter was a small boat 12 to 15 feet long with what looked like a much smaller engine than it should have had. They must have been made to ply the harbor. They would bob like a top as they rode the waves of the larger ships, but their operators did not seem to mind.

We also saw garbage collectors. They consisted of watercraft with reels in front that picked up boxes, bottles, and other debris floating in the harbor. They were constantly at work and would roam about the harbor in no apparent pattern to sweep it of any debris.

One morning as we ate breakfast while overlooking the harbor, a large passenger ship several stories high came past the hotel close to shore. That was an awe-inspiring sight.

I had never heard of Kowloon before my visit there. Greater Hong Kong consists of Hong Kong Island, which includes Hong Kong city, and Kowloon Peninsula, which includes Kowloon city.

Hong Kong Island is about 10 miles long and four miles wide, but its shape is irregular. Kowloon Peninsula is attached to mainland China, across the harbor from Hong Kong Island, and is seldom thought of as part of greater Hong Kong. Kowloon is divided into two sections – the New Territories in the north and the peninsula in the south.

Great Britain gained control of Hong Kong Island in 1842 and Kowloon Peninsula in 1860. On July 1, 1898, China leased to Britain the New Territories and the rest of the more than 235 islands that make up greater Hong Kong. The entire colony, including Hong Kong Island, was returned to China when the lease expired on July 1, 1997. The Chinese now call greater Hong Kong a "special administration region" of their country. So when Patti and I were there, greater Hong Kong was still under British governance.

I hope the shopping in Hong Kong is still as remarkable as it was when we were there. If you wanted a dress or shirt or coat or suit, you would first pick a style that you liked. The clerk would take several measurements, and then you would return a few hours later for a fitting. The next morning you could return again and pick up your perfectly fitted garment.

Bob Roberts met us in Hong Kong, where a coin show was in progress, and hosted us to dinner at a restaurant atop the Regent. It was a marvelous dinner unlike anything I had ever been treated to before. Patti's menu was presented to her tied up in a ribbon. She saved it and carried it half way around the world with her on our return trip but then forgot it in the Denver airport.

Our stay in Hong Kong facilitated our entering Australia on its west coast. From Hong Kong, we flew to Singapore and then boarded a connecting flight to Perth. What an elaborate terminal that was in Singapore! I wished we had planned a layover in Singapore because our flight from Singapore to Perth was long – eight to nine hours – on top of the earlier flight from Hong Kong to Singapore and then waiting time between flights.

By the time we got to Perth, the traveling had gotten the better of me, and a sinus condition I have fought all my life flared up. So my first call in Perth was a doctor, who gave me the antibiotic I needed. Twenty-four hours later, I was up and at 'em again, but poor Patti had to wait out my recovery.

An acquaintance of mine picked us up the next day and took us to lunch by the ocean, near the shipping docks. Perth is the only major harbor on Australia's west coast.

Sheep raising is an important industry in western Australia, and sheep are an important export. As we approached the harbor, a giant sheep boat already out in the ocean appeared like a giant building. Sheep have to be shipped above deck; the ship's hold has to be filled with ballast. This ship had several stories of sheep above deck.

The ship left well before our arrival, but its aroma still lingered in the harbor. It may have been helped by a west wind pushing it back at us. The ship was headed to Saudi Arabia. Upon arrival there, the sheep would be butchered in the morning and had to be consumed that same day because of an Arab custom to always eat meat the same day of its slaughter.

Later that afternoon, Patti and I boarded a train, the India Pacific, that would take us east to Adelaide, a journey of about 1,300 miles. We had compartments across the aisle from each other, so we had our own spaces but could still readily converse. The trip took the better part of three days; it was interesting at times and boring at other times. It was not until we got home and I took time to read the literature we brought back with us, as well as some library references, that I fully appreciated where we had been.

As we left Kalgoorie, we headed across the desert of the Nullarbor Plain. I was told it rained there once every 15 years or so, but it could be up to four inches at a time. The rain sprouts seeds in the ground, and the desert becomes a sea of yellow flowers. As they mature and go to seed, grasses that grow three to four feet high take over. The grass, in turn, goes to seed and then dies for lack of moisture. Insects then hatch and reproduce several times over. They proceed to bury the grass seeds and straw in the ground until they, too, die for lack of moisture. The seeds lie dormant until the next rain, when the cycle starts all over again.

When Patti and I traveled through the land, it was dormant, so we did not see all of the underlying life. What we saw looked like moon rocks and sand.

We began to see signs of life again as our train made its way east. There were evergreen trees that looked like our pine but appeared to grow with great difficulty, their stems knurled and crooked. We also saw emus, which I can best describe as two-toed ostriches, and kangaroos. The "roos," as they are called locally, come in a wide variety of sizes – some as small as a rat.

At one point, our train traveled across the plain in a straight line for 275 miles. At times it stopped at small villages that dotted the land. There were no roads to these villages; their residents depended on trains for all goods and services, at a high cost. All worked directly or indirectly for the railroad. Doctors and other health providers rode the trains, stopping at a village for a day or two before getting back on the train and moving on to the next town.

We got off the train in Adelaide and spent some time in the city. That was a wonderful stop; it was our first chance to rest since leaving Hong Kong.

We visited the zoo, which had howling monkeys. They must have known we were coming because they were in great voice that day.

We ate at a McDonald's restaurant. I ordered a hamburger, and the waitress asked me if I wanted "chase." She repeated it several times, but I couldn't understand what she was saying. Finally, Patti said "cheese." The waitress was asking me if I wanted cheese on my hamburger.

Our purpose in getting off the train in Adelaide was to catch an airplane to Alice Springs, about 800 miles northwest of Adelaide, and see Ayers Rock. Australia is about the same size of the United States. If you compared the geography of the two, Perth would be San Francisco, Adelaide would be New Orleans, Sydney would be Washington, D.C., Melbourne would be Tallahassee, Florida, and Alice Springs would be Denver.

There were DC-9 flights every day from Alice Springs to Ayers, but there was a high-profile trial going on in Ayers at the time, and all of the flights were filled with news media and jury members. The trial was the basis for the movie "A Cry in the Dark", about a dingo stealing a baby. I tried to charter a light aircraft but was not having much luck. Finally, I received word that a television crew was returning to Alice Springs on a small plane and we could climb on board for the return to Ayers Rock after it was serviced.

We made it to Ayers Rock in time for lunch. Our pilot was a bit of a tour guide and pointed out several spots of interest in the desert below. On our approach to Ayers Rock, we flew over The Olgas mountains before landing.

After lunch, we boarded a tour bus for a ride around the rock, which, as I remember, is five miles long, a mile wide, and 1,000 feet high. It looks like a round lump of sugar. Patti and I climbed to its top with the help of a pipe railing going up the rock. At the top, you could see The Olgas, about 15 miles west. The Olgas were rocky outcroppings to Americans who are used to rocks, hills, and mountains. There was no habitation there.

Ayers Rock had a good visitor's center and a reception, motel, and restaurant area. It also had ants two inches long.

Our return trip to Alice Springs was in the evening, and we were happy to return to civilization. We spent some additional time in Alice Springs before flying to Sydney. You could gamble in Alice Springs; our motel had a facility. Not being a gambler, however, I did not try my luck.

We walked to the business section of town one day and encountered Aborigines standing in semicircles in the shade of trees. We were told that they would follow the shade around the tree as the day progressed, occasionally moving from one group to another. At night, they would just lie down and sleep wherever the shade left them in the evening. When they awoke the next morning, they would stand in the shade again. I have no idea what they ate or where, or what they did when nature called.

The main street in Alice Springs was much like an American main street but without cars. In fact, we saw few cars in this part of the country. Gasoline and maintenance had to be expensive. Plus, there were not many places to go except work or across town, which was not very far.

We did, however, see "truck trains." These consisted of a Mack truck pulling a regular semi trailer plus two or more two axle trailers. They were loaded with 40-foot containers brought by rail from Adelaide. Each truck train was almost 250 feet long.

They traveled a gravel road to Darwin, a seaport on the north shore of Australia, about 1,000 miles from Alice Springs. They moved at about 70 miles per hour. If you met one while traveling in a car, it was best to pull over until it passed because the gravel it churned up could damage a car. Plus, the truck trains had the right of way.

One afternoon, Patti and I were relaxing at a picnic table behind our motel and reflecting on where we had been and what we had seen. If you are from Iola, Wisconsin, and you are sitting in Alice Springs, Australia, you are about as far away from home as you can get, except for maybe Mongolia, which I have never been to or hope to get to.

Ayers Rock.

The next day we flew to Sydney, which is a modern, metropolitan city with a beautiful natural harbor. Its distinctively styled opera house, which opened in 1973, is a worldwide landmark. Its zoo is one of the best in the world and a must-see for visitors to the city. Bob Roberts was again our host in Sydney. Patti took advantage of the shopping opportunities to purchase a ring for herself and another one for her cousin Kris Shurson of Colorado.

Patti's father (my brother Neil) was in Australia for a time during World War II, stationed north of Sydney. He used to talk about what great friends the Aussies were and why. The British army consisted of troops from throughout the commonwealth, including Australia and New Zealand. Because Australia was under the threat of an attack from the Japanese, the country felt its troops should return to protect their homeland but Great Britain didn't allow them to return. But the United States responded to their cries for help. The U.S. Navy was sent to guard the entrance to the Sydney harbor, and U.S. bases were set up in the country. Those bases were later used to train troops for the Allied offensive war. Australia was, is, and probably always will be an American friend.

From Sydney, we went to Christchurch, New Zealand. The country consists of two large islands – North Island and South Island. They are separated by Cook Strait, which is only about 20 miles wide at its narrowest point.

North Island is much like we Americans might envision New Zealand. South Island is long and narrow, and extends south well into the cold that we associate with places like Alaska and Newfoundland. A mountain range, the Southern Alps, run north and south on the west coast of the island and rise about 12,000 feet. The prevailing winds are from the west, off the Tasman Sea, which separates South Island from Australia. The west winds pick up moisture from the sea and deposit it in the form of snow on the high peaks of the Southern Alps, providing year-round winter sports.

East of the mountains is the Canterbury Plains, a desert that receives only a few inches of rain annually. Christchurch lies north of the Canterbury Plains, on the eastern shore of South Island. The city has an excellent international port that receives ships from Europe and Asia. It is also the closest port to Antarctica.

Christchurch seemed quite independent. Most residents were engaged in commerce and relied on foodstuffs from abroad. Little international news hit the airways or the local papers. Almost everything we saw or read was local.

While there, we walked around the heart of the city, which today has a population of about 344,000, the second largest city in New Zealand. There are two or three car museums in Christchurch, and I made it a point to visit each one. A lot of pre-1930 cars were preserved. In light of Christchurch's isolation from the rest of the world, the initial cost of an automobile must have been high, along with the cost of maintaining it and the cost of gasoline. As a result, cars were preserved instead of being sent to the scrap yard.

I stopped in Auckland on my trip home so I could visit Bob Madgwick again. Our stay there was too short, but when you plan a four-week tour that covers as many miles as we did, you don't always have enough time at some stops.

From Auckland, we started our journey home. Our first stop was Honolulu, where we rested for a few days. Although Honolulu is a major tourist destination, it was rather anticlimactic for Patti and me. I had also been there before, but the chance to rest was welcomed.

Patti and I took in a luau on the beach. We took a boat tour of Pearl Harbor, which provided a good narration of what happened there. A coin-collector friend of mine named Norris Johnson of Ventura, California, was a naval pilot stationed at Pearl Harbor during the attack of December 7, 1941. He once gave me a firsthand account of what happened. On another occasion, John Hotvedt, a retired Navy pilot and an Iola native who served in the Korean Conflict, guided me around the harbor.

While Patti rested one day, I visited the U.S. Army Museum of Hawaii at Fort DeRussy.

Notable among the museum's items was a World War II M-15 half-track. The M-15 was an anti-aircraft weapon. It had a turret with a 37-caliber gun and 50-caliber machine guns on either side. My anti-aircraft unit in the Army used 40-millimeter guns.

I am told the M-15s were not good weapons. They were refurbished in Texas by placing a quad 50-caliber mount on the chassis. Also, about eight inches of its rear armor was fitted with hinges so it would fold down. The refurbished unit was called an M-16A1, which was far superior to the M-15. I owned one once.

I had tried for several years to find an M-15 to buy for my collection of World War II anti-aircraft equipment but finally learned that the sole known survivor was in this museum. I had to leave it that day knowing that I would never own one.

Our route home from Honolulu included a stop in Denver, where we met Kris Shurson, my niece and Patti's cousin, and Patti gave her the ring she had purchased for her in Sydney. It was great to see a familiar face after a month away from home. After an overnight stay in Denver, we made the last leg of our journey back to Appleton, Wisconsin, via Chicago.

Our long adventure was finally over, but the memories from it remain with us today.

Chapter 16

Back to Luxembourg

As documented previously, my first tour of Europe started in the fall of 1944 and ended in the spring of 1945 and was at Uncle Sam's expense. I even got paid for it. In the spring of 1992, I and four other members of my old Army unit and their wives retraced some of our World War II travels with the 565th Anti-Aircraft Battalion. I put together the 1,100-mile tour with the help of a travel agent in Luxembourg.

Joining me on the tour were Kelton and Betty Herndon of Gallatin, Tennessee; Millie and George Harber of Macon, Georgia; Imogene and Craig Rudisill of Marshall, North Carolina; and Patricia and Harris Dake of Flat Rock, North Carolina. Upon our return, Harris wrote a narrative of our trip, which I had printed into a 12-page booklet along with pictures. The booklet was sent to all of the 565th veterans. The following recollections of that trip are based largely on Harris' writing.

We left Kennedy International Airport in New York on April 28 and flew to Reykjavik, Iceland. It was the first time Betty and Kelton Herndon and Imogene Rudisill had flown, so they logged plenty of miles on their first venture into the skies. The next day, we flew to Luxembourg International Airport and transferred to our headquarters at the Hotel Nobilis in the heart of the city. It was only two or three blocks from our old battalion command post and the railroad station and three bridges that were central to our defense assignment during the war.

That first evening in Luxembourg, we learned how appreciative and gracious the local people were for the U.S. Army's liberation and defense of the city during the war. As we were leaving the hotel dining room after dinner, three men about our ages, who were seated at a table adjacent to the exit, stood up, extended their hands, and said, "Thank you for saving us and our country." We were all taken aback by their gesture and at a loss of words for a response.

April 30 was our first day of touring in Luxembourg. We were led by two people. The first was Tilly Kimmes-Hansen, who was secretary of the Cercle D'etudes Sur La Bataille Des Ardennes, or CEBA. This was a group dedicated to preserving Battle of the Bulge history. As part of that mission, it organized receptions for groups like ours – U.S. veterans returning to visit the areas where they served. Tilly was a retired school teacher who was attending college in Luxembourg at the time of the German occupation. She was outgoing, exuberant, and well informed.

Our second leader was Guy (pronounced Gee, with a hard G) Bartholme, who owned and operated our 32-passenger, German-made tour bus. Guy could speak five languages and had a nice sense of humor. He was also efficient, hard working, and punctual, and he made sure we did not lack for local traditions and comforts. He took care of lodging, meal, and sightseeing arrangements, and did a great job retracing our routes of 1944-1945.

We first toured parts of Luxembourg City, including General George Patton's headquarters, the Pescatore, where Patton was given his famous prayer for good weather in December 1944. Cold and snow had prevented Allied forces from mounting a counterattack to the German offensive that drove into Belgium and laid siege to the city of Bastogne. Patton asked his chaplain to compose a prayer for good weather. Apparently,

it worked, because shortly afterward, the weather broke and Allied forces were on the move.

During the city tour, George Harber, who served in D Battery, was able to locate the battery's gun position, which was now a school site. Several nearby houses were also familiar.

After touring Luxembourg City, we proceeded to a historical museum at Diekirch, passing by a statue of Patton and a Sherman tank at Ettlebruck on the way. The museum was small but well stocked with military artifacts, including a Sherman tank near the entrance. The museum was dedicated to the liberation of Diekirch and the Sauer River crossing by the 2nd Infantry Regiment and the 50th Field Artillery Battalion on January 18, 1945. It was one of the fiercest and most costly battles in the liberation of Luxembourg.

We then motored to Clervaux. For the most part, the highway followed a high ridge parallel to the Our River. The German border was about 10 miles to the east as we traveled north. We stopped prior to descending the deep and narrow valley to the Clerve River and Clervaux. The view was like being in a low-flying aircraft as we looked down on the picturesque scene. It was difficult to imagine that this quiet, beautiful village of 1,000 people had borne the initial brunt of the German offensive that would become known as the Battle of the Bulge. It was easy to see how difficult it must have been for the 110th Regiment of the 28th Infantry Division to defend the village against the 2nd German Armored Division – like shooting fish in a barrel. It was eventually liberated by the 26th Infantry Division on January 26, 1945.

CEBA hosted a reception for us in the dining room of a feudal castle in Clervaux. CEBA President Camille P. Kohn gave a speech that talked about how much the people of Luxembourg suffered during the Nazi occupation, their joy at being liberated, and their continuing gratitude to the United States and its veterans. His remarks were very touching and emotional for us. I gave a response on our behalf. After the speeches, Moselle wine and camaraderie flowed freely.

On May 1, we visited the Luxembourg American Military Cemetery and Memorial. This was another emotional experience for us. I laid a bouquet of flowers at the base of an altar in the memorial's chapel. The altar is inscribed with the words "I give unto them eternal life and they shall never perish."

We then visited the Victory Memorial Museum at Arlon, which was by far the largest and most complete museum of those we visited. An extensive presentation of military machinery and armament was displayed in lifelike tableaus.

From Arlon, we motored to Bastogne and visited the Bastogne Historical Center, another excellent museum. It was divided into three parts: (1) an account of the Battle of the Bulge; (2) a collection of uniforms, weapons, and material from both sides of the battle; and (3) a montage of film shot during the battle. A few yards from the historical center was an American memorial. Like the historical center, it was built in the shape of a five-pointed star with an open

As we traveled, we felt like the clock had been turned back almost 50 years.

rotunda in the center. The outer and inner walls of the star points bore the names of the states and units involved in the Battle of the Bulge.

On our return to Luxembourg City from Bastogne, we stopped to see the Radio Luxembourg facility near Junglinster. The 565th's C Battery was assigned to defend the facility's three towers during the war. BBC and Voice of America radio broadcasts were used to send messages in code to underground networks and the people of occupied countries. Even the German people listened, at the risk of their lives, to try to find out the truth about the war's progress. At the time of our 1992 visit, three more towers had been added. Unfortunately, we were not able to enter the facility's buildings, but we were able to walk around outside and take pictures.

After resting from our long day of touring on May 1, we left Luxembourg on the morning of May 2 and headed for Boppard, on the Rhine River. On the way, we stopped at Hausbay, another site of our battalion headquarters. At Boppard, we stayed at the Bellevue Rheinhotel, established in 1887, with a beautiful view of the river.

The next day, we enjoyed a wonderful 4 1/2-hour cruise up the Rhine to Bingen. The scenery, consisting of old castles and steep vineyards, was spectacular. We recognized the site of the pontoon bridge defended by A, B, C, and D batteries at Lorch. Upon arrival at Bingen, we took a bus back to Boppard. The next morning, we departed for Eisenach.

On the way to Eisenach, we followed the Rhine to the vicinity of Mainz and then turned north through the western outskirts of Frankfurt. About halfway between Bad Hersfeld and Eisenach, we crossed into what had recently been East Germany. Guy pointed out the border checkpoints and the huge ditch that was dug by the Soviet Union to separate the two Germanys. The barbed wire and fortifications along it were now torn down, and the ditch was being filled in.

As we traveled, we felt like the clock had been turned back almost 50 years. Roads, homes, utilities, railroads, and businesses were in disrepair. Except for the absence of the carnage of battle and military equipment, it looked much as it did in the spring of 1945. We proceeded a short distance north of Eisenach to Behringen and fairly accurately located an airfield and the positions D Battery used to defend it.

In Eisenach, we stayed at the Hotel Hellgrafenhof, which had been newly built by an Italian family. So in the heart of Germany, we enjoyed some great pizza and spaghetti. We left Eisenach the next morning, May 5, and turned off the main highway to make our way up a steep, winding mountain road to visit Wartburg castle. We got off the bus and had another long climb by foot to the castle entrance. From there, we had another spectacular view of Eisenach. Craig Rudisill and I were the only ones who had enough energy left to climb to the top of the watch tower.

After much picture-taking, we boarded the bus again and headed for Weimar and the

Buchenwald concentration camp. Returning to this site that we had first visited right after its liberation was eerie and uncomfortable for many in the group. We decided to forego a detailed tour of the many acres of buildings and markers that now cover the area.

We then went to a little village called Linda, where Harris Dake and some other GIs had been held as prisoners of war until they were liberated by a Russian army unit. We visited a little café where Harris and his fellow prisoners were when the Russians entered the village. Harris fulfilled a longtime dream of drinking a victory beer in the place.

Late that same day, we arrived at the Hotel Moskau in Chemnitz, where we enjoyed a nice dinner and some welcome rest. We were on the road again the next day, traveling south from Chemnitz to Forchheim and then on to Erlangen for a stay at the Hotel Rokokohaus. On May 7, we visited sites at Erlangen and Nürnberg, including the huge stadium where Adolph Hitler gave many of his rousing speeches from high atop a speaker's platform. Some of those in our group took a picture of me waving from the same spot.

Another nearby area brought back memories of seeing a USO show there that featured Jack Benny, Ingrid Bergman, and other celebrities. George Harber even remembered some of the jokes.

Our travels on this day continued southeast from Nürnberg to Regensburg, located at the confluence of the Regen and Danube rivers. We had a leisurely stop there, which included lunch at a sidewalk café across the street from St. Paul's Cathedral, some shopping at a street fair, and ice-cream cones. We then got back on the bus and continued on to Straubing, also located on the Danube not far from the Czech border. There was more shopping here, and Kelton Herndon and I found the hotel where we were billeted during our stay in 1945.

May 8 was a long day of travel as we started to work our way back to Luxembourg City, but we did stop at Schwarzenberg Castle at Scheinfeld on the way. This was where we had celebrated V-E Day and found the basement full of good German beer. It was also where Kelton Herndon and I had fixed the clock in the castle's tower. The castle was now a home for teenage boys and girls who were wards of the court, but the clock was no longer working.

That night we stayed at the Hotel Scandic Crown on the banks of the Moselle River near Trier. The next morning, we went into downtown Trier for some more shopping and walking before continuing our last leg of our return to the Luxembourg airport and a 1:50 p.m. return flight to Reykjavik. At the airport, we said goodbye to Guy, who had been an outstanding driver and guide during our two weeks of motor touring.

We arrived in Reykjavik on time and had dinner that evening at the Naust restaurant, about two blocks from our hotel. The restaurant featured nautical décor and good food, although some in our group were shocked by the high cost of living in Iceland.

On the morning of May 10, prior to our departure for New York, we took a bus tour of the city and island. We learned that heating for homes and other buildings in Iceland comes from underground hot springs. We stopped and watched people swimming in a pool as steam rose from the water and snow fell from the sky.

We had a 4:40 p.m. flight to New York. We spent that night at a Hilton hotel and had a farewell dinner together that evening. Missing from the group, however, were Millie and George Harber, who had reservations at a different hotel thanks to a miscommunication somewhere along the line. The next morning, May 11, we said our farewells and were on our separate ways to our homes.

At different times, the retracing of our war route from Luxembourg City into Germany was fun, eerie, emotional, and nostalgic. I look back on it today with many fond memories and appreciation for the opportunity to take the trip with some of my fellow veterans.

Chapter 17

North to Alaska

In addition to my overseas travel, I have visited all 50 states, including three trips to Alaska, which makes that state something special to me. My last trip, just to Anchorage and back in 1976, was made to present a Numismatic Ambassador Award. This award was created by Krause Publications to bring national recognition to grass-roots contributions promoting the numismatic hobby, such as those who help at club-sponsored coin shows.

On a couple of my trips to Alaska, I had a wonderful tour guide named Russell Anderson, who was from Iola originally and served as head of the Alaskan Civil Air Patrol for 18 years. He seldomly received a visitor from his hometown, so he treated me like royalty whenever I visited. He knew Anchorage like the back of his hand. On one occasion, he took me up in his own airplane and showed me around the whole basin of Anchorage. What a treat that was!

I knew another Iola transplant in Alaska named Glenn Bergen. He was in the fish business

there, buying salmon from independent fishermen and then shipping it to Seattle for canning.

Stops on my first trip, in June 1967, included Kotzebue and Nome, both on the northwest coast. I and another gentleman were the first tourists of the season, arriving from Fairbanks on Alaska Airlines. Kotzebue lies at the tip of a peninsula in Kotzebue Sound. Ice forms a bridge across the water surrounding the peninsula for much of the year. In that area, the ice would not just form overnight. Instead, it would flow down from the Arctic Ocean, arrive unannounced, and then leave the same way.

At Kotzebue, I saw firsthand what Eskimo life was all about. The Eskimos made their living from the sea. In contrast, the native Indians lived inland and made their living from the land. The two had little interface with each other. Red meat was hardly heard of in Kotzebue, but the salmon and shellfish were great and fresh.

The local people would ice fish through the flows. They would drill holes four to six feet deep and jig for sheefish. One could stroll down the beach and see a bunch of holes in the ice with a jig pole by every one. The shiny hook was an oddity to the fish, and they would attack it. When the fisherman felt a tug, he would pull the line up through the hole. The hooks were barbless, so the fish would almost fall off once it was above the ice.

The fishermen took advantage of the natural refrigeration and just left their catching lying on the ice. When a family needed a meal, they would walk onto the ice and pick up however many fish they needed.

I was the only guest at my hotel. One day I observed out my window what appeared to be three generations of an Eskimo family. The grandmother was sitting by the door to her house, maybe 40 feet from the ice on the beach. Her teeth were worn down to the gums from biting leather to make moccasins. A younger woman, who appeared to be the grandmother's daughter, was bustling about doing family chores. A teenage girl – apparently the granddaughter – was dressed in newer clothes and high heels. I was told most people bought their clothes by mail order from Sears, Roebuck and Co. in Seattle.

From Kotzebue, I flew to Nome, a name much more familiar to me. Nome is located southwest of Kotzebue on the Seward Peninsula. The Arctic Circle runs between the two towns. Nome became famous during the gold-rush days of the 1800s. There was still an old dredge on shore, and those who panned for gold still found a few minute pieces.

At that time, the buildings in Nome were better than those in Kotzebue but not by much. And they were not up to the standards of the

"South 48," as Alaskans called the continental United States. There were two churches in Nome, and both were painted – the only paint I saw in the Arctic.

Both of the churches stood straight and erect, a challenging achievement in those parts. Most buildings just sat on the ground, and the thawing and refreezing of the soil would shift them about. There were two ways to prevent this when constructing a new building. One was to dig a trench around the perimeter of the building site and install refrigeration coils in it. In the summer, the coils would be turned on and keep the top four feet of soil frozen.

Another was to drill holes about 40 feet deep and about four feet apart around the perimeter of the building site. Pilings were driven into each hole, and the new building was constructed on top of the pilings. The two churches – one of each method – were the only buildings in town constructed this way. Perhaps better or more widely used methods have been developed since.

My second trip to Alaska consisted of leading a numismatic tour group of 11 people in spring of 1969. The tour was the brainchild of Ed Rochette during his time as an editor at Krause Publications. We also put together numismatic tours of Mexico and Europe but found them quite time consuming for the gain we enjoyed.

My mother joined me for this Alaskan tour, which made it that much more special for me. The tour formed at a Seattle hotel. Rather than fly there, Mother and I flew to Minneapolis and then transferred to a Chicago Northwestern train for a ride across the northern Great Plains and the Rocky Mountains. Trains were the common form of long-distance travel for Mother during the pre-automobile era, and I had not traveled by train since my return from the Army in 1946. I had been doing a lot of business travel in the late 1950s and all of the '60s, so it was a wonderful opportunity for the two of us to have some extended time together.

When we got to Seattle, it was my duty to make sure the other nine tour members had arrived. I then briefed them on a few simple rules of tour travel. All of our luggage had to be properly tagged and then set out in the hallways outside our rooms before breakfast. They were then picked up by the bellhops while we were eating. This routine changed when we got to Barrow, Alaska, where they had never heard of bellhops. Everybody was responsible for toting their own luggage there.

From Seattle, we flew to Prince Rupert, British Columbia, where we claimed our staterooms on a ferry. As the term implies, the vessel hauled automobiles, too. In southeast Alaska, we stopped at Ketchikan, Wrangell, and Petersburg. We then disembarked at Juneau, the capital. At each stop, we were able to get off the ship and travel into the city or village for a short time while the ferry was unloaded and reloaded. Some of the other travelers on the ship – those not in our group – would unload their cars and spend a day or two at the port community before boarding the next ship and traveling on to another destination.

The most memorable parts of the trip for me were traveling among the islands of the Tongass National Forest, which formed an intercoastal waterway, and the tremendous tide. I believe it was 33 feet. It was not unusual for us to tie up at a dock, leave the ship for two or three hours, and come back to find it several feet below the dock.

One might expect the approach to Juneau to be from the south, but in fact, it is from the north. Directly west of Juneau is Douglas Island, with a bridge across the Gastineau Channel connecting the two. A large sandbar allowed only smaller boats to enter and arrive from the south. So our large ferry had to travel up the west side of Douglas Island and then turn and come in from the north to dock at Juneau.

Although it's the state capital, Juneau has an approximate population today of only 31,000. It is located on the narrow strip of the state that extends south along the Pacific Ocean and borders Canada's Yukon Territory and British Columbia. Someone living in Barrow, at the far northern tip of the state, would have to travel more than 1,000 miles to get to the capital, and that is as the crow flies. Ketchikan is another 225 miles.

Among the things that stand out in my memory of the trip were the Alaskan golf courses, which did not have greens because grass does not grow well that far north. The greens were made of a highly compacted sand. After a group of golfers putted out, they would drag the "greens" with a plank to smooth them out for the next group. Winter rules always prevailed in the roughs.

The Alaska State Museum in Juneau was crowded with exhibits and rich in quality in depicting the life and history of southeast Alaska. We learned about the Tlingit Indians and how totem poles are carved. We also saw real seal-skin

Mother stands by the train we took from Minneapolis to Seattle, through the Great Plains and the Rocky Mountains.

money, the likes of which I had not seen before and have not seen since.

The Mendenhall Glacier, just north of Juneau, was outstanding. It is not the biggest one in the world, but it is still large. One could drive a car right up to it. It was not unusual to see huge pieces of ice fall from its upper reaches, maybe a couple of hundred feet high. I was told there was another 400 feet of glacier lying below the surface.

Our next stop was Skagway, about 90 miles north of Juneau. It was not a big town – about 900 people today – but a great jumping-off spot for the nearby Klondike Gold Rush National Historic Park. Skagway was at the southern terminus of the White Pass and Yukon Route narrow-gauge railroad, which hauled people and supplies to Whitehorse in the Yukon. It made a round trip

to Whitehorse every other day. So we traveled up to Whitehorse one day, spent the next full day there, and then caught the next train returning to Skagway. On the return trip, we stopped at Carcross for lunch. Another train traveling in the opposite direction on another track had done the same thing, but the trains were timed so one was leaving just as the other was coming.

The train trip to Whitehorse and back through the mountains was awesome. It was filled with hairpin turns, like an automobile highway through the mountains, but they were a piece of cake for the train. At one point, I was able to look out my window and see our locomotive across a deep ravine as we made a horseshoe turn. At another point, if we could have opened a window, we could have leaned out and seen straight down

Mother and I are bundled up for a stop in Barrow, Alaska. Joining us in the photo are Mr. & Mrs. Emery Rogers from Marion, Wisconsin, near Iola, whom we met along the way.

several hundred feet. There was just enough rock split off the near-vertical mountain face to allow the train to pass. The outside wall of the train must have extended over the cliff.

We made our way back to Juneau and then flew to Anchorage, which was a hustling and bustling city even in the 1960s. We could still see damage in the city from the devastating earthquake of 1964.

Anchorage offered a lot for tourists to do. One of our side trips was to a state ski area, where we rode the lift to the cold top. It was 80 degrees at the bottom and 32 at the top. We were given blankets to help ward off the cold.

The next morning, we boarded a train to Fairbanks. We made an overnight stop at the little community of Denali, about 40 miles east of Denali National Park. We checked into the

National Park Hotel and, shortly after midnight, boarded buses for the park. It was broad daylight in the land of the midnight sun.

On the way, we saw caribou that had yet to leave their winter habitat and Dall sheep, which were perfectly white. But the most amazing thing we saw were a couple of lone grizzly bears grazing in the Denali meadow. Apparently, they had been unmolested by man because they showed no signs of aggression.

We traveled to an observation point to view Mount McKinley, but it was cloudy. Even an occasional opening in the skies was not enough to get a good look at the peak, which rises more than 20,000 feet.

We returned to the village of Denali in time to continue our train ride north. Fairbanks is much smaller than Anchorage – about 30,000

Our Alaska tour group gathers for a photo. I am in the back row, third from the right, with Mother standing to my left.

today compared with Anchorage's 260,000. The city had a special flavor to it. Lawns were just plain dirt – no grass to cut or shrubs to trim – and it is dark for much of the time in the winter. But the residents still enjoyed living there.

Our side tours included the Tanana River, a main branch of the wide Yukon River. I was told the riverboat captains had to stay alert because the river's course can change daily. Here we saw fish reels, which were used to catch salmon. They looked like waterwheels that somehow scooped up the fish and deposited them in nets. A boat would then come by, gather up the fish, and haul them to market, which was a cannery in Fairbanks.

A must stop is the museum at the University of Alaska near Fairbanks. This was truly an Arctic museum, with plenty of space to display everything properly. If the weather cooperates, which it did on the day I was there, you can even see Mount McKinley from the site.

We also got to see the famous peak as we flew out of Fairbanks for our homeward journey back to Seattle, where our tour-group members said their goodbyes. Alaskans like to say that Texas is one of the larger intermediate-sized states, and those in our group liked to repeat that saying. We were all richer in knowledge for having visited the country's largest state.

Chapter 18

My Russian Friends

My involvement with Krause Publications created many friendships over the years. Oftentimes they started as business relationships and then turned into friendships. Sometimes they stretched across borders – the aforementioned Cale Jarvis of Toronto, for example. Other times they stretched across oceans and into lands with which few U.S. citizens have had contact.

An example of the latter was Igor Victorov-Orlov and his wife, Lucy. Igor and Lucy both had doctorate degrees and were on the faculty of Chelyabinsk State University in the Russian city of the same name. Igor was chairman of the language department. At some point, he started supplying us with information on Russian coins and paper money, which we used in the *Standard Catalog of World Coins* and other volumes in the *Standard Catalog* series. The information he gave us was excellent, and he certainly deserved to be paid for it. But we were unable to send him a check or money order, or transfer funds by wire.

The only way we could get money to him was to slip a $20 or $50 bill in the mail. This was risky because the Russian post office X-rayed incoming foreign mail. If a postal worker detected money in an envelope, he would open it, pocket the money, and throw out the letter. So we would wrap the cash in carbon paper. That way, the X-ray would just show a big black blob. The Russian postal workers who processed our mail must have hated us.

To further compensate him for his efforts, we also promised Igor and Lucy a trip to America. We made good on that promise in the summer of 1994. To Igor and Lucy, Krause Publications was a giant locomotive with a free run on all the tracks in America. Russia is a much larger country but was not available for them to see because of lack of funds.

Bob Wilhite, who was Krause Publications' U.S. coin-market analyst, drove to New York City in my 1987 Lincoln Town Car. We picked up

Lucy and Igor Victorov-Orlov of Chelyabinsk, Russia, on their visit to Iola in 1994.

Igor and Lucy at Kennedy International Airport. After a night in downtown New York, we went to the Russian embassy so Igor and Lucy could get visas allowing them to travel to Canada.

Once that was accomplished, with a bit of extra effort, we all piled into the Town Car and headed for the Adirondack Mountains in northern New York state. From there, we followed the Lake Ontario shoreline to Niagara Falls and then on to Buffalo, hometown of Colin Bruce, editor of the *Standard Catalog of World Coins*. I then flew back to Wisconsin, while Bob, Colin, Igor, and Lucy continued on to Toronto. A couple of days later, they reentered the United States at Detroit, where they attended the American Numismatic Association convention. I rejoined the group there, and after the convention, we motored back to Wisconsin via Michigan's Upper Peninsula.

Once in Iola, several members of the *Standard Catalog* staff who had communicated with Igor in the past served as his hosts and local tour guides. Igor and Lucy stayed at the Thorson House, a 19th-century farmhouse adjacent to the Krause Publications grounds, which the company owned and maintained as a guest house after an extensive renovation.

I or someone else on the staff slipped Igor a handful of U.S. currency to spend while in America, but they did not need it for many of the souvenirs he and Lucy took back to Russia with them. They took full advantage of the displays of free tourist brochures we happened upon in restaurants and other places. They loved fast food, and we ate at McDonald's several times. They always kept the paper cups with the McDonald's logo on them. They also kept any napkins with logos on them.

I do not know what all of America went back to Russia with them, but when we saw them off at O'Hare International Airport in Chicago, they each had a large suitcase full of stuff. Fortunately, this was prior to today's more intensive airport security checks, or we might still be there. To us, it was stuff we routinely throw away. To them, it was part of America and material for some great show-and-tell sessions back in Russia.

Prior to their departure from O'Hare, Igor, Lucy, and Colin attended a convention for collectors of orders and decorations, or what we more commonly call military medals in the United States, in Rosemont, Illinois, a suburb of Chicago. I flew to Chicago to join them. Our stay coincided with the St. Patrick's Day celebration in Chicago, so we took the train downtown to see the Chicago River dyed green. Igor and Lucy had heard about this tradition but, of course, had never seen it.

The next morning, Colin and I broke bread with Igor and Lucy before their flight from Chicago to New York and then on to Moscow. All of us sat there trying to find words that would ease their way back to Russia. Their visit was great for us because the Krause Publications staff was able to interface with Igor and Lucy in person rather than just through the mail. For Igor and Lucy, their once-in-a-lifetime trip to America was coming to an end – a trip that Krause Publications had facilitated. I hoped we had done a good job, and I think we did.

Fortunately, though, in the summer of 1996, I had a chance to see Igor and Lucy in person again. This time, I traveled to Russia, and they were my tour guides.

I had some health problems leading up to the trip, so I wanted to have someone with me who was familiar with my health history and could take the appropriate action if the problems were to reoccur. That person was to be Bob Julian of Logansport, Indiana. Bob was another contributor to the *Standard Catalog of World Coins* and a longtime freelance writer for Krause Publications' numismatic periodicals. Russian coins were one of his specialties. Bob taught himself how to read Russian, which would come in handy for the trip, but he was unable to speak it.

But at the last minute, Bob had to back out of the trip because of some health problems of his own. I did not want to postpone the trip because the arrangements in Russia were prepaid and not refundable. So, health problems aside, I ventured out alone. Fortunately, language – not my health – proved to be the only significant challenge during the trip. I made it over and back, and returned with a much greater knowledge of Russia and its people.

I also benefited from some pretrip advice from Bob. He recommended I take a roll of toilet paper with me because the Russian version is a first cousin to sandpaper. He was right.

I flew from New York's Kennedy airport to St. Petersburg via Delta Airlines. It proved to be the most pleasant of the three major hubs of my visit. The other two were Moscow and Chelyabinsk. St. Petersburg was by far the most attractive of the three. The city lies on the delta of the Neva River. It had scores of bridges, all built eons ago, but they handled the residents' needs just fine and added to the city's charm. I stayed at the Moskvia (Moscow) Hotel. The accommodations there were nice compared to some I endured later in my visit. I recommend St. Petersburg for anybody who has just a limited time to spend in Russia.

I had an excellent tour guide there, thanks to Bob Julian, who had made the arrangements before his last-minute cancellation. Her name was Ludmilla Goborova, and her friend drove us around in his car. I would have liked to have purchased some new spark plugs for that car. Several times we returned to the car to find Ludmilla's friend searching through a bag of plugs that should have been in a museum, trying to find the best ones. Sometimes he was successful; others times, only three of the car's four plugs worked properly.

But I must have been special to them because Ludmilla invited me to her sister's apartment for a meal one night. Three of the five people in the group spoke English, so I was able to have a nice conversation with them.

Ludmilla, who was Orthodox Christian, asked me if I would like to accompany her to a worship service. I said I would if it was proper for me to do so. She assured me it was, and I enjoyed the experience a great deal. I remember everyone at the service stood rather than sat in pews and, to some degree, changed positions as if in a crowd. Ludmilla and I circulated freely toward the back of the crowd, lit some candles, and then departed after about half an hour. That seemed to be the routine of the others, too.

Yuri Bursky, also a coin collector, who was especially kind to me, also guided me during my stay in St. Petersburg. He and his wife hosted me for dinner at their apartment one day. We used public transportation during our travels through the city because that was how Yuri traveled.

He took me to see the national coin collection at the Hermitage Museum. The main building at the Hermitage is the Winter Palace, which was once the main residence of the Russian czars.

I was received at the national coin collection as if I were a special person because I was the Krause of the Krause-Mishler *Standard Catalog of World Coins*. But I did not know how to act the part. All of the vaults were opened and at my disposal. I believe the curators there thought I knew all about the coins in the collection, but truth be told, I did not. Cliff and I compiled the *Standard Catalog*, but we did not write it. We relied on people like Bob Julian for their expertise in specialized areas. My attempts to explain this fell on deaf ears, so I had to accept being an important person for a couple of hours.

This happened again when Yuri took me to a coin bourse one Sunday. I was asked by many of the people there to autograph small denominations of world paper money for them.

My Aeroflot flight from St. Petersburg to Chelyabinsk was a whole new experience for me. The plane was Russian-made and a bit worse for the wear. It looked like it had been repainted several years before, and springs were sticking up through the upholstery of my seat.

For the first time since leaving the United States, I realized what a lonely feeling it is to not be able to read the language. I really did not know what time we were supposed to arrive in Chelyabinsk because it was written in Cyrillic letters and I had not taken the time beforehand to have it translated.

The plane landed, and as I set foot on the tarmac, I asked if this was Chelyabinsk. The reply sounded like "you American." I was ushered into what turned out to be a second-floor VIP lounge; I thought I might be headed for a Russian court. I showed someone there the name Igor Victorov-Orlov, but it was not written in Cyrillic, so they could not read it.

Meanwhile, Igor and his son-in-law, Sergei, were scurrying about the airport looking for me. They tried valiantly to have me paged in English but failed. Finally, after an hour, Sergei came upstairs to the lounge and found me. He did not speak English, but I could still interpret the joy in his greeting. We went downstairs and found Igor, who responded with another greeting of joy and relief.

Chelyabinsk is located about 800 miles east of Moscow and is an industrial city with many smokestacks from coal-fired factories. Stalin bulldozers were made there. They were rugged-looking machines operated with winches and cables, but they could never be exported with that name.

I was billeted at the Belgrade Hotel. I was told a lot of tourists from Romania and Yugoslavia stayed there. I think I was the first American to stay there and, I hope, the last. The bill of fair for breakfast was again written in Cyrillic, so it was of no help to me. I was given a slice of cold liver and a small slice of bread for breakfast. "Uffda," as the Norwegians in Iola say. After a couple of days of that, Igor straightened things out for me and I was given "blintzes," a kind of pancake, for breakfast after that. It was a rather tasty morsel after eating cold liver.

After breakfast, Igor, who was now retired from the university, would arrive and we would either walk to some place of interest or Sergei would drive us somewhere. We always ate at the home of Igor's daughter, Jane. She was a very nice young woman who could speak English and served as an interpreter for local industries doing business with Americans and the British. She said she never had much trouble communicating with the Americans and British except for one particular Texan with a thick drawl. She had to withdraw from the job and turn the guy over to another American who spoke Russian.

Jane would serve us a nice lunch that always included a shot of vodka – sometimes two. Igor and I, however, were the only ones who drank. Afterward, I figured out there was not enough to go around. After lunch, I was retired to a room that included a couch, at which I was to take a two-hour siesta.

Chelyabinsk has a population of more than 1 million, but I saw no evidence that they had spent any money on street repair for several years. Potholes were 20 feet wide and 50 feet long. The side streets were not paved at all.

One of our sightseeing trips was to a beach on the Miass River. Public beaches in America are usually equipped with restrooms and trash containers. Not in Russia. A grove of second-growth trees about 100 yards behind the beach was the relief station for men and women alike. The rain was the flush tank.

The beach was littered with trash of all kinds, including broken glass. I asked why there were no trash containers, and I was told that someone would have to tend to them and haul the trash away. The wind took care of the paper, and during the flooding season, the river took care of the rest of it.

On another occasion we traveled west toward Europe, and I had my picture taken straddling the marker dividing Europe and Russia.

Another excursion took us east of Chelyabinsk into Siberia, where we stayed at a summer camp Igor had helped found several years previously but in what capacity I do not remember. En route there, we passed through a city inhabited by White Russians. They had blonde hair and were descended from Mongolians that emigrated to Russia, same as the people of Belarus, which was called White Russia in my earlier years.

The camp consisted of cabins that accommodated four people each and was quite adequate. A common kitchen served the entire camp.

Igor warned me about the camp's toilets and their stench. He said they were the worst toilets in the world, and he was not far from wrong. Sergei and I did a little investigating and found some toilets on the other side of the camp's

fence that nobody seemed to be using, so we took advantage of those. I do not remember much about the food at the camp, but I know it was a lot better than cold liver.

The road back to the city was a new stretch of blacktop, the only one I saw in Russia. It was a lonely road, and Sergei took good advantage of the lack of traffic.

Many Chelyabinsk residents have what they call "dachas," or summer homes, not unlike America. Igor and Lucy's dacha was about 35 to 40 miles from the city and was set back maybe 300 feet from a lake. They had a garden between the home and the lake. When Igor, Sergei, and I arrived for a visit, Jane and her mother were tending to the garden.

I was served a great home-cooked meal. The next morning, we walked along the single street in the area and whiled away the time. But in the afternoon, we were hit with a straight-line wind that wreaked havoc with the new steel roof on Igor and Lucy's dacha. The wind tore most of the roof off and sent it into the street. Once things calmed down, Igor and Sergei began recovering the corrugated steel and brought it back inside the board fence that separated the property from the street. Igor and Sergei did not want me, their guest, to help, but I did anyway because it needed to be done and I felt I should help. It turned out Igor and Sergei were most concerned about someone stealing the roofing material.

We retired for the night without a roof over most of the house, although I still had a roof over my upstairs bedroom. I drifted off to dreamland but awoke about midnight when it started to rain.

The rain was accompanied by thunder that was so loud it shook off some of the bricks that had been put on the house the summer before.

The water found its way into my room and started to soak the bed. The electricity was out, so I had to find my way downstairs in the dark in an unfamiliar house. When I got downstairs, my hosts looked like drowned rats. Igor, Sergei, and I got in the car, and they hustled me back to my hotel. Igor and Sergei then went home and changed into dry clothes. They gathered up some dry clothes for the women and went back to rescue them. It was a bad storm, but we got through it without a bump or bruise.

Later that day, we all gathered at Jane and Sergei's home for dinner. Then the next day, I went back to the damaged dacha with the men to recover some of their belongings. Some of the bricks from the walls of Igor's dacha fell against his neighbor's fence. She wanted him to fix it. I was quite amused when he told her that he did not put the bricks there and she should collect from whoever did. I spent the rest of our time there helping to recover the fallen bricks.

The next day Igor and Sergei picked me up at my hotel, and we drove to the airport, where Igor and I boarded an Aeroflot flight to Moscow. Upon arrival in Moscow, we took a taxi into the city. Moscow had taller buildings than St. Petersburg and Chelyabinsk and more of a metropolitan feel. I was told that was why cities like Chelyabinsk looked so rundown, because the dictatorship spent all the money keeping up Moscow.

Igor made arrangements with the curator of the Moscow History Museum, and one of its employees volunteered his time on a Saturday to be our personal guide. I was told that when dignitaries from European countries visited Russia, they brought gifts with them. The gifts were accompanied by an invitation for a return visit to the dignitary's country. When the Russian dignitary made the return visit, he would bring a gift of greater value than the one received. The gifts brought to Russia were displayed at the museum. It was well worth a trip to Moscow to see.

Red Square is not like a town square in America. It occupies a couple of long city blocks on a wide street. At one end is the domed, multicolored building that is its trademark. I remember it as a seven-sided building, with a mosque occupying each side. The Kremlin was just off Red Square. There was a lot of construction going on in downtown Moscow during my three or four days there.

Igor could no longer drive because of a degenerative eye condition, so he was used to walking a lot. One day, he decided that we should walk back to the hotel, which was about two miles from Red Square. Like any big city, Moscow had its seedy side, and we walked through a couple of blocks of it. I was a little apprehensive, but Igor calmed my fears by telling me that we were just a couple of old men and it was broad daylight.

Igor returned to Chelyabinsk by train on the day before my departure from Moscow. I had a 9 a.m. flight the next day, so I wanted to be sure there would be a taxi available to get me to the airport on time. Most of the hotel staff spoke English, so communicating was not a problem this time.

I was told I would need a reservation for a taxi if I left before 7. A desk clerk said I would need to leave at 5:30 or 6 to give me plenty of time to get to the airport and clear customs. He made some calls and finally arranged a taxi for me for 4:30 a.m. I don't know why the lead time was so long; I should have had Igor make the arrangements for me. And the next morning when I stepped outside the hotel, there were several taxis stationed in front.

I was to fly from Moscow to Helsinki, Finland. I had scheduled a six-hour layover in Helsinki so I would have time to tour the city's downtown. I got to the Moscow airport in plenty of time to check in and clear customs. But as we were about to board our Delta Airlines flight, I and a number of other Helsinki-bound passengers were told that we would have to take a later flight. To wait out the six-hour delay, we were sent to a Marriott Hotel and given a room and lunch.

After my sometimes spartan accommodations in Russia, the Marriott seemed like I was back in mid-America. The ambiance was cheerful, and the food was made to order and geared to the American palette. The beds had mattresses and were made up with sheets, as opposed to the feather beds I endured in other parts of the country.

Upon our return to the Moscow airport, we were sent through the lines with expedited service and put on a direct flight to New York.

I returned to New York and then Chicago and eventually Iola safe and sound. I suppose I should not have been traveling alone in light of the

My visit to Russia included some time in Moscow and Red Square.

medical problems I experienced before the trip. I carried with me my full medical history and what should be done if certain conditions arose, but fortunately I did not have any problems.

It was a most interesting trip, despite some of the language problems I encountered. I learned a lot about the Russian culture, and I also learned why so many people in the world want to visit and live in America.

Chapter 19

My German Friend

My acquaintance with Ernst Battenberg of Munich, Germany, was another one of those friendships that transcended business and borders. It, too, started as a business relationship focused on the *Standard Catalog of World Coins*. Ernst also owned a publishing company bearing his name, which published German-language numismatic books. In the early days of Krause Publications' *Standard Catalog of World Coins*, I flew to Munich to talk to Ernst about his becoming the European distributor for our *Standard Catalog*. A follow-up trip to seal the deal included an excursion to his mountain home at Riesle, near the foot of the Alps.

Subsequent travels together in the ensuing years took us to Spain; France; up the Ruhr River valley and into the western Alps to see Mont Blanc (White Mountain); Luxembourg; northern Germany; Copenhagen, Denmark; and Oslo and Kongsburg, Norway. On one of my European trips, I also incorporated a visit to an island in Eastern Friesland to visit Alan Herbert and his

wife, Lisa, who was German. Alan is another longtime contributor to Krause Publications' numismatic books and periodicals who lived on the island at the time.

Ernst was also on my list of stops in April 1988, when Krause Publications faced some difficult challenges marketing the *Standard Catalog* in Europe. At the time, the U.S. dollar was so strong compared to European currencies that our normal discounts to distributors were still higher than the book's retail price in the United States. We did not want to lose the European market, so we sold the books to distributors at the previous year's prices. To reassure our distributors, I scheduled a two-week tour of Europe that took me to London, Amsterdam, Oslo, Stockholm, Munich, Milan, and Rome. About three days at each place gave me time to meet with our distributor in each city and also squeeze in a little sightseeing.

Ernst was my guide for many of these European travels, and I returned the favor a number of times when he and his wife, Gitta, visited the United States. We had a simple agreement: When I was Ernst's guest in Germany, I never paid for board, room, or transportation. I extended the same courtesy when he and Gitta came to the United States.

On one occasion, they flew into Phoenix, where I met them, and we overnighted at a motel near the airport. Ken Buttolph, our market analyst for *Old Cars* weekly newspaper, purchased on my behalf a 1949 Packard at an auction in Scottsdale, Arizona, and handed the keys over to me. The Packard provided the transportation for a tour of the Southwest.

The next morning, we stopped at a local restaurant for breakfast. Ernst read English well, but Gitta had some trouble comprehending American menus. She did not understand "hash browns," "American fries," or "over easy." She hesitated to try ordering on her own. I explained to our waitress that my guests were from Germany and did not understand the American breakfast menu. She responded, "Well, if they are going to eat here, they better well learn it." How do you tip somebody like that? She should have given me a tip just for putting up with her.

Through my friendship with the Battenbergs and in my travels to Germany, I found that Germans loved to eat beef – at all three meals when they had the chance. That is what Ernst and Gitta did during their time in America. Farmland is precious in Germany, so the farming focuses on dairy cows rather than beef cattle. Thus, beef is a delicacy. When it comes to beef, what we Americans think of as expensive is cheap to Germans.

The Battenbergs wanted to see the Southwest because one time I told Ernst that in west Texas you could see farther and see less than any other place in America. So from Phoenix, we motored east in the old Packard on Interstate 10 to El Paso, Texas. There, a coin-collecting friend named Larry Hanks was our host. He showed us the city, and we also went across the border into Mexico for lunch. Gitta would have purchased a pickup load of crafts at the local market there if she could have carried them back to Germany.

From El Paso, we traveled southeast into the Big Bend area of Texas. Ernst enjoyed this part of the trip immensely. He got to see the wide-open country that I spoke of, and he also got to see oil wells planted in hills like a corn field.

Our eventual destination was Houston, where we visited the space center. We approached the city from the southeast, through Galveston. I was somewhat familiar with the area because Camp Wallace, Texas, which was west of Texas City and Galveston, was my first port of call after being drafted. We used to use the Galveston water tower to sight in our 90-millimeter anti-aircraft guns, but I never got to fire one because I was shipped out to Camp Stewart, Georgia, and mechanics school before my training was complete.

There is a spot along the Gulf of Mexico where all of the cottages and homes sit on stilts to protect them from the rising water during storms. I was cruising along at about 65 mph without a taillight in front of me or a headlight in my rear-view mirror. All of a sudden, my mirror was filled with flashing red lights. Apparently, this traffic officer was hiding between the stilts of a house, and I was the only prey available.

*My travels with Ernst Battenberg once took me
to Rudlice, Austria, where my grandmother
Maria Theresa Pelz Krause was born.*

Ernst Battenberg on the streets of Rudlice.

When I got home, I called the town's justice of the peace, who referred me to the mayor. I paid the fine, but they never notified Wisconsin of the violation, which would have cost me six of the 12 points I am allowed if I want to keep my license.

The space center was great. I probably would have never seen it if the Battenbergs had not wanted to go there.

My guests flew home from Houston, but I drove the Packard to Shreveport, Louisiana, to visit Paul Whitnah, another coin-collecting friend. At that time, Paul was head of American Airlines' operations at the Shreveport airport. About 14 miles from my destination, I ran out of gasoline. Fortunately, I was at a rest stop, and a pay phone there saved the day. I called Paul, who arrived a short time later with a couple of cans of gasoline.

Paul and I each consumed a pound of crawdads for lunch, and I was on my way again, this time heading north, back toward Wisconsin. I got as far as Memphis, Tennessee, and so far, the old Packard had not given me any trouble. But the farther north I went, the colder the temperature got. One morning, I planned to get an early start on the day's travels, but the old car would not start. Luckily, I had a couple of cans of starter fluid (ether) with me. I was able to get the car started by manually depressing the starter and feeding starter fluid into the carburetor. Later, I discovered there was a crack in the intake manifold, which allowed air instead of gasoline into the cylinders. Apparently, the starter fluid plus a small amount of gasoline warmed things up so the crack closed.

When I got home, a new manifold fixed the problem. I sold the car at a loss, but it was still less than the cost of a rental car from Phoenix to Iola.

I hosted the Battenbergs again in July 1988. Herman Gjertson, who was our longtime head of maintenance at Krause Publications, and his wife, Donna, drove my Lincoln Town Car from Iola to Denver, where they met me at the Denver airport. We then awaited the arrival of Ernst and Gitta, who were flying in from Munich.

We overnighted in Denver and then headed west for Seattle, where Ernst wanted to visit a former classmate who was now a professor at the University of Washington. We motored west on Interstate 70 toward Salt Lake City, Utah. We stayed overnight there, and Ernst and Gitta and Herman and Donna went to a performance of the Mormon Tabernacle Choir. I was not feeling well, so I stayed behind at the hotel to rest.

Our route northwest took us through Boise, Idaho, and the desert of eastern Oregon on our way to Bend, in the west-central part of the state. From Bend, we continued west to Albany and then north to the small town of Aumsville, near Salem. We stopped in Aumsville so I could visit the gravesite of my Aunt Anna, my father's sister, and her husband, Chris Godahl. We then doubled back to Albany, where I visited Jim McGruder, who was the publisher of the *Western Stamp Collector*. The publication later became part of the Krause Publications lineup of periodicals and was renamed the *Stamp Collector*.

From Albany, we turned north toward Seattle with a brief stop in Puyallup to visit some of my cousins, who treated us to a wonderful cookout. We overnighted nearby, and the next day, Ernst went to see his friend. While those two caught up on old times, the rest of us drove to Vancouver, British Columbia, I think mostly so Gitta, Donna, and Herman could say they had been in Canada. We had lunch in Vancouver and then returned to pick up Ernst in the evening.

The next morning, we began our trip back to Wisconsin via Spokane, and somehow we found the proper route to Glacier National Park in northern Montana before clearing the Rockies. Heading toward Great Falls, Montana, Ernst remarked about how many rich people must have lived there because of the great expanse of wheat fields, which were in the early stages of harvest at the time.

Our route back took us to Devil's Tower National Monument in northeast Wyoming, the Black Hills of South Dakota, Mount Rushmore National Memorial, Badlands National Park, and the Corn Palace in Mitchell, South Dakota. By the time we returned to Iola, we had covered 5,000 miles, which seemed unreal to our guests from Germany.

Germans who want a fine automobile in which to travel the Autobahn or other roads in their country usually buy a Mercedes or a BMW, but Ernst did not like them. So to outdo his fellow countrymen, he decided to buy a Cadillac limousine – not a highly stretched version, but the shorter seven-passenger variety with two jump seats in front of the rear bench seat. So it became my job to order one on his behalf and take delivery of it. All went well, and General Motors delivered it on the day it was promised. I then contacted a shipping company in New York and arranged delivery of the car to Munich.

I called Ernst to tell him his car had arrived, and he and Gitta flew to Wisconsin. After a brief stay in Iola, we climbed into Ernst's new Cadillac limousine and headed for New York to deliver the car to the shipping company. Ernst could not drive in America because he did not have an international driver's license, so I took the wheel of the big "Caddy," as Ernst loved to call them.

The first leg of our journey took us to Chicago, where we met a friend of mine for dinner and an evening at a White Sox game. Baseball was strange to Ernst and Gitta, and although I knew what was going on, they did not have a clue. Of all things, the game included a grand slam. I have probably seen only a dozen pro baseball games in my life, but even I recognized what it was and how rare it was to see one.

The next morning, we left Chicago and drove to Pittsburgh, where we found a motel for the night. At dinner, Ernst asked me how far we had traveled. I said about 500 miles. Ernst likened that to traveling the greatest length of Germany without a stop sign. We, of course, had all interstate highway driving from Chicago to Pittsburgh.

The next day, we drove from Pittsburgh to New Jersey. The next morning, we timed our departure for metropolitan New York to avoid as much traffic as possible. We encountered a detour on the way, which caused a little nervousness on the part of my German guests. Detours are not that long or involved in Germany.

We went through the Lincoln Tunnel into lower Manhattan. I turned north onto one of the avenues and went all the way up to 56th Street. I then turned right and headed toward Seventh

Avenue. I turned right onto Seventh Avenue and, three blocks later, pulled up to the front door of the Sheraton Hotel and Towers with all the grace of a professional limo driver but without the proper hat. Honestly, though, it gave me the willies to drive that big car into the heart of Manhattan.

Ernst and Gitta went inside to register. I took a claim check for my luggage and proceeded to deliver the car to the shipping company's parking lot on 34th Street. I parked the extra-long vehicle with no problems and crossed the street to the company's office. I got a signature on some paperwork for the car and then caught a taxi back to the hotel.

That afternoon, Ernst, Gitta, and I visited some mutual friends. The next day, I bid *auf wiedersehen* to my German friends and new Caddy limousine owners, as they departed for the airport and their car departed for an ocean crossing.

I last saw Ernst again at a hotel near the Newark, New Jersey, airport. I had been in Florida and made the trip up the coast to meet him there. Ernst and his sister were on a round-the-world cruise, but he took sick aboard the ship and got off at New York. They flew back to Germany from New York. A few months later, I learned that Ernst had died after a short battle with cancer.

I lost a most interesting and cavalier friend. Our travels together in Europe and the United States were a joy and a most enriching learning experience.

Chapter 20

"Chet & Cliff"

"Chet and Cliff" was a common reference for many people in the numismatic community, the Iola community, and the community of Krause Publications employees. "Cliff" referred to Cliff Mishler, and our names were often linked in matters related to the communities listed above. Although I retained majority ownership of Krause Publications until the Employee Stock Ownership Plan bought me out in the 1990s, Cliff was my partner in managing Krause Publications starting in the mid-1960s and a trusted adviser on business and community matters.

Cliff's start with the company, however, was non-descript. In fact, I did not even meet him until his first day of employment with Krause Publications.

Cliff grew up in the little town of Vandalia, Michigan, about 20 miles northeast of South Bend, Indiana. He also spent some time in Kalkaska, Michigan, where his father, Nelson

Mishler, was in the business of manufacturing and building concrete stave farm silos. Cliff became interested in numismatics in the early 1950s when he was about 11 years old. A friend of his collected stamps and tried to get Cliff interested in stamps, too, but the stamps did not do much for him. In looking at his friend's hobby magazines, however, Cliff became interested in coins. Like me and a multitude of other coin collectors, Cliff started by searching circulation coinage for Lincoln cents and placing the keepers in a Whitman holder. By this time, though, the holders were blue folders instead of the big "penny boards" that started me in coin collecting in the 1930s.

By the mid-1950s, when he was only a teenager, Cliff started buying uncirculated coins in auctions and from dealers to fill in the dates and mint marks he could not find in circulation. He also became interested in medals and tokens and world coins because he liked the variety in their designs. In the late 1950s, he started issuing medals himself. His first one jointly commemorated the granting of statehood for Alaska and Hawaii.

He also started self-publishing an annual booklet that listed and illustrated commemorative medals and tokens issued throughout the United States and Canada that year. That caught the eye of Ed Rochette, who was Krause Publications' senior editor at the time. Ed and Cliff then met for the first time at the 1961 American Numismatic Association convention in Atlanta.

In early 1963, we planned to increase the frequency of *Numismatic News* from twice monthly to every other week and needed more editorial staff. So in early February, Ed called Cliff and asked him if he would be interested in moving to Iola and joining the *News* staff full time. The two talked, and a few days later, Cliff responded with a three-page, single-spaced typed letter that, in a word, said yes, he would be interested in a position with the *News*. I have often said that Cliff could take a one-page story and turn it into a three-page story.

Cliff and his mother, Lilly Mae Mishler, drove around the bottom tip of Lake Michigan, through Chicago, and then north to Iola one Saturday in February 1963 so Cliff could interview with Ed. I was in Toronto at the time meeting with Cale Jarvis on the launch of *Canada Coin News*. At the end of the interview, Ed offered Cliff a job on the *Numismatic News* editorial staff for $110 a week with a promise of a $10 a week raise after one year. Cliff said he would think about it and get back to him.

I don't think there was much for Cliff to think about, however. Cliff got good grades in high

Cliff's role with the company expanded in the 1970s as the company diversified into other hobby fields.

school, where his elective course work included such diverse subjects as journalism, business classes, and mechanical and architectural drawing. He also worked on his high-school newspaper and yearbook, but that was about the extent of his experience in publishing. There were also, of course, his self-published references on medals and tokens. Altogether, Ed thought Cliff demonstrated the necessary numismatic knowledge and writing skills to join the *News* staff.

After high school, Cliff enrolled in the Northwestern University School of Business in Evanston, Illinois, but he lasted only two semesters. His enrollment was more at the urging of friends and relatives rather than his own initiative, and small-town Cliff and a major university were not a match. His grades were OK, but his heart just was not in it.

After dropping out of college, Cliff landed a job as supervisor of the re-manufacturing department of a lumber yard near Vandalia in which his father held ownership. The job lasted 2 1/2 years until the department's major customer went out of business. He kicked around at some other factory jobs and was even a beach bum in Florida for a while before Ed called that day in February 1963. So I think the chance to join *Numismatic News* and work in a hobby he enjoyed greatly was the first time since graduating from high school that Cliff found something to which he was truly dedicated.

He started with Krause Publications on March 10, 1963, and pursued his new job aggressively, maybe too aggressively at first. Friction soon developed between Ed and Cliff, and after a year, the two were barely talking to each other. One day, Cliff walked into my office and related that Ed had promised him a $10 a week raise after a year of employment. It was now more than a year, and he had not heard anything from

Ed Rochette (right), Krause Publications' senior editor at the time, hired Cliff in 1963.

Cliff (left) was my second in command and trusted adviser for most of his 40 years at Krause Publications.

Ed. The communication between the two was so bad that Cliff did not feel comfortable approaching Ed on the subject. I told Cliff that if that was what Ed promised, then that was what he would get. I made sure Cliff's next paycheck included the $10 raise.

I am happy to report that whatever the problems were between Ed and Cliff, they got resolved soon after that and the two got along fine and still do today.

Also during this time, Cliff started to get my attention as a reliable and hard worker. I noticed those traits in him early on in his employment with Krause Publications. Thus, Ed and I could tend to other business, leave Cliff in charge of the *News*, and we never had to worry about whether he would get the job done. For example, we published a book called *Coins Questions and Answers*. Many on the

editorial staff contributed to the project, but Cliff coordinated the whole thing and got it through production on time. So in 1964 we promoted him to editor of the *News*.

I promoted him again, to numismatic editor, in the fall of 1966, when Ed left to become editor of *The Numismatist*, the American Numismatic Association journal. That put Cliff in charge of the editorial of all of our periodicals, which covered just coin collecting at that time. He took care of the editorial and production parts of the operation, allowing me to focus on the promotional and financial parts.

As documented in a previous chapter, this was at the depths of the economic challenges of the mid to late 1960s. The coin-collecting hobby collapsed, and so did our advertising and subscription revenues. The cash flow was not even sufficient to meet payroll, so I sold some coins and paper money from my collections to inject some cash into the business.

Cliff and I really started to mesh as a management team during this time. I would come into the office on Saturday mornings and usually found Cliff there, too. During this time, we would talk about what could be done to pull the company out of its financial crises. It would be quiet in the office during this time, and there were no deadlines bearing down on us. So the creative ideas flowed freely.

Sometimes I would hit on an idea for a subscription or advertising promotion. Cliff would take my concept, turn it into words, and then hand it off to Doug Watson. Doug would take the words and combine it with graphics to turn it into an attractive presentation. It a matter of a week or so, the idea would have been taken from concept to ready for publication.

It was also during these Saturday-morning sessions that we talked about the need to diversify – both within the coin hobby and outside of it. With his interest in world coins, Cliff was a key figure in conceptualizing the *Standard Catalog of World Coins*. I was hands-on in gathering listings and photos for the first edition, but Cliff took over with the second edition and, as always, immersed himself in the work. That continued until we corralled Colin Bruce to edit future editions.

Cliff was also a key figure in the decision to diversify into old cars. Although he was not an automotive hobbyist, Cliff had the ability to analyze different hobby areas and provide some valuable input into which one would be the best fit for Krause Publications. Ultimately, we decided on old cars in 1971 because that hobby did not have a news and trader publication – a la *Numismatic News* – at the time.

Cliff had the ability to combine practical knowledge and common sense with the more creative and academic aspects of hobby publishing. I attribute the practical knowledge and common sense to his background in the construction business – working first with his dad and then later in the lumber business. That, of course, was something we had in common.

Cliff (far right) and I pose with past recipients of Krause Publications'
Numismatic Ambassador Award at our 1976 building dedication.

I attribute the hobby knowledge to simply his love of numismatics. I believe that love extends beyond the hobby itself and into the hobby community. I think Cliff has always enjoyed being part of that community and associating with others in it. He seems to make friends easily in the hobby, and others, in turn, like him.

Thus, in 1975, once we emerged from the economic crises of the late 1960s, I named Cliff executive vice president and publisher of the numismatics division. In 1978, I expanded his role as executive vice president to include oversight of all Krause Publications publishing divisions.

Cliff remained a valued adviser during Krause Publications' rapid expansion of the 1980s. He and I would visit a potential acquisition and examine it together. He always asked the critical questions and raised the important concerns with bringing a new product into our fold.

So in the early 1980s, when I started thinking about the future of Krause Publications and its eventual life without me, it was logical for me to turn to Cliff first. I always envisioned him taking over as president and even majority owner. But when I approached him on the subject, he backed away. He said he liked to be involved in the hands-on aspects of the business, such as product development. He was not interested in being the No. 1 person and assuming all of the responsibilities involved with it. I brought up the subject several more times in the ensuing years, but Cliff's answer was always the same.

So I had to look outside of the company and eventually hired Don Nicolay in 1986. But when Don left just four years later, I again turned back to Cliff. He was still reluctant to become president, but this time he agreed that if a suitable candidate could not be found outside of the company, he would take the job. Also, the Employee Stock Ownership Plan was well in place by this time, which took care of the ownership aspect.

When the suitable candidate was not forthcoming, Cliff was named president of the company in December 1990, effective January 1. As written in a previous chapter, it was a popular choice among the employees. We did not call Cliff "interim president," but that is how Cliff viewed the job. He accepted the title of president with the condition that he would find and groom his successor for the future. That person turned out to be Roger Case, whom we promoted up through the ranks of the company. When Roger became president in 2000, Cliff was named chairman of the board.

Through the years, Cliff has been a valued member of the Iola community, too. For many years, he was the de facto general chairman of the Iola Old Car Show and Swap Meet, until a not-for-profit corporation was formed to manage the show in 1985. He has been active in the local Lions Club and historical society. Most recently, he headed a fundraising effort to construct a building to house the society's three pieces of antique fire-fighting equipment that were once used in the village. The building's design was patterned after the village's original firehouse, which still stands today.

Cliff's most lasting legacy in the community, however, will probably be the Iola-Scandinavia Fitness and Aquatics Center, which is adjacent to the Iola-Scandinavia High School building in Iola. Cliff and Sally, his wife, brought the idea forth to the community, made a major donation to get the project started, and then headed the effort to raise the remaining funds necessary to complete the project.

The completed building was dedicated in 2001 and has since become a focal point of the community. It features a four-lane swimming pool, a leisure pool with zero-depth entry, a water slide, whirlpool, gymnasium, fitness center with aerobic and weight machines, and community meeting rooms. Area residents of all ages use the facility and benefit from Sally and Cliff's vision in conceiving the idea and then their hard work in making it happen.

In reflecting on Cliff's career, I find it interesting how closely it followed mine. At Krause Publications, he followed me as publisher of the numismatics division, then president of the company, and then chairman of the board.

I received the Farran Zerbe Award, which is the American Numismatic Association's highest honor, in 1977. Cliff received the same award in 1984. I was named to the ANA's Numismatic Hall of Fame in 1990. Cliff received the same honor in 2004.

I have written in these pages about some of the Iola community projects in which I was involved, and I have documented above how much Cliff has meant to the local community. Cliff was raised in a small town and remained a small-town boy at heart through the years; he and Iola are a good match.

So that is the story of how we became "Chet and Cliff." Cliff remained loyal to the company and to me personally during Krause Publications'

Although he accepted the role reluctantly, Cliff became president of Krause Publications in January 1991.

financial crises of the 1960s, when it may have seemed to be in his best interests to go elsewhere. I, in turn, looked past some of Cliff's youthful indiscretions in his early years with the company because I saw how hard the guy worked and what he contributed to the organization.

I employed many dedicated and hard-working people who contributed greatly to the success of the company, but I cannot imagine having owned and managed Krause Publications through its expansive growth from the early 1970s through the 1990s without Cliff Mishler.

Chapter 21

Gifts & Awards

There are many things an individual can give. Thanks and kindness rank high on my list. So do time and talent. And then, of course, there is money. I have been blessed with plenty of money to share with others. I have met and heard of a lot of people who seem to be so busy accumulating money that they never get into the spirit of giving. That is a shame.

As a coin collector, I am reminded of three Bible stories, each with a numismatic angle, that illustrate the spirit of giving. The first concerns the "tribute penny." In Matthew 23:17-22, the Pharisees attempt to entangle Jesus in his talk by asking him if it is lawful to pay taxes to Caesar. Jesus asks for a sample of the money used to pay taxes, and he is handed a coin. He asks, "Whose likeness and inscription is this?" The Pharisees respond, "Caesar's." Jesus then replies, "Render therefore to Caesar the things that are Caesar's, and to God the things that are God's."

Scholars believe the coin Jesus was handed was most likely a denarius of Emperor Tiberius. In the King James Version of the Bible, it is called a "penny" because that was the contemporary English coin that most closely corresponded to a denarius. To me, the story of the tribute penny symbolizes worldly material wealth and the giving of money to try to cover up other transgressions.

The second story involves the thirty pieces of silver that Judas Iscariot received for betraying Jesus (Matthew 26:14-15). Scholars say these were probably shekels of Tyre. To me, this story symbolizes the greedy – those who can always find an excuse not to give.

The last story is the familiar tale of the widow's mites. Mark 12:41-44 says Jesus sat in a temple in Jerusalem and watched people putting money into the treasury. "Many rich people put in large sums," the story says. "And a poor widow came, and put in two copper coins, which make a penny. And he [Jesus] called his disciples to him, and said to them, 'Truly, I say to you, this poor widow has put in more than those who are contributing to the treasury. For they all contributed out of their abundance, but she out of her poverty has put in everything she had, her whole living.'"

The coins referred to in the story are believed to be mites, or leptons, minted in Judaea. They were the smallest coins available in the region at the time. The story has a great moral, but I do not believe that I could in good conscious solicit or accept a gift that was all someone had. If I did, I would find a way to see that the person received something back worth twice as much.

The material wealth that resulted from a successful business has allowed me to make gifts ranging from modest to sizable. The Marshfield Clinic in Marshfield, Wisconsin, has benefited from my gifts because I believe in the work of the clinic's research facilities. In the case of the Rawhide Boys Ranch in New London, Wisconsin, I believe in the ranch's giving of love and discipline to otherwise wayward boys.

I have supported the Maxi Fund, created by former Green Bay Packer Max McGee, to try to find a cure for juvenile diabetes. I have several good friends who have suffered from diabetes all their lives.

I have also been a longtime member and supporter of the Iola chapter of the Lions Club, whose motto is "We Serve." Lions clubs worldwide, including the Iola chapter, have supported and promoted sight-related causes.

The local Lions Club's big fund-raising event each year is the Iola Old Car Show and Swap Meet, held during the second full weekend in July on the car-show grounds in Iola. The Lions Club used to sponsor a chicken roast in the village park each year. In 1972, when Krause Publications was in the early days of publishing *Old Cars*, I invited some fellow automotive hobbyists to display their old cars at the chicken roast as an added attraction. A couple of dozen of them accepted and received a free chicken dinner in appreciation.

It took a few dollars of subsidy for a few years, but the show continued to expand in subsequent years. Today, it is one of the largest old-car shows and swap meets in the country, and many other civic organizations from Iola and surrounding communities provide volunteer labor for staging the show. In return, they each get a piece of the $250,000 in annual earnings provided by the show.

The show is managed by Iola Old Car Show Incorporated, a not-for-profit organization governed by a board of directors consisting of representatives from the major groups involved in the show. The Iola Lions Club is still one of them, and they still serve grilled chicken at the show.

The most recent community project to which I have given financial and moral support has been Living Oaks, a new 24-unit residential care apartment complex in Iola. It was built and is managed under the auspices of Iola Living Assistance Incorporated, which provides rehabilitation, skilled nursing, and housing facilities. My support of Living Oaks was a bit of a guilt trip for me. I have given to many smaller projects in Iola over the years, but others collectively have funded the larger benevolent activity. So I jumped on the bandwagon in a major way because I am at the point where I need such a facility and a lot of my friends will, too. It became my home in December 2007. My sister Mary Klug moved there earlier in the year.

When I have announced major gifts to groups, I have often said, "They say you should give until it hurts. Well, I feel great." My greatest joy in benevolence is giving to those who really need help. A gift of any amount can help civic projects and worthy causes get over the top. I have done this for people I have known and some I have never known. Either way, it is a wonderful feeling.

It is a wonderful feeling also when organizations that I have supported over the years provide formal recognition of those efforts. I have been the fortunate recipient of many honors and awards over the years. Among them was the Marshfield Clinic Heritage Foundation Award, which was established in 1997 to honor individuals who have made significant contributions to the community, government, civic leadership, education, medicine, law, or business.

The inaugural recipient was Melvin R. Laird, a former U.S. representative from Wisconsin and defense secretary during the Nixon administration. Other recipients have been clinic physicians Dean Emanuel, Russell F. Lewis, and George E. Magnin; former Wisconsin governors Lee Sherman Dreyfus and Tommy G. Thompson; Robert F. Froehlke, former National Advisory Council chairman and Army secretary under Defense Secretary Laird; and David R. Obey, U.S. representative from Wisconsin's 7th Congressional District.

I was honored to have received the award in 2001. Leading up to the award, I had served on the Marshfield Clinic National Advisory Council and was involved in fund-raising for the original Laird Center and then the Laird Center for Medical Research. When my term on the council was complete, I was given emeritus status, which means I can still attend meetings and contribute to the discussions but I can no longer vote. Speakers at my award presentation included Mel Laird, Max McGee, and John Gillespie, who is the co-founder with his wife, Jan, of Rawhide Boys Ranch.

Besides a plaque, recipients of the Heritage Foundation Award also receive a green sport coat, which we are expected to wear at all National Advisory Council functions. I do and proudly.

In some cases, the honors I received were more a reflection of Krause Publications than me personally, but I was the person whose name was attached to it. I consider that to have been the case in 1977 when I received the Farran Zerbe Award, which at the time was the highest honor of the American Numismatic Association, a national organization for coin collectors. The presentation was made at the ANA's annual convention that year in Atlanta.

Because Krause Publications was founded with coin-collecting periodicals, the company and its representatives did a lot of traveling within the hobby and were active in different aspects of the hobby – at the national and even world level on down to local clubs. The Zerbe award reflected that involvement, and I consider it the first great award I received.

Subsequent to that, I received the ANA's Lifetime Achievement Award, and then in 1990, I became the 55th inductee into the ANA

Numismatic Hall of Fame. My portrait, along with those of other Hall of Fame inductees, is displayed in the Edward C. Rochette Money Museum at ANA headquarters in Colorado Springs, Colorado. I cherish those honors greatly, because coin collecting was my original hobby interest and I have spent most of my active hobby life in numismatics.

In early 2007, I received another cherished hobby honor when I was the honoree at the annual dinner gala of the American Numismatic Society, which is another national organization, based in New York City. The dinner and accompanying dance and benefit auction was held in the Empire Room of the Waldorf-Astoria Hotel in New York.

Another honor that had my name on it but again was more reflective of a company accomplishment came in 1990 when I was named the Wisconsin Small Business Person of the Year in an awards program sponsored by the U.S. Small Business Administration. Thanks to the efforts of others, I was selected for the award before I even became aware that I was nominated.

Tom Godfrey, a retired businessman in nearby Waupaca, Wisconsin, served on the SBA's local district board at the time. He approached Iola attorney DeLyle Omholt about nominating

Krause Publications produced this brochure to commemorate my winning the Wisconsin Small Business Person of the Year Award in 1990.

1990 Wisconsin Small Business Person of the Year

Presented by the Wisconsin Small Business Administration
May 11, 1990
Marc Plaza
Milwaukee

Chester L. Krause
Founder and Chairman of the Board
Krause Publications
Iola, Wisconsin

I receive the Wisconsin Lions Foundation award from Dewey Carl of Manawa, a Lions district governor.

me for the award. DeLyle then contacted Don Nicolay, who was president of Krause Publications at the time. Don and Greg Loescher, who worked in Krause Publications' marketing department, completed the nomination paperwork.

The nomination had to document success in staying power, growth in number of employees and revenues, innovativeness in products or services offered, response to adversity, contributions to community projects, and demonstration of initiative in an area of national interest.

The SBA awards week in early May 1990 was a whirlwind time. First, we were off to

Washington, D.C., where we joined the winners from the 49 other states plus the District of Columbia and Puerto Rico-Virgin Islands. "We" were my nieces Patti Krause, Sue Helgeson and Beth Meagher; and Beth's husband, Bruce. We stayed at the Hotel Washington, across the street from the Treasury building and just a short distance from the White House. Our stay in Washington included a reception hosted by Gannett Newspapers and lunch on Capitol Hill, where many of our representatives and senators joined us.

On the afternoon of May 8, we gathered in room 450 of the Old Executive Office Building, where the winner of the national Small Business Person of the Year Award was announced and President George H.W. Bush briefly addressed the gathering.

"The strength of America lies with those who are willing to take a chance in small business and build for the future," the president told us. "And it's here you find the determination and the ingenuity and the vision that have created the enterprises which drive our economy and enrich our lives."

The national award, won by the Iowa state winner, was presented by Susan Engleleiter, a former Wisconsin state senator and head of the national SBA at the time. Also during the week, I was interviewed by a writer for *Entrepreneur* magazine for an article that appeared in the September 1990 issue.

After the events in Washington, Patti and I flew to Milwaukee, while the rest of our entourage headed back to Iola. I formally received the state

Small Business Person of the Year Award at a luncheon May 11 in a ballroom at the Marc Plaza Hotel in Milwaukee. Governor Thompson was keynote speaker for the event, which was attended by more than 400 business people and politicians. Included in the crowd were about 50 family members, friends, and Krause Publications staff members.

Many years later, as I reflected on this award, it made me pause a bit to think of how great it was to be selected for this honor. This and the many other honors that have come my way are a reflection of the great people I have surrounded myself with over the years.

Rawhide Boys Ranch founder John Gillespie and I stand by the sign for the Chester L. Krause Fieldhouse at Rawhide. I was honored to have the building named for me in appreciation for my gift toward its construction.

I was the inaugural recipient of the Meguiar's Award, sponsored by the car-care product company of the same. Subsequent honorees have included entertainer Jay Leno, to my right.

Chapter 22

Public Service

When it comes to public service, large gifts of money often get the most publicity. But gifts of time and talent can be equally important. Over the years, I have volunteered or have been asked to serve on a number of boards or councils, and have been involved with the charitable works or public service of other organizations. A few were mentioned in previous chapters; following are a few more that stand out in my memory.

Those who are not coin collectors or are not familiar with U.S. numismatic traditions have probably never heard of the U.S. Assay Commission. The commission had its roots in 13th-century England. The Royal Mint created an independent annual jury charged with checking a random sample of English coins to see if they conformed to the required specifications. The trial pieces against which the sample was judged were delivered to the jury in a small box called a "pyx."

Thus, the process became known as the Trial of the Pyx.

The sample coins were first counted to make sure the proper number were provided. They then were weighed – individually and in bulk – to see if they were within the tolerance standards. Finally, the coins were assayed to determine if they were of the proper fineness, or purity, and composition. The jury would then report to an official of the king or queen on its findings. The tradition continues today in Great Britain.

In this country, Congress provided for a similar body and process when it passed the original act establishing the U.S. Mint in 1792. The first U.S. Assay Commission met March 20, 1797. Like England's Trial of the Pyx, it counted, weighed, and assayed a sample of U.S. coins, compared them to the standard, and reported to the government on its findings.

I was appointed to the Assay Commission in 1961. At the time, members were recommended by

I am pictured here with my fellow Lake Iola Estates developers. To my left are Jim Twetan, Al Langland, James Olson, and Ed Thoe.

U.S. representatives and approved by the Treasury Department. Ed Rochette, editor of *Numismatic News* at the time, arranged for my appointment through Representative Harold Donahue of Massachusetts, who was from Ed's hometown of Worcester. Ed headlined a subsequent issue of *Numismatic News* with "Publisher Appointed to Assay Commission." My appointment started a steady stream of coin collectors who were nominated in ensuing years. New commission members were appointed every year. There were 11 of us who served in 1961.

The commission met annually in February at the Philadelphia Mint to go through the ritual of weighing and assaying a sample of U.S. coins. The year I served, there had been a big snow storm in Philadelphia a few days before my arrival. When I got to town, the streets still had plenty of the white stuff piled up on them.

My fellow commissioners and I reported to the mint building on Spring Garden Street. This building opened in 1901 and was the third Philadelphia Mint building in history. The fourth and current building is located at the corner of 4th and Arch streets and opened in 1969.

An official from the Commerce Department's Weights and Measures Division provided us with the official weights to be used in testing the coinage samples. We appointed someone to chair our group, and then each of us was assigned to a particular committee: counting, weighing, or assaying.

During the year, the Mint was required to set aside one coin for every so many produced. These coins that were put aside were called "counters" and provided the sample the commission used to compare with the standard. The commission members on the counting detail had to count the

An aerial view of the Iola Country Club golf course, looking northwest. Today, the course is known as Glacier Wood.

counters, which were in stacks of equal height. A number of coins were then selected from the counters for weighing and assaying.

I was on the weighing committee. As I recall, we weighed 10 dimes, 10 quarters, and 10 half dollars. They had to weigh within a small tolerance of the standard. We hoped to find at least one coin that matched the standard weight perfectly, but we did not. After weighing, the coins were sent to the assaying committee, which tested them to see if they conformed to the composition standard of 90-percent silver and 10-percent copper.

After our duties were complete, we were guided around the mint building. My guide was U.S. Mint Chief Engraver Gilroy Roberts. Gilroy worked on the designs of a number of U.S. coins but is probably most famous for designing the obverse of the Kennedy half dollar. I had met

Gilroy previously, so he took me to many special parts of the mint building and made a special effort to introduce me to the many coin collectors who worked there.

When the duties at the mint were complete, we returned to our hotel for a dinner hosted by Philadelphia Mint Superintendent Rae V. Biester. At the dinner, commission members each received a medal commemorating their service. My original one was later stolen, but I was able to replace it by purchasing one at an auction.

The last public meeting of the Assay Commission was on February 11, 1976. The Carter administration discontinued the practice as a cost-saving move. The actual cost to the government, however, was minimal – a dinner or luncheon for commission members, the medals, and staff time. Commission members paid their own way to Philadelphia.

The commission continued to meet after 1976 but with government officials appointed to the group instead of public members. The commission ceased meeting altogether under the Reagan administration. Some say the commission became a mere formality when the country switched to base-metal coinage in 1965. Others, however, felt it was an important tradition that should be carried on and could be carried on at little cost to the government.

The commission does live on, to a degree, through a group called the Old Timer Assay Commissioners Society, which was formed at the 1969 American Numismatic Association convention in Philadelphia. It is mostly a social group – we have no bylaws or officers, for example – made up of those of us who served on the commission. We continue to meet annually at the ANA conventions, but time is taking a toll on our numbers.

Closer to home, I served on another government board in the 1960s that was better known locally but was not popular – the local draft board. I don't remember exactly how I came to be on the board, but I considered it an extension of my Army service during World War II. Serving on the board was not too bad in the late 1950s and early 1960s, but it became worse as the Vietnam War dragged on in the mid-1960s and the country's anti-war feelings grew.

To a large degree, serving on the draft board was a clerk's job. In Waupaca County, that clerk was Luella Johnson, who later worked for Krause Publications. She had a set of federal rules to follow and was a de facto member of our board.

She told the board members what needed to be done.

Draft registrants automatically fell into one of five categories designated by the numbers 1 through 5. There were subcategories within the numbered categories designated by various letters. A registrant designated 1-A was a prime candidate for being drafted. A 4-F was not eligible, oftentimes for medical reasons. A 5-A was over the age of liability for military service.

A 2-C classification designated an agriculture-related deferment. A 2-S designated a student deferment. Luella would send a form to those eligible for these deferments, which they would be required to complete. She would then present the required documents to the board. Board members would review the documents and then vote on the registrants' status.

There were some registrants who did not qualify for deferral or who did not agree with their classification and requested a personal appearance before the board to plead their cases. As one can imagine, these proceedings were oftentimes filled with emotion. Sometimes a father and son would appear together. Sometimes the father was a farmer who felt he needed his son to stay home and help with the farm. Other times a student would request a few months of deferment so he could complete a semester of work. And still other times a registrant would plead that his parents were ill or had become disabled and they relied on him for support.

I remember one case in particular. A local fellow named Dennis Biederman received his notice to report four days before he found out his wife, Judy, was pregnant. After 1966, married men and fathers no longer automatically qualified for a deferment. In considering hardship cases, board members had some criteria passed on to us that we would follow, and we established our own criteria in an attempt to be fair to everyone. But in Dennis' case, there was nothing we could do about it, although we wished otherwise.

I am happy to report that Dennis completed his service and made it back home safe and sound. He is still a good friend of mine, and when we meet today, we occasionally reflect on the situation we found ourselves in some 40 years ago.

As I reflect today on my service on the draft board, I consider it a job that had to be done, and somehow it became my lot to do it. It was an interesting job but a difficult one at times, too.

Another interesting but sometimes difficult project was my involvement in the development of Lake Iola. The village of Iola is located on the south branch of the Little Wolf River. In the mid-1800s, when the area was first being settled, a dam was built on the river to power a grist mill, which created a millpond. By the 1960s, however, the mill was out of operation and had long since stopped using the water power created by the dam. The water in the pond had become stagnant and weeds had taken it over, making it almost impossible to navigate the upper part of the pond.

Jim Olson, who ran a heating business in the village, dreamed of one day draining the water from the pond, removing the stumps and debris from the open-water area, and improving the shoreline. His dream started to become reality when he convinced James Twetan, a local insurance agent; Al Langland, owner of Iola Plumbing and Heating; Edmund Thoe, a local chiropractor; and me to form a development corporation that we named Lake Iola Estates.

We first purchased the old mill, which still stands today on South Main Street, from Frederick Wipf. We then acquired all the land flooded by the dam and adjacent property. After getting the blessing of the Iola village board and the state Department of Natural Resources, we began lifting the planks on the overflow dam so the pond would drain. When the dam is in place, the water backs up for a couple of miles, so we removed the planks gradually to limit the amount of additional water that flowed downstream. We were anxious to get rid of the water and start cleaning up the pond bed, but we had to be patient. The first year was non-productive in terms of cleanup, except for a few spots.

After we eventually drained most of the pond, water was still trapped in low areas, and the river channel was full of silt, which did not allow the river's tributaries to empty. One Sunday afternoon, Jim, a couple of other volunteers, and I donned waders, armed ourselves with rakes and pitchforks, and started trudging upstream. As we went, we dislodged brush and snags that held the silt back. Several times when we dislodged the debris, 100 to 150 feet of channel silt would let go and we would proceed to the next section of the river. As each section of the river channel was cleared, the tributaries would release their trapped water.

Finally, we reached a spot called Indian Point. That was where the river channel ran closest to the shore of the pond. We pulled ourselves ashore, took off our water-filled waders, and stretched out on the ground to rest. It was a hard Sunday afternoon of work. Of all the effort that was put into developing the lake, I always considered those four hours to be the most productive. Of course, I was part of it, so my view is probably biased.

After the water was drained, we could start removing stumps. The lake bottom is firm sand with no sinkholes, which allowed us to bring in heavy machinery along the shoreline for removing the stumps. Carl Waller owned a service station in town, and we used his wrecker to pull the stumps ashore. We had to leave one behind – and it is still there today – because we could not find a way to pull it out.

As the lake began to take shape, we brought in surveyors and began plotting waterfront and back lots. Nearly 100 frontage lots were established. Roads to the lots had to be built and sewer lines had to be brought in, but as homes were built on the lots, the village increased its tax rolls considerably.

Today, Lake Iola provides year-round fishing opportunities and a waterfront setting for two parks. Anybody driving by on a summer evening will usually see anglers fishing from the banks and one or more small boats out on the water. In the winter, ice-fishing shanties dot the frozen water.

Five of us served on a board that developed the lake. We did not always agree, and I was usually at the center of the problem because I was a take-charge person. When I did take charge, I occasionally caught hell from the other four. It

would serve no purpose to rehash those differences of opinion today because it is all water under the bridge. In the end, we got the job done, and Lake Iola has been a wonderful addition to the community.

At about the same time we were working on the Lake Iola project, John Greiner, manager of the Central Wisconsin Electric Cooperative, and local attorney DeLyle Omholt were planning the construction of a nine-hole golf course that would abut the eastern edge of Lake Iola. Although the golf course and lake development were two separate projects, they complemented each other and were an enhancement for both.

I joined the organization developing the course and supported it, but golf has never been my thing. After the course was built, I did, however, assemble some clubs and whacked my way around the course a few times. But I tried to avoid doing that whenever a good golfer was around.

The course originally was known as the Iola Country Club. Several years ago, it was expanded to 18 holes, a new clubhouse was built to replace the old one after it was damaged by fire, and the course was renamed Glacier Wood Golf Club. It was one of 17 Wisconsin golf courses listed in the book *Best Places to Play 2004-2005*, published by *Golf Digest* magazine.

The Lake Iola and golf-course developments are two projects from the late 1960s that have endured today and have given an added boost to our small community.

Chapter 23

Thank You

In a way, I have come full circle. Much of my time today is spent in my retirement office in the building I originally constructed in 1957 to house the growing operations of *Numismatic News*. I repurchased the building in 2002, did some remodeling and renovating, and moved in. I share the building with the law office of Bruce Meagher, the accounting office of Iola Bookkeeping & Tax Service, and my assistant, Chris Williams.

I am there during most business hours – 8 a.m. to 5 p.m. Monday through Friday – but those hours are subject to personal appointments elsewhere and the whims of independence, like a two-hour noon break. When I am there, I greet visitors who stop in, take care of business related to the Krause Family Foundation, continue some collecting-related interests, and just have fun.

Those collecting interests have waned in some regards in recent years but have strengthened in others. Being realistic, I know that to leave everything I have collected to the person that would have to liquidate it would be a full-time burden to that person.

At its zenith, my collection of World War II military vehicles and equipment totaled 45 to 50 pieces. They included everything from a Sherman tank that weighed 65,000 pounds to jeeps built by Ford and Willys that were so much alike parts from one would fit the other. The collection also included an M-26 Dragon Wagon. In English, that was a tractor-trailer rig with 34 tires – half of which were tandem – that could haul the Sherman tank. It weighed 92,000 pounds. My mechanic, various other helpers, and I loaded the tank on it once and took it to a parade. We were invited to never come back after marking up the road pretty badly. The Dragon Wagon now resides at a museum at Fort Snelling, Minnesota.

Besides the heavy equipment, I also owned seven 2 1/2-ton GMC 6x6 trucks. General George S. Patton credited that type of truck, jeeps, and DC-3 airplanes with winning the war in Europe. I started my military collection by acquiring anti-aircraft equipment of the type used by my battalion. That included a 40-millimeter automatic

My World War II military collection focused on the type of equipment used by the anti-aircraft battalion in which I served. An example is this 40-millimeter anti-aircraft gun.

gun and an M-51 quad 50. The latter consisted of four 50-caliber machine guns mounted on a turret that could traverse 360 degrees and elevate to 90 degrees – straight up. It was as wicked a piece of equipment as the Army had at the time. When I owned it, however, the guns and all of the other weaponry had been demilitarized and could no longer fire.

After acquiring the guns, I began buying other anti-aircraft ordnance – searchlights, generators to run them, a 90-millimeter gun, and a tractor to pull it.

While interesting as all get out to an anti-aircraft artillery veteran, the collection was difficult to sell. Some of my close friends knew of my dilemma, and a series of contacts turned up interest in the collection from a military museum in Holland. A transaction was completed, and soon most of the pieces were headed for Europe.

Over the years, I also assembled a large collection of collectible cars, civilian trucks, tractors, and antique gasoline engines. Those were sold June 5, 2004, in a 176-lot sale conducted

in Iola by Aumann Auctions of Nokomis, Illinois. The highlight of that sale was an early International Harvestor tractor – one of the first built. It sold for $125,000.

I kept a few cars and trucks from the collection: a 1903 Ford Model A, which was the first car in Waupaca County and now is in the Dean Oakes Museum in Iowa City, Iowa; a 1912 Sears Runabout, which I subsequently sold; a 1914 Case touring car; a 1929 Packard touring car; a 1939 Ford Marmon-Herrington half-ton pickup truck; a 1957 Chevrolet Bel-Air four-door hardtop that was my aunt's car; and a 1970 Chevrolet utility truck.

I still collect military vehicles, too, but with a different focus. I was sad to see my previous military collection go, so I decided to try to assemble a collection of one example of every type of military jeep produced. I once saw a picture of 11 different jeeps and thought that was all that were made. I was familiar with World War II jeeps from having served as an auto mechanic in the Army, but I had not kept up with models produced

This World War II Sherman tank once resided in my military vehicle collection.

for the Korean and Vietnam wars. Today, my jeep collection consists of 23 vehicles extending into 1960s and '70s models. The collection includes a 1941 Bantam BRC prototype, a 1941 Ford GP four-wheel-steer prototype, and a 1944 amphibious Ford GPA.

Coin collecting was my first passion, and although I have liquidated some holdings there in recent years, too, I still own and continue to acquire numismatic pieces. "Numismatics" deals with anything that is money or represents money. That includes coins, paper money, and things that substitute for money, such as tokens, scrip, and paper chits.

Privately issued tokens have a long history in this country as substitutes for coins. Many were issued during the economic depression of 1837 and are known today as Hard Times tokens. I had a large collection of these but sold them several years ago to concentrate on other areas. Tokens were still used in modern times by public transportation systems and casinos, but electronic debit cards are

taking over many of those duties.

Scrip is a paper substitute for money. It is little used today, but it was more common in the 1930s when coins and paper money were scarce. Businesses would sometimes pay their employees with scrip, which other businesses in the community would honor.

I still have most of the coins I collected in the 1950s and '60s in blue Whitman folders. Like many others, I cut my collecting teeth on Lincoln cents, starting as a youth. I started with a circulated set and improved it over the years. Today, I own a nice set of Lincoln cents in grade MS-60 (uncirculated) or better. Several years ago, I obtained a set of two-cent coins, a short-lived series from 1864 to 1872.

I bought 19 proof Liberty Head nickels from my longtime collecting friend and employee Art Christoph before he died. I have since acquired the 13 other proof Liberty Head nickels Art did not have, so I now have a complete set. I also bought Art's proof sets from 1936 to 1964 and his mint sets from 1934 to 1964. So I have examples of nearly all U.S. coins from 1934 to date.

I also have complete sets of U.S. commemorative coins and Standing Liberty quarters in grade MS-60 or better, including the rare 1916 and the 1918/7 overdate.

Perhaps the rarest and most expensive coin I ever owned was a Canadian 1936 "dot" cent. In 1937, the obverse portrait on Canadian coins changed from King George V to King George VI. The new portrait, however, was not ready when production of 1937 coins was supposed to begin, so the Canadian mint continued to strike 1936 coins but placed a small dot under the date to indicate that they were struck in 1937. Only a handful of the 1936 cents with the dot under the date are known to exist.

John J. Pittman of Rochester, New York, another longtime collecting friend who was well known in numismatic circles, previously owned my example and two others. He always promised to sell one of them to me, but he died before we could get the job done. So when his collection was sold at auction and this lot came up, I held up my bidder's card until it was mine. I have since sold it myself, but it was a pleasure to have owned it.

I collected stamps, too, as a youth, but those were destroyed in our house fire when I was in high school. In later years, however, I started to build a collection of U.S. uncirculated singles. The first stamps I purchased was the Great Americans series, which started in 1980 and which I still have. I stayed current with new stamps and also started working my way back in time. I remember how great it was to complete a mint

set of the Columbian Issue, a series of 16 stamps commemorating the 1893 World Columbian Exposition in Chicago. At today's values, I am glad I did.

I tried to keep up with new issues, but there are so many now that it is a full-time hobby by itself and I have too many other collecting interests.

In most recent years, Wisconsin paper money has been at the forefront of my numismatic collecting interests. I collect Wisconsin territorial bank notes and scrip (1836-1848), Wisconsin state bank notes (1853-1865) and scrip (1853-1900), Wisconsin large-size National Bank notes (1862-1929), and Wisconsin small-size National Bank notes (1929-1935). I have been an avid collector of this material since the early 1960s, and I believe I have the largest collection existing today.

I have also started collecting some lesser-known examples of Wisconsin paper numismatic items. Among them are canal bonds and scrip. These were used to finance the construction of a canal from the upper Fox River to the Wisconsin River at Portage. The Wisconsin River flows from the northern part of the state south into the Mississippi River; the Fox River flows north into the waters of Green Bay. So the canal created a navigable waterway connecting the Mississippi with Green Bay and the Great Lakes. It was used until 1951, and remnants of it still exist today.

I also own bonds issued by the Sturgeon Bay and Lake Michigan Canal Company. This company built a 1.3-mile canal that connected Sturgeon Bay, part of the waters of Green Bay, and Lake Michigan about half way up Wisconsin's

I bagged my first wild turkey with the help of Gordy Krahn, a Krause Publications outdoors editor at the time.

Gerry Blair, a former Krause Publications outdoors editor who resided in Arizona, and I once had a successful coyote hunt near Wickenburg, Arizona.

Door Peninsula. This allowed vessels traveling from ports on Green Bay to lower Lake Michigan to avoid the dangerous waters between the peninsula's northern tip and Washington Island, about five miles north of the peninsula. The early French explorers named this passage "Porte des Morts," or Death's Door. The canal also knocked about a hundred miles off the trip.

Extending beyond Wisconsin, I also collect bank notes and scrip, including mining scrip, from Michigan's Upper Peninsula, World War I Liberty Bonds, and postage-stamp envelopes of 1862. These envelopes were another response to tough economic times in the country. Postage stamps were used in transactions instead of small change, but they stuck together and became worn when handled so much. So companies in New York and Massachusetts produced small envelopes of about 2 1/2 inches by 1 1/2 inches to house the stamps. The amount contained in the envelope was printed on it. Sometimes a merchant paid to have his advertising printed on the envelope.

Apparently, the envelopes were not saved to any extent. As they became worn, they were thrown away. I have bought them at auction and have paid as much as the price of a nice coin for some examples.

I also completed a type set of Confederate currency, which I sold at an auction conducted by R.M. Smythe & Company of New York City.

What makes a person so passionate about collecting? It is hard to nail down and put into words. Perhaps it is the same thing that makes some people good writers or carpenters or auto mechanics or doctors or artists. A coin collection can provide an outline of a chain of historic events. It can also provide economic lessons. Assembling it gives the collector a sense of anticipation, and completing it gives the collector a sense of accomplishment. When I acquire a piece of paper money I have sought, I feel like a kid with a new toy.

As for my non-collecting interests, I am still able to enjoy hunting now and then, although I no longer venture far from home to do it. In the late 1940s, I visited my Uncle Willie's ranch near Rochelle, Wyoming, in what today is known as the Thunder Basin National Grassland, and shot a deer and an antelope there. In the 1960s, my brother Neil and I made several trips to Montana and hunted with Joe DeSaye, a major *Numismatic News* advertiser at the time who lived there. Our mission was to help reduce the population of prairie dogs – a rodent that digs and tunnels through the ground and disrupts ranching operations.

We also hunted on the Belknap Indian Reservation in north-central Montana, which required special permits. Neil and I made at least a half-dozen hunting trips to Montana before Neil died in 1980. I went back about as many times after that.

I consider myself an able marksman, a skill I learned from my dad and both of my brothers. They taught me the basics of hunting and how to navigate through the woods.

In my early years of deer hunting (1946-1960), we went "up north" to hunt – the land that extends from Shawano County, just north of Waupaca County, to the border with Michigan's

Upper Peninsula. There was no deer season in Waupaca and many other counties in central and southern Wisconsin at the time because of overhunting in previous decades. I can remember even before the war going to the Willow Flowage area in north-central Wisconsin to hunt deer. I also remember several deer hunting trips farther east of there near a little town called Alvin, which is east of Eagle River and just a short drive south of the U.P. border. That was great training country for becoming a good woodsman, but few deer made their homes there.

One morning, however, I saw a couple of does on a bluff about a mile east of our camp. So I staked out the location and hoped they or others might come down the same path, but it was all to no avail. I had decided earlier to walk to the southeast and cross a swamp of spruce trees maybe half a mile wide. The forecast was for sun that day, but instead, it started to snow. The half mile of swamp was a pretty large area to undertake in a snow storm, but off I went. I headed toward a clump of higher trees, which I was able to keep in sight despite the snow. I made it, but then the question was, where do I go from here?

Because of the snow, I could no longer see the hill from which I came, so I could not use that for a landmark. I got out my compass and decided to continue walking southeast. I made it out of the spruce swamp and into some lowland with taller trees and tag alders. Those are about as miserable a bunch of brush as there is, but they usually mark the transition from a swamp to higher ground. I fought my way through the brush, only to have my wits scared out of me by the snort of a buck.

I was not able to see it well enough, however, to get off a shot, so I sat down for a moment or two just to get my bearings again. I looked at my watch – it was 10:30 a.m. – and just then the sun came out. I set my visual course due south again, and in a few minutes, I was at the base of a hill replete with tall timber. I continued to head south until off in the distance I could see the distinctive red coat of a hunter from a neighboring camp. That confirmed that I was where I set out to be.

Out in those woods by myself, I was truly lost for the first time in my life, but I made it back and passed a lasting lesson on contending with the outdoors.

I never shot a deer in that area despite about 10 years of hunting there, but one year I did get the prize of the forest – a timber wolf. At that time, there was still a bounty on wolves. They were a protected species for many years until restrictions were loosened more recently.

It was late one afternoon, and I was about ready to head back to our camping trailer. I did not have much time to shoot and had a small target aperture on the rear sight of my 30-06 Enfield that Neil and I had converted to a sporting rifle. But I got a good look at the wolf and hit him low in the belly. He retreated from whence he came, but I found him after tracking him a few hundred yards.

I began my trek back to camp with my wolf, only to be met by other members of our group coming to help drag a buck home. Neil and I were known for making our first shot count, and a single shot was a sign of success. I was successful on this deer-hunting trip, but in an unexpected way.

Our hunting trips to Wisconsin's Northwoods region ended when deer hunting opened in our own Waupaca County as wildlife populations were restored. Now, we were just a few minutes away from hunting land that had been part of our farm but was kept when we sold the farm and moved into the village. Sometime in the late 1950s, I bought another 40 acres of land east of Iola, and that became my hunting grounds. Sometimes Neil, Ben, or some acquaintance would join me, and I would let Krause Publications employees hunt on the land, too.

George Aanstad, who was Iola's postmaster, owned land adjacent to mine, and he let me personally hunt his land, too. On the eastern slope of what we call Aanstad Ridge is a big rock. It must be 15 to 20 feet wide and 12 feet tall. It made an excellent landmark when traveling through the woods and a great deerstand. It was a productive area; I shot about a dozen deer there.

Today, my nephew Carl Krause owns land with a home on it about six miles east of Iola. One can sit on the porch of his house and watch wild turkeys and deer go by. One April day in 2007, I went to Carl's land and sat from early morning until breakfast time. I had breakfast served to me at Carl's house, took a two-hour break, and sat again until noon. I then came in and ate lunch, drove back into town, and returned at about 4:30 that afternoon. At 6:15 p.m., a two-year-old "jake" – a young male wild turkey – came close enough for me to get a shot, and I bagged him. He had three-quarter-inch spurs and weighed 23 pounds, 4 ounces.

I would love to hunt the Belknap with Joe DeSaye again, but I don't think either one of us is up to it physically anymore. I am fortunate, though, to have good hunting opportunities just a few minutes from my home.

"Fortunate" describes a lot of aspects of my life. I was fortunate to have a good upbringing with parents and older siblings who taught me valuable lessons about life that have stayed with me to this day. We were not blessed with material wealth on our little farm during my youth, but as I look back on it today, we were blessed with so many other things that were much more valuable.

I was fortunate to get through one of the great wars in world history with hardly a scratch on me and return to my family and home. Many others were not as fortunate, and I and my fellow battalion veterans have annual reunions and keep them in our thoughts and memories.

I was fortunate to have work waiting for me when I got back from the war and to be successful in my first career – carpentry. I was fortunate that my idea for a little trader publication for coin collectors took off and became my life's work. In doing so, I was fortunate to surround myself with good people who worked hard for our company and helped it grow. I was fortunate to have subscribers and advertisers who supported our efforts to deliver quality products to them. In many instances, those relationships advanced beyond employer-employee or business-customer and into cherished friendships.

I was fortunate to accumulate some material wealth as a result of success in business and to put that wealth to work for the community and charitable causes. I have been fortunate to be part of a great community inhabited by great people who care about it and continually work to make it an even better place to live.

The Iola Winter Sports Club operates Norseman Hill, about six miles northwest of the village. It provides ski-jumping hills ranging from 5 meters to 60 meters and 15 kilometers of top-flight cross-country ski trails, including four miles of lighted trails. Glacier Wood is a beautiful 18-hole course today and compares favorably to some of the top courses in the state. The Iola Old Car Show and Swap Meet continues today as one of the top automotive events in the country. The Iola-Scandinavia Fitness and Aquatics Center provides recreational and fitness opportunities for all ages and has become a focal point of our community. Iola Living Assistance and its newest venture,

Living Oaks, provide quality care for those in need of skilled nursing and rehabilitation services and housing options for our senior citizens.

Those are just a few of the places and groups that make Iola special. My apologies to the many others who also deserve mention.

I am fortunate today to have an extended family – nieces and nephews – who keep watch over me and care for me, and provide me with the love and companionship that can only come from family.

I have often said that the two most powerful words in the English language are "thank you." So to everybody who has made my life fortunate, thank you.

This massive Nichols and Shepherd steam engine was part of my collection of antique tractors.

This 1938 Reo fire truck did postwar service for the Iola Fire Department. The truck's box and firefighting equipment were fabricated and installed by Rhinehard Anderson of Iola. After residing in my collection for many years, the truck is now owned by the Iola Historical Society along with a 1924 Ford fire truck and a horse-drawn pumper that once served the village.

This 1903 Ford Model A was the first car in Waupaca County. It was one of a handful of vehicles I kept when I liquidated my auto collection.

This Ford GPW was the first collectible jeep I purchased. About 750,000 were produced, making them the most common jeep used in World War II.

Along with the 40-millimeter gun, my military collection also included two searchlights and a number of 2 1/2-ton trucks, one of which is shown in the background in this photo.

The early touring cars were among my favorites in my auto collection. Pictured is a 1912 Case.

Part of the Krause Auto Collection, which was liquidated at auction on June 5, 2004.

Trail King Industries
Mitchell, South Dakota
Gordon Thomsen, 62

Thomsen was not new to the trailer business when he started Trail King Industries back in 1974. His career had included sales positions with many of the top agricultural equipment companies in the Midwest, and over the years, he helped build them into profitable operations. "Finally, one day my banker said to me, 'Look, you're making everyone else a success; why don't you go out and do it for yourself?' " Thomsen recalls. Today, Trail King Industries is a $40 million company.

The "Trail King" trailer was originally manufactured by another company, but the manufacturer couldn't keep up with all the sales Thomsen was generating for the product. Thomsen ultimately bought

Photo Courtesy: G.F. Thompson & Associates

him out. "He's still my plant manager," Thomsen says.

Steve Connolly Seafood Co. Inc.
Boston, Massachusetts
Steve Connolly, 64

In the 350-year-old world of the Boston seafood industry, Steve Connolly, who's been in business for nine years, is a relative newcomer—but he certainly knows his fish.

Connolly had 37 years experience managing other seafood businesses before starting his own. "I wanted to prove to the world that we could build a better mousetrap—offer an excellent quality fish at a moderate cost," he explains. Steve Connolly Seafood Co., now sells fresh fish, lobster and crab to hotels and restaurants worldwide, with annual sales of $25 million.

Conn
prosp
a pro
under
indus
peop

produ
recer
Squar
made
"It's
claim

Taquan
Ketch
Jerry

had h
not o
too: A
we ce
says

The
on an
Alask
emplo
airpla
Taqua
to ret

Krause Publications Inc.
Iola, Wisconsin
Chester Krause, 66

Photo Courtesy: Krause Publications Inc.

Any little kid could have told his parents that baseball card collecting was a hot hobby. Chet Krause listened, and in 1980 added baseball card periodicals to his impressive list of hobby and trade publications. Now they account for nearly half of Krause Publications' estimated $37 million in sales.

Krause, who was born and raised five miles from his Iola, Wisconsin, office, has worked in publishing for 38 years. "Back in 1952, [publishing] was an unusual business for this area; now, it's everywhere," he says.

Krause worked as a freelance carpenter after serving in World War II. At the same time, he began producing his first newspaper, which linked coin collectors, buyers and sellers through classified ads, on his parents' kitchen table. Now, he has more than 240 employees and publishes 26 periodicals and 50 book titles.

Photo Courtesy: Taquan Air Service Inc.

ENTREPRENEUR **13**

sites . . . even
gure Tom
livia Newton-
want to go.
e beginning.
Alaskan
nake enough
ertificate.
arket his

people I knew
A "supportive
elped him

Inc.

Photo Courtesy: Steve Connolly Seafood Co.

have told his
rd collecting
Krause
ded baseball
npressive list
ications. Now
half of Krause
$37 million in

orn and raised
Wisconsin,
blishing for 38
oublishing]
for this area;
he says.
a freelance
in World War
began
paper, which
uyers and
d ads, on his
Now, he has
more than 240 employees and
publishes 26 periodicals and 50 book
titles.

Photo Courtesy: Taquan Air Service Inc.

ENTREPRENEUR **13**

176 *Entrepreneur magazine profiled me and other state winners of the Small Business Person of the Year Award in 1990.*

USA TODAY
Money

TUESDAY, FEBRUARY 11, 1992

MONEYLINE
A QUICK READ ON THE TOP MONEY NEWS OF THE DAY

Coming Wednesday
The Economy in the '90s: Paying for the Party
A four-page Special Report
▶ The road to recession 1980-1991: a year-by-year look at how we got where we are today
▶ Where do we go from here? Answers from some top economists

DOW UP: The Dow Jones industrial average rose 19.68 points to 3245.08. The NASDAQ composite index dropped 1.74 points to 633.21. Yields on 30-year Treasury bonds rose to 7.79%, from 7.76%. The discount rate on three-month Treasury bills rose to 3.71%, from 3.73%. Comex gold rose 90 cents to $355.90 an ounce. Light sweet crude oil dipped nine cents to $19.78 a barrel on the N.Y. Merc. The Tokyo market is closed today for a national holiday. *(Market Scoreboard, 3B.)*

RECOVERY AHEAD: Despite recent signs of weakness, the economy will be in a modest recovery by summer, a survey by *Blue Chip Economic Indicators* newsletter found. The 50 economists surveyed forecast that the economy will grow at an annual rate of just 0.5% this quarter after growing an anemic 0.3% last quarter. For the year, the economists expect growth of about 1.6%. Robert Eggert Sr., editor of the newsletter, said the economy continues to teeter near recession, but the consensus suggests a recovery by summer. *(Brady's outlook, right.)*

EGGERT: Modest rebound by summer.

UAL CUTBACKS: United Airlines announced a cutback in airplane deliveries Monday that will reduce its capital spending by $6.7 billion the next three years. The biggest cuts affect deliveries of Boeing 737 and 757 jets, news that sent Boeing stock down 1⅜ to $48. But Boeing pointed out that orders weren't canceled — the delivery schedule was just reworked. United is Boeing's biggest U.S. customer. United said it will take delivery of 156 jets from 1993 through 1995, 122 fewer than planned. Last month, United reported a record loss of $252 million for the fourth quarter.

CREDIT CRUNCH: Two government surveys out Monday showed that the credit crunch showed no signs of easing in last year's final quarter. A Federal Reserve survey of 60 U.S. banks and 18 foreign banks found that virtually none had changed their credit standards for approving business loans since the previous survey, in October. The Fed also said demand for business loans weakened last quarter despite a drop in interest rates. Demand for consumer loans also fell. Many economists say stricter government regulations have caused banks to tighten loan standards, causing a credit crunch.

GM, FORD RECALLS: GM and Ford announced safety recalls affecting about 764,000 cars and trucks. GM is recalling about 414,000 1991 Chevrolet Cavalier and Lumina, Pontiac Sunbird and Grand Prix, Buick Regal and Oldsmobile Cutlass Supreme cars to inspect guide loops for shoulder safety belts. Ford is recalling about 350,000 1992 light- and medium-duty F-Series trucks, Broncos and Rangers because of a potential problem in door latches.

TREASURY AUCTION: Interest rates on short-term Treasury securities fell in Monday's auction to the lowest level in nearly 20 years. The Treasury Department sold $10.4 billion in three-month bills at an average discount rate of 3.72%, down from 3.86% last week and the lowest rate since May 1972. It also sold $10.5 billion in six-month bills at an average discount rate of 3.8%, down from 3.93% last week and the lowest since March 1972.

MONEY HOT LINE: 1-900-555-5555
Call 24 hours a day for stock quotes, CD rates, interest calculations, updates on investments and used-car prices. Stock instructions, 6B; other services, 8D.
Cost: 95¢ per minute

By Donna Rosato

Inside MONEY
Amex, OTC	6B	Mutual Funds	6-7B
Market Scoreboard	3B	New York Exchange	5B
Money Bookshelf	4B	Travel Solutions	8B

USA SNAPSHOTS®
A look at statistics that shape your finances

Takeover pace falls
After a slump early last year, corporate takeover activity picked up in summer and fall. The number of takeovers announced each quarter.

Source: Merrill Lynch Business Brokerage and Valuation

By Bob Laird, USA TODAY

Recess[ion]

By Kevin Anderson
USA TODAY

What's more painful than [the tax] season? Tax season during [a reces]sion?

Nearly every economic [means] of coping with hard times [has] consequences, many of [them new] territory to longtime middle [income earn]ers. How to treat unemploy[ment bene]fits? Job-hunting expenses? [How are] pension distributions or [severance] packages given to workers [laid] off the payroll? Cash from [...]

Such questions domina[te USA TO-]DAY's eighth annual Tax [Hot Line] Monday. For 12 hours, [...]

Krause's

COLLECTOR'S COLLECTOR: Chet Krause amassed 25 publica[tions before he retired in 1988.]
Now, he's working on a collection of World War II equipment. He's [...]

COVER STORY
Brady: Recovery has begun

By Mark Memmott
USA TODAY

The economy is turning from recession to recovery, Treasury Secretary Nicholas Brady told USA TODAY reporters and editors Monday.

Brady said he sees "compass points" that make him believe a recovery has begun. They include:

▶ Healthy earnings increases at many corporations, including Coca-Cola Co. and Johnson & Johnson.
▶ Goodyear Tire & Rubber's recent announcement that it will recall 300 laid-off workers. And, Brady said, "the president of Goodyear called me and said he thinks it's going to be closer to 900."

Brady bristled at suggestions that administration officials and economists thought a recovery was under way last summer and were wrong. "I don't think the compass points ... were there," he said. And he doesn't believe the recovery will falter. "I don't think that's the way it's going to turn. I really don't."

Brady also said:
▶ Democrats should not throw darts at the president's economic-recovery plan until they've got a plan of their own. "Where is the opposing plan? Is there some other plan?" he said. "I'm sure the president would be glad to adopt any other sensible suggestion."
▶ Now is not the time to consider a sweeping change in the tax system. But Brady leaves the door open to a shift from income taxes to consumption taxes — a national sales tax, for example — in the future.

Such a change is "not something ... that in an election year is helpful to put on the table," Brady said. "I think it's an idea that ought to continue to be looked at, though."

▶ Interview, 11A

Krause's collectibles empire

CHER: NO SONG AND DANCE
CHER DOESN'T SING IN EQUAL AD, BUT NUTRASWEET FINDS HER TESTIMONY VALUABLE. ADVERTISING & MARKETING, 8B.

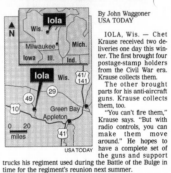

By Anne Ryan, USA TODAY
COLLECTOR'S COLLECTOR: Chet Krause amassed 25 publications before he retired in 1988. Now, he's working on a collection of World War II equipment. He's sitting in a 1944 Ford jeep.

COVER STORY
Magazines find success among silos

By John Waggoner
USA TODAY

IOLA, Wis. — Chet Krause received two deliveries one day this winter. The first brought four postage-stamp holders from the Civil War era. Krause collects them.

The other brought parts for his anti-aircraft guns. Krause collects them, too.

"You can't fire them," Krause says. "But with radio controls, you can make them move around." He hopes to have a complete set of the guns and support trucks his regiment used during the Battle of the Bulge in time for the regiment's reunion next summer.

Krause, 68, isn't just any collector. With his longtime associate, Clifford Mishler, Krause has parlayed his love of collecting into Krause Publications Inc., a publishing empire with $47 million in revenue last year. If you collect, Krause Publications probably has a magazine or guidebook for you. Coins? *Numismatic News.* Baseball cards? *Baseball Card News.* Comic books? *Comic Buyer's Guide.* Old cars and trucks? *Old Cars.* Old toys? *Toy Shop.*

The company is as full of surprises as Krause's ware-

Please see COVER STORY next page ▶

By Anne Ryan, USA TODAY
RURAL CONVERTS: 'Comic Buyer's Guide' editors Don, Maggie Thompson welcomed the move from Cleveland to Iola, Wis.

Krause Publications was profiled in the February 11, 1992, issue of USA Today.

Friends & Acquaintances

The preceding pages contain the names of many people who have touched my life. In addition, I am proud to have known the following people. Some of the names may be familiar to the reader; others may not. Some I have known well; others were a brief meeting. But in each instance, a million thanks go to those who have made my life joyful, richer, and meaningful.

Burnett Anderson

The National Football League used to conduct its annual draft of college players in the basement of the Park Central Hotel in New York City. I know that because the Metropolitan New York Coin Show used to follow the NFL at the Park Central. The hotel staff would be cleaning up from the NFL meeting as dealers and other exhibitors, such as Krause Publications, were moving in for the coin show. The location was also memorable because the Carnegie Delicatessen – the best in the world – was a short walk from the hotel.

I met Burnett on the bourse floor of that show in 1980. He was retired after 27 years with the U.S. Department of State foreign service. His foreign-service career started in 1952 as press officer for the Marshall Plan agencies in Germany. In ensuing years, he served in many other European countries as well as Iran. A life-long interest in numismatics brought him to the coin show.

We struck up a conversation because Burnett, too, was a native of Wisconsin. He grew up in Grantsburg, a small town in the northwestern part of the state, south of Superior. Burnett retired to a home in Washington, D.C., not far from the Capitol.

Burnett had been press secretary for Governor Harold Stassen of Minnesota, a newspaper reporter after that, and then an information officer while in the foreign service. His writing background, his location in Washington and knowledge of the various government agencies, and his interest and knowledge of coin collecting made him a great fit for Krause Publications.

Upon my return to Wisconsin, I gave his name and phone number to Cliff Mishler. Burnett and Cliff subsequently met and worked out a deal in which Burnett would cover hobby happenings in Washington for Krause Publications. Burnett often said that he and Cliff sealed the deal with just a handshake and that it was the best contract he ever had. Burnett turned out to be a great asset to the company, giving us firsthand coverage of coin-collecting news out of Congress, the U.S. Mint, and the Bureau of Engraving and Printing, which prints U.S. paper money. After just a year or two, we started billing Burnett as chief of our Washington bureau.

As an information officer with the foreign service, Burnett was stationed at the U.S. embassies in the various countries in which he worked. Part of his job was to escort American government officials visiting the country and fill them in on the host country's state of affairs. He got to meet and know many important U.S.

government officials as a result.

One of his longtime friends was former U.S. Chief Justice Warren Burger. The two had met when Mr. Burger, a native of St. Paul, was a young attorney in Minnesota and Burnett was working for the governor.

Burnett and the chief justice regularly had lunch together, and on one of my visits to the capital, Burnett invited me to join them. I asked Burnett how I should address a person of such stature, and he said I should call him "Chief." I was also concerned about what I should talk about. Burnett told me not to worry because "Chief" would do all the talking. So at lunch, I addressed him as "Chief," and Burnett was right: He did all the talking.

Burnett's wife, Pia, was Swedish, and the two met in that country. She worked for a division of the United Nations in Sweden. She could take dictation in five languages, but more important, she was also a gourmet cook. I enjoyed many meals at their table.

Burnett died in 1998 after a brief battle with cancer. He was a great friend and represented Krause Publications well. His image was that of ours. I miss him, Cliff misses him, and the hobby misses him.

Cliff gave a eulogy at Burnett's funeral in Washington, and Burnett was buried in the family plot in Grantsburg. *Numismatic News* staffers Dave Harper, Bob Wilhite, and I chartered a small airplane and flew to Grantsburg for the graveside services.

My life has been a lot richer for having known Burnett.

Charles & Joel Anderson

I have known brothers Charles and Joel of Florence, Alabama, since the early 1960s. They are avid coin collectors to this day, and their father, Charles W., was the founder of Anderson News, which bills itself as the largest sales and marketing company for books and magazines in the United States. The elder Charles was also a friend of Senator John Sparkman of Alabama.

I tapped that connection to gain access to the senator in 1966. The Coinage Act of 1965 eliminated mint marks from coins to streamline production in response to a coin shortage. But by this time, the shortage had abated, and I and others in the hobby felt it was time to restore mint marks to U.S. coinage. Mr. Sparkman was potentially a key figure in this effort because he was chairman of the Senate Banking and Currency Committee at the time.

I set up a lunch meeting in Washington with U.S. Mint Director Eva Adams and also plotted to meet Senator Sparkman. In advance of my trip, the younger Charles wrote Senator Sparkman a letter in which he said, "In a few days, a Mr. Krause will be coming to your office to ask a favor. If my father were still alive, he would want you to treat him as his son." Those were pretty strong words.

So off I went to Washington. Before my meeting with Eva, I found Senator Sparkman conducting a hearing on a bill. During a break in the hearing, he stepped out into a hallway, and I followed. I introduced myself to him and quickly stated my business. He asked me what the Treasury Department thought of the idea. I replied that I was having lunch with the Mint director and would find out. The senator said that after my meeting with the director I should report to the Banking and Currency Committee office and ask for a Mr. Odom and report to him on the results of my meeting.

So during lunch, I asked Eva, as we commonly called her in personal contact, what she thought of restoring mint marks to U.S. coins. She replied, "Oh, I like those little D's and S's. Don't you?" I volunteered a "yes" and changed the subject.

Making my way back to Capitol Hill after lunch, I found Mr. Odom's office and stated my business. His first question in response was, "What does Miss Adams think of mint marks?" I said she liked them.

In a matter of days, Senator Sparkman introduced legislation to restore mint marks to U.S. coinage. When the bill made it to a House committee hearing, Eva did not disappoint the chairman. She did a great job testifying to how great mint marks were. The bill eventually passed, and mint marks returned to U.S. coins, much to the delight of coin collectors.

All of this was made possible by the Andersons introducing me to Senator Sparkman. I am glad to have had their friendship all these years and to be their guest for lunch whenever I am in Florence.

Mark Anderson

Burnett and Pia Anderson had two sons – Mark and Lee. Lee lives in Washington, D.C., and is a photographer. He often helped his dad by supplying pictures to go with Burnett's reports on numismatic events in the Washington area. The favor was greatly appreciated; I doubt if the rates we paid Lee were anything near what he got for work he did for publications such as *USA Today*.

Mark lives in New York City. He apparently has a vast intelligence network that does not allow me to step foot in the city without his knowledge. I still love to go to New York after nearly 50 years since my first visit there. So in the twilight of my life, it is nice to have someone to report to when I go there.

Mark was in the banking business in New York. He started as a loan officer for European American Bank, which at one time was very visible in Manhattan. He was promoted to senior vice president before Citigroup Incorporated bought out European American. Today, Mark works at R.M. Smythe & Company auctioneers, who specialize in state bank notes. I have purchased notes at Smythe auctions, and the company has also auctioned some of my duplicates along with a type set of Confederate currency.

Mark has dinner or lunch with me at least once during my every visit to New York, and he has either met me or dropped me off at LaGuardia Airport. Like his father, he has traveled to Iola. When he does, Grantsburg usually works its way into the trip. His grandfather – Burnett's dad – was a banker in Grantsburg and signed some National Bank notes from that community.

Mark collects National Bank notes from Wisconsin and, to a lesser extent, state bank notes. Although I have been collecting bank notes a lot longer than Mark has, he has teased a couple of Grantsburg pieces away from me and now has the better set. But that is as it should be; as age creeps up on me, I will have to sell them anyway.

I had a great friendship with Burnett Anderson, and it is a joy to have another great friendship with his son.

Oscar C. Boldt

Oscar is chairman of The Boldt Group Inc., whose holdings include Oscar J. Boldt Construction, a family-owned firm founded in 1889. The company is based in Appleton, Wisconsin, but has 13 offices throughout the country. Oscar went to school with John Bradley (see Ann Walsh Bradley and Mark Bradley) and served in World War II.

We met through our mutual involvement in the new Fields of Honor Military Veterans Museum in Oshkosh, Wisconsin, which is planned for a site adjacent to the headquarters and museum of the Experimental Aircraft Association. Despite his prominence in business, Oscar is one of the most down-to-earth fellows you will ever meet.

Ann Walsh Bradley & Mark Bradley

Many Americans have probably never heard of John "Jack" Bradley, but chances are they have seen his picture. He was from Appleton, Wisconsin, and he is one of the servicemen in the famous World War II picture of the flag being raised on Iwo Jima. Mark is Jack's son. Mark's brother Jim is co-author of the book *Flags of Our Fathers* and author of *Flyboys*. I saw the movie based on *Flags of Our Fathers*, and I have heard Jim speak. His inspirational talk is by far the best.

I met Mark, an attorney with Ruder Ware in Wausau, Wisconsin, through our service together on the Marshfield Clinic National Advisory Council. He introduced me to his wife, Ann, and I have since had the pleasure of visiting with both of them at clinic functions. When Ann is wearing a black robe, she is known as the Honorable Ann Walsh Bradley as a justice on the Wisconsin Supreme Court. They are a great couple and very down to earth.

Jimmy Carter

For whatever reason, the president was scheduled to speak at a high school in Wausau, Wisconsin, so my niece Patti Krause and I decided to go. A friend of ours and her husband decided to join us, but we got a late start because of them. We were the last ones to arrive at the event and had to walk a long way to get a seat on the top row of the bleachers in the school's gym.

We had tickets for a private event afterward, which included the chance to shake hands with the president. Our traveling companions did not, but somehow they ended up in the receiving line ahead of us.

It was great to shake the president's hand, but it was quite an unnecessary hassle to do it.

Joe DeSaye

Joe lived on a ranch in Turner, Montana, a little town about 10 miles south of the Canadian border in east-central Montana. He bought and sold U.S. and Canadian coins as J&G Sales.

Into the 1960s, the U.S. government bought and sold silver as needed to keep the metal's price at $1.29 an ounce. A silver dollar contains 0.77344 ounces of pure silver. So at $1.29 an ounce, the precious metal in a silver dollar was worth just under a dollar. By the 1970s, however, with precious metals eliminated from U.S. coinage, the government discontinued its practice of controlling the price of silver in the open market. The price rose, and the precious metal in a silver dollar became worth much more than a dollar.

There were thousands of silver dollars in Montana banks. So Joe bought them at a profit to the banks and resold them to buyers of bags of coins at a profit to himself. He knew every bank in Montana and every dealer of bulk silver in the country. He was also able to cherry pick many of the scarce coins from the bulk quantities he bought from the banks and either keep them for his collection or sell them individually to collectors.

Joe was a good advertiser in *Numismatic News*, and although I knew him by name, I did not handle his account personally nor had I ever met him. Then one day I was waiting at a gate at O'Hare International Airport in Chicago for a connecting flight to Toronto, where I was to attend a coin show. I overheard a guy talking to the fellow next to him and soon determined from the conversation that the guy was Joe DeSaye. When the fellow sitting next to Joe got up and left, I slipped into the empty chair.

Soon Joe began talking to me. I responded to him reservedly at first but let a little bit of my identity slip into the conversation now and then. Finally, Joe put together the pieces of the puzzle and figured out who I was. After a good laugh, we began talking numismatics and continued to do so all the way to Toronto.

We were both going to stay at the King George Hotel in Toronto – a monstrous building – but when we got there, they did not have a room for Joe. So I offered to share mine with him, and I had a roommate for the balance of my stay. We had breakfast together each morning but then went our separate ways during the day, each attending to our business at the show.

Joe and I became great friends and remain so today. I made several trips to Montana to visit him, and we often hunted together. On one occasion, I was accompanied by my brother Neil, who was the real marksman in our family and a gunsmith. Joe collected guns as well as coins, so the three of us got along great.

On various subsequent visits, I was accompanied by my mother and two of her sisters. Joe and I also hunted together in western North Dakota and western South Dakota.

In later years, Joe and his wife, Carol, have spent their winters in Mesa, Arizona. I visited him whenever I attended winter car auctions or meetings of the Marshfield Clinic National Advisory Council, both in nearby Scottsdale. At one time, there were up to eight people – old business friends and other acquaintances – in the area that I called on during those visits.

I saw Joe and Carol in March 2007 in South Dakota; they were already en route back to Great Falls, Montana, for the summer. Five of their six children live in the Great Falls area, so they have lots of family there. Our hunting days, however, are over. Jostling about the prairie is not for someone my age. I still look forward, however, to seeing Joe and Carol again in Mesa in the winter.

To Chester
Best wishes
Buddy Ebsen
June '87

Buddy Ebsen

The actor and entertainer was most famous for his role as Jed Clampett on *The Beverly Hillbillies* and the lead role in the *Barnaby Jones* television series. He was also a coin collector. When his collection was sold by Superior Galleries of Beverly Hills, California, I had the chance to meet him and his wife, Dorothy, at a pre-auction cocktail party.

Dr. Dean Emanuel

Like me, Dr. Emanuel has not moved around a lot. He still lives in the house in Pittsville, Wisconsin, in which his parents raised him. I first met Dr. Emanuel when I started going to meetings of the Marshfield Clinic National Advisory Council.

Dr. Emanuel is credited with having found the cause of "farmer's lung," a form of chronic pneumonia that was more prevalent in Wisconsin when the state had more farms and smaller farms than today. He discovered it was caused by inhaling spores from moldy hay. A similar ailment was caused by spores found in the dead bark of logs at sawmills. That is why the bark is stripped from the logs or the logs are used when they are still green. Dr. Emanuel's work in this area was the Marshfield Clinic's first big research project and led to the formation of the Marshfield Clinic Research Foundation and the National Farm Medicine Center.

In addition to being a great cardiologist, Dr. Emanuel is one of the finest gentlemen anyone could ever meet.

Gerald Ford

I first met the former president when he was still a U.S. representative from Michigan. There was some kind of shindig in Philadelphia dealing with Benjamin Franklin. My exact memory fails me, but it may have been promoted by Joe Segal of the Franklin Mint.

At the time, the Franklin Mint was an up and coming company headquartered west of Philadelphia in the small town of Media, Pennsylvania. As an early promotional outlet for the company's goods, *Numismatic News* received thousands of dollars worth of advertising a year from Joe and his company. In appreciation, someone from Krause Publications attended just about every event he sponsored, and there were a lot of them.

Mr. Ford was the keynote speaker for the evening. I knew personally the U.S. representative from my district, Melvin Laird, and I knew he and Mr. Ford were close buddies. So I introduced myself to Mr. Ford. Because the pre-dinner and program were not demanding of his time, Mr. Ford and I broke into a lengthy visit – one I have cherished through the years.

In more recent years, Mr. Ford attended a Marshfield Clinic event because of his friendship with Mel Laird and because of Mel's involvement with the clinic. I had the chance to say hello to Mr. Ford at that event, too.

Robert F. Froehlke

Bob is the former president of Sentry Insurance, based in Stevens Point, Wisconsin, and, as documented in my section on Melvin Laird, a key person on the Marshfield Clinic National Advisory Council. He was one of the council's first members and its chairman during my time with the group. He ended his career as president and chief executive officer of IDS Mutual Fund Group in Minneapolis.

He served in the European Theater of Operations as an Army infantry captain during World War II and later served as secretary of the Army when Melvin Laird was secretary of defense. He once took a trip around the world, which included a trek on the Trans-Siberian Railroad, something I would have dearly loved to do. One of his stops was Chelyabinsk, where I spent 11 days in 1996.

Bob and his wife, Nancy, spent summers on Long Lake on the Waupaca chain of lakes, about a 20-minute drive from Iola. They would invite me to dinner every year before they left for their winter home in Scottsdale, Arizona. Bob also loved to play the Iola golf course, known today as Glacier Wood. When he came to Iola to play golf, he would stop to see me. It was always a great thrill and uplifting experience.

Bob and Mel should have been included in Tom Brokaw's book *The Greatest Generation*. Together with Nancy, they rank as some of the greatest people I have ever known.

Harold Froehlich

Harold Froehlich first entered my life in 1973 when he was elected to the U.S. House of Representatives from the Wisconsin district that included Waupaca County at the time. He is from Appleton, Wisconsin, originally and served in the state legislature prior to his election to Congress.

Cliff Mishler and I were in Washington renewing old acquaintances and making new ones shortly after Harold took office. Harold was on our latter list of stops. In fact, when we walked into his office, it was bare of any furniture. As a freshman congressman, Harold had to wait until the more senior representatives claimed their furnishings.

Harold served just one term in the House but was appointed an Outagamie County circuit court judge in 1981 and continues to serve in that capacity today.

Frank Gasparro

Frank succeeded Gilroy Roberts as U.S. Mint chief engraver. He designed the Lincoln Memorial reverse that has appeared on the one-cent coin since 1959, the reverse of the Kennedy half dollar, and both sides of the Eisenhower and Anthony dollars.

One time at a numismatic event in Washington, D.C., Frank mentioned to me that he had never seen the Lincoln Memorial in person, even though he had designed its image on the cent. So at 11 o'clock one evening, I toured the Lincoln Memorial with the man who created an artistic rendition of the structure that is seen by millions of Americans every day.

I also mentioned to him in the late 1960s that it was time to update the Lincoln-cent obverse – particularly Abe's hairdo. And he did. A comparison of a 1968 or later Lincoln cent with an earlier issue shows Abe with a full head of hair instead of what previously looked like a cheap wig.

Jan & John Gillespie

Jan and John are the founders of Rawhide Boys Ranch in rural New London, Wisconsin, which provides counseling, academic, and vocational training for court-referred and at-risk youth in a residential setting. I first met Jan and John at a political rally. He was there because it was in Rawhide's best interests to be on good terms with public officials regardless of their party affiliation. I was there because a friend wanted me to go.

During our conversation, Jan and John outlined the merits of Rawhide but lamented how their time was spent raising funds rather than focusing on Rawhide's purpose – to help troubled young men get their lives together. I was sympathetic to all their needs.

Rawhide gives young men a chance to become productive citizens through love, discipline, and leadership. We all have to have a little of each to succeed. I learned that young men who come to Rawhide probably have never had anyone put their arms around them, hug them, and say "I love you" and mean it. Rawhide is a Christian camp, so the boys also learn about God and what He means to their lives.

From a practical standpoint, when I met Jan and John, the ranch was in debt about $200,000. It was a favored customer of a bank, which charged the ranch minimal interest. Nevertheless, the debt was an outflow of cash that could be put to better use. I told Jan and John that this debt could and should be eliminated and that there was free money lying all over the place to do it. I was not whistling Dixie either, as I had given money to charities as well as solicited contributions from others. To prove my point, I made a sweep around Waupaca County and collected a few thousand dollars for them.

As it played out, it was time well spent. Rawhide not only paid off the debt, but was able to fund a new building with cash and in-kind donations. Later, I contributed the funds to build a new field house at Rawhide, which was named the Chester L. Krause Field House, an honor I cherish.

Jan and John have since retired from Rawhide and now run a fundraising consulting business that helps churches help themselves. They are still very good friends who make Iola a port of call whenever their travels bring them in the vicinity.

Mark Green

Mark joined Krause Publications as a numismatic editor after graduating from the University of Wisconsin-Eau Claire. He was with us for only nine months, however, when he gave notice that he was leaving to enroll in the University of Wisconsin Law School in Madison. At the time, he also indicated an interest in politics.

After law school, Mark was elected to the Wisconsin state legislature, representing a Green Bay-area district, and then successfully ran for Congress. He represented Wisconsin's 8th Congressional District, which included Waupaca County for a time during his term. In 2006, he gave up his congressional seat to run for governor but fell short in his bid to unseat the incumbent.

Throughout his various campaigns, Mark remembered his employment roots with Krause Publications and spoke at the company's 50th anniversary celebration in 2002. He was appointed ambassador to Tanzania by President George W. Bush in the spring of 2007.

Leonard Haroldson

Len has been a great friend for many years. He and his cousin Gerald Kitzman used to come to our house and help stuff the first issues of *Numismatic News* into envelopes on the very table on which these words were written. Only one house separated ours from the house of Len's parents, Leo and Leona. Recently, he returned the bottom four feet of a pair of stilts I once made for him. When I had made them in 1952, I walked over to his house on them.

One day when he was in high school, Len shot a nice buck in the woods adjoining the village, perhaps a quarter mile from town. He let it lie in the woods so he could get to school on time. After school, we went back into the woods, field dressed the deer, dragged it out, loaded it into the back of a pickup truck with help from his father, registered it, and brought it home.

Leonard followed in his father's footsteps as an electrician. Although the elder Haroldson worked independently in the Iola area, Len was a foreman for a large contractor in Appleton. Len is now retired and lives at the west end of North Lake, about six miles north of Iola, with his wife, Irene. Both are pictured above.

Len sets a fine example by his actions and is one of the great men that walks quietly among us in Iola.

John J. Keller

I first met Jack in the early 1960s when he and his wife, Ethel, came to an open house at Krause Publications' new building at 160 North Washington Street, the building that houses my office today. Ethel and Jack founded J.J. Keller & Associates in Neenah, Wisconsin, in 1953, just one year after I started *Numismatic News*. The company offers consulting services and publications that help a number of industries manage risk and liability and comply with government regulations.

Until his death in 2007, Jack still maintained an office at Keller as founder and chairman emeritus. His two sons continue the business. Ethel died in 2004.

Jack, Ethel, and I interfaced in recent years through our support of Rawhide Boys Ranch. At about the same time I contributed funds to build a new field house at Rawhide, Ethel and Jack contributed funds to build a new school at the ranch. In addition to growing a business, Jack and Ethel benefited Wisconsin's Fox Cities through their benevolence as well.

Dave Krieg

Dave was born in Iola and attended the now defunct Milton College in Milton, Wisconsin. He played quarterback on the Milton football team and, after graduation, signed as a free agent with the Seattle Seahawks. A long shot to even make the team, he went on to become the Seahawks' starting quarterback. He played for the Seahawks from 1980 to 1991. In all, he played for 19 seasons in the National Football League and passed for more than 38,000 yards.

Although his family moved from Iola to the Wausau area when Dave was very young, they still maintained some contacts in the community. Because of his connections to Iola, I got to know Dave, who now resides in Phoenix, after his rise to fame in the NFL and still see him occasionally.

Melvin Laird

I first met Mel Laird when he was campaigning for U.S. representative from Wisconsin's 7th Congressional District in 1952. He and Bob Froehlke, who managed all of Mel's campaigns, came through Iola, which at that time was part of the 7th. Bob and his wife, Nancy, and Mel were high-school classmates in Marshfield, Wisconsin. Mel and Bob are also World War II veterans. It was no accident that they all later became associated with the Marshfield Clinic, despite gaining great fame in fairly distant places.

As a U.S. representative, Mel sponsored the legislation that established the Communicable Disease Center and was a key figure in other health-related legislation. He also represented America at several international medical events.

Mel became defense secretary under President Richard Nixon and in that capacity was the point man in bringing the Vietnam War to a conclusion.

In more recent years, Mel and Bob were both on the Marshfield Clinic National Advisory Council when I joined the group at the invitation of Dr. Tom Nikolai.

I joined the group as it was completing fund-raising for the Lawton Center, a laboratory and research facility on the Marshfield Clinic campus. The council's members then started talking about construction of the $11-million Laird Center, which was to house the National Farm Medicine Center, Center for Human Genetics, and Epidemiology Research Center. Most of us on the council just sat back and found a few dollars while Mel and Bob tapped Mel's Washington friends for about $8 million.

We were about to have a ground-breaking ceremony but were still short $2 million. Area money was tight, and Mel had run out of friends who could donate large sums of money.

I shared all of this with Cliff Mishler. I also related to Cliff that they wanted to get Harry Quadracci's private train to make a whistle-stop tour from Waukesha to Marshfield as a means of getting publicity for the fundraising effort. Harry was founder of Quad Graphics, a large printing company based in Pewaukee, Wisconsin, and Krause Publications was one of its customers. Among his outside interests was collecting vintage railroad cars, which made up the train.

Cliff called Harry, and Harry referred Cliff to his trainmaster. It was a done deal in a matter of minutes. I reported back to the council that we had secured the services of Harry Quadracci's private train. Talk about earning my stripes, and I had not done a thing. It was a shocker even to me and another example of how Cliff has been such an invaluable asset to me over the years.

We got on the train on the day of the groundbreaking and began our journey north. Harry got off in Fond du Lac so he could travel to the Kentucky Derby but not before he pledged $100,000 toward the project.

There was still the matter, however, of being $2 million short of our fundraising goal for the Laird Center. At the ground-breaking ceremony, I shared the dais with Mel, Bob, U.S. Representative David Obey of Wisconsin's 7th Congressional District, former Secretary of State Lawrence Eagleburger, and a host of other dignitaries from the Marshfield Clinic. Mr. Eagleburger went to high school in Stevens Point and graduated from the University of Wisconsin-Stevens Point. He served under the first President Bush.

Bob called me to the microphone in about the middle of the program. Only he and Dr. Nikolai knew what I was going to say. I announced that if the council could raise half of the remaining $2 million, the Krause Foundation would contribute the remaining $1 million.

Over the years, Mel and I have often met on National Advisory Council business, and his greeting is always warm and sincere. He is really a great man.

Photo Courtesy of Krause Publications

Bill Louth

Bill was head of Medallic Art Company and was another personality that was very much a part of my hobby life in the 1960s and '70s. Medallic Art Company was a fixture in the field of producing high-relief medals. The company made a wide array of high-quality medals in different sizes and shapes, but its typical issue was three inches in diameter and featured deep engraving. It had to be struck several times with a high-pressure press.

Bill, who died recently, was special because he knew how to make high-quality medals and he was a gentleman of the first order. He represented an old-time firm that made products with old-time quality.

Dr. George Magnin

I knew of Dr. Magnin during my days on the Marshfield Clinic National Advisory Council, but I got to know him better after he received the clinic's Heritage Foundation Award in the fall of 2000. I learned that many other doctors turned to him when answers failed them. He is the type of doctor that has made Marshfield Clinic so respected in the medical world.

I am glad I got to know Dr. Magnin and that he got to know me. A cordial welcome between us is always in the offing whenever we meet.

Max McGee

Max was a fifth-round draft choice of the Green Bay Packers in 1954. He left the team to serve as a pilot in the Air Force in 1955 and 1956 but returned in 1957 and played 11 more seasons with the Packers as a wide receiver. He was one of the stars of the first Super Bowl and had a reputation for liking the nightlife, much to the chagrin at times of his coach, Vince Lombardi. I suspect Vince had his hands full with Max.

After retiring from football, Max went on to become a successful businessman and was also the color commentator on Packer radio broadcasts. I met Max through Dewey Sebold, who was a member of the Marshfield Clinic National Advisory Council during my time on the council. Max had two young sons at the time, one of whom was diagnosed with juvenile diabetes. Max and his wife, Denise, established The Maxi Fund to raise money to find a cure for juvenile diabetes. In 1999, their efforts resulted in the opening of the Max McGee National Research Center for Juvenile Diabetes at Children's Hospital of Wisconsin in Milwaukee.

I think Max was shy about asking people to contribute to the fund. Dewey called me one day at Krause Publications and asked me if I would be interested in donating to the fund. He set up a meeting with Max and me. Prior to the meeting, I gave the request considerable thought. So when Dewey asked at the meeting, "How much would you like to give," I responded, "Half a million." I do not think Max and Dewey expected an answer that quickly and to that magnitude. Each of them immediately came to their feet and reached for my hand.

I was Max's guest several times after he retired from the Packer broadcasts. On three occasions, he hosted me and others at a Lambeau Field skybox given to Children's Hospital. Max also introduced me to Denise and their sons. Max, who died in October 2007, was a great man indeed.

Hyde Murray

Hyde's father, Reid F. Murray, was from Ogdensburg, Wisconsin, a small town six miles southeast of Iola. Reid Murray was the U.S. representative for Wisconsin's 7th Congressional District from 1939 until his death in 1952.

Hyde was born in Iola and graduated from Little Wolf High School in nearby Manawa and from the University of Wisconsin-Madison. He later earned his law degree from Georgetown University. When I first met Hyde, in 1965, he was serving as the minority counsel for the House Agriculture Committee. Hyde let me hang my hat in his office as I made my way around Capitol Hill on numismatic-related matters. He gave a lot of his time to guide me on congressional matters through his advice and counsel. And I had some success, too.

Hyde and his wife, Nancy, returned to Waupaca County upon his retirement. I am still able to visit him at Iola Living Assistance.

Dr. Thomas Nikolai

Dr. Nikolai, an oncologist with the Marshfield Clinic, came to see me. Usually, it is the other way around when you see a doctor. I did not charge him a cent, but in the end, it cost me dearly through a series of benevolent contributions.

He came with Bill Matthews, who was one of our local bankers in Iola, to ask me to serve on the Marshfield Clinic National Advisory Council. I said yes and served for four years – a year longer than the usual three-year term. The extra year came because Dr. Nikolai wanted me to stay on until the Laird Center was dedicated. Shortly afterward, the council changed its bylaws to create emeritus members, and I was the first one.

Dr. Nikolai, like Dr. Dean Emanuel, was an ex-officio member of the council. My association and conversations with both were most enlightening to me.

Dave Obey

Dave succeeded Melvin Laird as the U.S. representative from Wisconsin's 7th Congressional District, which encompasses much of central and all of northwestern Wisconsin. Iola was once in the 7th but was moved to the 8th, then the 6th, and now back to the 8th again. Although he no longer represents the district in which I live, Dave remains a good friend, and I still have contact with him through our involvement in the Marshfield Clinic.

To a small degree, I helped elect him the first time. I will never forget how we tramped through the snow at a ski-jumping event at the Iola Winter Sports Club one February as he met and greeted people and campaigned for votes. Dave was dressed in low shoes, and I had rubber foot gear. He may have ended up with pneumonia, but if he did, he recovered well. He has now served in Congress with distinction since 1969. He is chairman of the House Appropriations Committee, and his face often turns up on national news reports.

Tom Petri

Tom once represented Waupaca County when it was part of Wisconsin's 6th Congressional District. He is still a U.S. representative, but Waupaca County is no longer in his district. Tom was an occasional visitor to Krause Publications during his time as our representative, and we remain friends today.

Cliff Mishler and I got to know him well when Congress was considering the authorization of coins to commemorate the 1984 Olympic Games in Los Angeles. Profits from the coins' sale were supposed to benefit the training of U.S. Olympic athletes, but Cliff and I, along with the rest of the *Numismatic News* staff, felt the proposed bill was written so private interests would skim off a major portion of the proceeds through distribution rights. We lobbied Tom that the U.S. Mint should distribute the coins with all profits going to the benefit of the athletes.

When the bill hit the House of Representatives floor, Tom led the charge to have it changed. He prevailed. Cliff and I were proud of the work we did on the bill and were grateful to Tom for taking up the cause of the athletes and the coin-collecting hobby.

David Prosser

In the 1970s, when Cliff Mishler and I were doing our heaviest lobbying in Washington on behalf of the coin-collecting hobby, we made a lot of get-acquainted calls on Capitol Hill. Among those on our list was our new congressman, Harold Froehlich.

There was not even furniture in his office when we walked in and were greeted by Dave, who was Representative Froehlich's top assistant. We sat on the window sills, had a good conversation, and found Dave to be a straight shooter. We used him as a source of information often in the ensuing years.

Dave himself ran for Congress in later years but was unsuccessful. He landed on his feet, though. Today, he is the Honorable David Prosser, a justice on the Wisconsin Supreme Court.

Harry V. Quadracci

Harry was the epitome of an entrepreneur. I first met him in the 1960s when he was a customer-service representative for W.A. Krueger Co., a printing company in which is father, Harry R. Quadracci, was a partner. Krause Publications needed a printer for *Coins* magazine. The Krueger company could do high-quality color printing and mail the magazine, too. Harry took care of the many details involved with our business relationship.

In 1971, Harry set out on his own. He mortgaged his house and started a small printing firm called Quad Graphics in Pewaukee, Wisconsin. Over time, it grew into the third largest printer in the nation, with plants in several locations.

Krause Publications grew, too, and I became reacquainted with Harry in the 1990s when we contracted with Quad to print several of our magazines. Despite the growth of Quad Graphics and his stature in the business, Harry had a policy of going to a customer to sign a new contract. So one day, Harry came to Iola, and we had a formal signing of the contract in one of our conference rooms.

Harry died in 2002. A finer gentleman never walked the face of the earth.

Ronald Reagan

I got to shake the former president's hand while he was campaigning for his first term as governor of California. I was at a coin show in the state, and Mr. Reagan was speaking at a luncheon in a room across the hall. One of the coin-show committee members knew him. He talked to a member of Reagan's entourage and got him to stop at the coin show.

Orville Redenbacher

He of popcorn fame once attended a coin show in Chicago. He knew a couple of the dealers set up at the show and came to see them. I was introduced to him. Orville was quick to offer me a handshake, as I did to him, too.

Gilroy Roberts

Gilroy was the U.S. Mint's chief engraver from 1948 to 1964. He is best known as the designer of the Kennedy half-dollar obverse. He was the first U.S. Mint chief engraver that I got to know personally and, in my opinion, the best engraver of my time.

I first met him in 1961 when I served on the

U.S. Assay Commission. He guided me around the Philadelphia Mint and made sure I met some of the coin collectors who worked there.

After his retirement from the U.S. Mint, he became chief engraver at the private Franklin Mint in Franklin Center, Pennsylvania.

I was in Philadelphia in December 1963, after President Kennedy had been assassinated and a new half-dollar design with his image was in the works even though the legislation authorizing the coin had yet to pass. I stopped at the mint to visit Gilroy, and he took me to the engravers' room, where they were working on the design. I saw the completed reverse design and was told the obverse would be based on Kennedy's official U.S. Mint presidential medal, the obverse of which Gilroy designed.

When I returned to Iola, I passed this information on to editor Ed Rochette. Ed was able to compose an image of the new half-dollar reverse design to the degree that I was able to describe it. He then modified the obverse of the Kennedy presidential medal to add the necessary features to make it a coin design.

Soon after the legislation authorizing the Kennedy half dollar was passed in the final days of 1963, *Numismatic News* and *Coins* magazine published Ed's projected image of the coin. It turned out to be remarkably close to the final version.

Gilroy died in 1992. I last saw him after he retired from the Franklin Mint and was being honored by several Philadelphia-area coin clubs. He was a great engraver and a great man. I am glad I had the chance to know him.

Orion Samuelson

Orion was born on a dairy farm near LaCrosse, Wisconsin, and started his broadcasting career in local radio. He was once farm reporter for WBAY-TV in Green Bay in the early days of television. He worked his way up in the business and became a farm reporter for WGN Radio in Chicago in 1960. His syndicated *National Farm Report* program is heard throughout the nation.

When Krause Publications acquired *Rural Builder* magazine in the 1980s, a trade show came with it. Orion was our keynote speaker one year when the show was held in Kansas City.

A winter storm hit during the show and

forced Orion to stay an extra day. So maybe for lack of something better to do, he got out his microphone and tape recorder and interviewed me for one of his future broadcasts.

D. David Sebold

"Dewey's" first remembrance of Iola is a summer job delivering Tombstone frozen pizzas to the town's establishments while he was a student at the University of Wisconsin-Stevens Point. He would load the back of a refrigerated truck with pizzas in Medford, Wisconsin, peddle pizzas until the truck was empty, and then return to Medford for another load.

After graduating from UWSP, Dewey served in the Navy and then worked in the pharmaceutical industry. One day, the president of Tombstone Pizza asked him to return to Wisconsin and become the company's general sales manager. Dewey accepted and brought the company to new highs in sales. He ascended to the presidency and eventually helped the founding family sell the company.

I met Dewey when I was a green punk – at least in terms of how medical clinics operated – from Iola on the Marshfield Clinic National Advisory Council and he was a veteran on the council. Dewey and I have been great friends ever since.

Joe Segal

I got to know Joe when his organization was originally known as the General Numismatic Corporation. It became the Franklin Mint, known for its high-quality gifts and medals. Joe had a dream, and he did not let anything get in his way. He even managed to get its location named as a U.S. Postal Service destination – Franklin Center – named for the company.

Some people disliked him for saturating the market with medals and knew him only after this occurred. They missed an important part of Joe Segal and did not know the same man I did.

The quality of Franklin Mint medals produced under his leadership were par excellence, and he did it with a bit of showmanship. The medals were produced in an absolutely clean environment. To enter the minting room, visitors had to don caps and gowns as if they were going to surgery. They then had to lift up the gown so forced air could blow away any dust and dirt that might come loose after entering the room.

Joe had three people who represented the Franklin Mint across the country: Ed Quagliana of Rochester, New York; Ralph "Curly" Mitchell of Fullerton, California; and Dan Harley, who was originally from San Jose, California, but was then stationed in Little Rock, Arkansas. Bill Krieg was the public-relations chief, who worked out of the Franklin Center office. They were all good at their jobs.

Joe also hired Rae V. Biester, former superintendent of the Philadelphia Mint, and Gilroy Roberts, former U.S. Mint chief engraver.

The Franklin Mint's cocktail parties at large numismatic conventions were some of the first I ever attended. The company even struck medals for the occasions.

Joe tried to start a secondary market for Franklin Mint medals but had little success. The company sold series of silver medals by subscription. There might have been 25 medals in a series that sold for $24.95 each. That was not a big monthly outlay, but a completed set was a $625 item.

There was some demand for individual medals, and I believe the secondary market would have blended into the existing market had not the price of silver gone through the roof in the late 1970s. When silver hit $50 an ounce, many Franklin Mint medals fell victim to the melting pot.

The Franklin Mint became a public corporation, so new officers were elected and Joe phased himself out of the company. The Franklin Mint now focuses on high-end gifts.

Joe Segal was a colorful guy, and I appreciate having known him.

Bart Starr

I first met the former Green Bay Packer and Hall of Fame quarterback at a function for contributors to the Rawhide Boys Ranch. Bart and his wife, Cherry, have been key supporters of the ranch since its founding in the 1960s by Jan and John Gillespie. The Starrs head a group of us who have assisted the Gillespies and Rawhide in their efforts to help troubled youth.

Because of their fame and charitable works, the Starrs are often in the limelight and rightfully so. What you see is what you get with Bart and Cherry. Bart is a man of his word and a great quarterback on and off the field. I consider him a very good friend — not because I have contact with him that often, but because we think alike on a number of matters.

Ed Sullivan

Former Krause Publications staffer Harry Becker and I were out for a walk in New York City, taking a respite from a coin show. At about 55th Street and Sixth Avenue, I said to Harry, "I think that's Ed Sullivan coming toward us. I'm going to introduce myself." I did, and he was very gracious.

When he found out we were from Wisconsin, he asked us if we were Packer fans and if we had been to the Ice Bowl — the subzero 1967 championship game against the Dallas Cowboys. I had, with my brother Ben and numismatic editor Bob Poeschl. Mr. Sullivan responded that I was the first person he had talked to who was actually there. It is a longtime joke in Wisconsin that a lot more people claim they were there than the stadium could actually hold.

Joe Theismann

I met Joe when he was the keynote speaker at our National Rural Builder Show at the Opryland Hotel in Nashville, Tennessee. He was a delight, much like Bart Starr. He arrived the night before his talk, and the next morning, he mingled with our booth holders and show attendees before speaking.

His message was outstanding. He spoke of overcoming the emotional disappointment of having his career as quarterback of the Washington Redskins end when he broke his leg in a game against the New York Giants. He was truly a delightful person to have for the job he was hired to do.

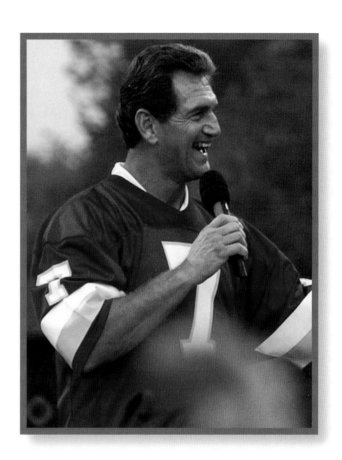

Tommy Thompson

Tommy served as Wisconsin governor for 14 years and then was Health and Human Services secretary under President George W. Bush. I first met him at a cookout at the home of Russ Rulau, who was a Krause Publications numismatic editor and active in Republican Party politics. Tommy had been a longtime member of the state legislature and, at the time of the cookout, was in the early but unannounced stages of running for his first term as governor. He struck me as a bright fellow, but I did not really know how bright at the time.

Later in his campaign, he was the keynote speaker at a Lincoln Day dinner in Waupaca. We offered him overnight accommodations at the Thorson House, Krause Publications' guest house. Dave Harper, another Krause Publications numismatic editor, showed him to the house and unlocked the door for him. That set off the security alarm at the house. As Tommy tells the story, two police cars came bearing down on the scene, and he and Dave had to do some explaining as to who they were and why they were there.

As governor, Tommy attended the Iola Old Car Show and Swap Meet several times and also came to the area in support of local politicians. Each visit provided lots of photo opportunities and was a great time. It has been exciting to know personally a longtime governor of our state who went on to serve in a cabinet post.

U.S. Mint directors

The U.S. Mint director is a political appointee of the president. The director reports to the U.S. treasurer, who in turn reports to the Treasury secretary.

I was not familiar with any of the directors or other Mint employees of the 1950s, other than one carryover into the 1960s. His name was Leland Howard, who was the senior civil servant in the department and the person in charge of actual coin production. I interfaced with him several times.

The first Mint director I met was Eva Adams, who President John F. Kennedy appointed. She was a good director, and the hobby generally liked her.

She came to coin conventions, and the office started to be seen and heard in the hobby. Her assistant was Roy Cahoon, who was a fine addition to the Mint staff.

Eva was a native of Nevada and had a master's degree in English. She taught at the University of Nevada-Reno before moving to Washington, D.C., and serving as administrative assistant to Nevada senators Pat McCarran, Ernest Brown, and Alan Bible. During this time, she also earned her law degree from American University in Washington and was admitted to practice before the Supreme Court.

During her watch as Mint director (1961-1969), the nation switched from precious-metal coinage to clad coinage in 1965. Eva allowed me to visit a cladding plant in St. Louis; I believe I was one of the few in the coin-collecting hobby to do so. At one time the factory was used to produce Winchester ammunition.

Eva continued to attend coin conventions after she left the Mint. She died in 1991.

President Richard Nixon appointed Mary Brooks, a native of Idaho, to succeed Eva as U.S. Mint director. Mary's husband, C. Wayland Brooks, had been a U.S. senator from Illinois, so she was right at home in the nation's capital. Mary, too, was good for the hobby. She traveled to the major shows, and I and others in the hobby got to know her as well as we did Eva.

When President Jimmy Carter was elected, he appointed Stella Hackel Sims from Vermont as Mint director. She seemed uncomfortable in the office and never warmed up to collectors as her two predecessors had.

One time she gave a talk at a coin convention in which she stated that mint marks would be removed from U.S. coinage. Rather than embarrass her in public, when I returned to Iola, I wrote her a letter stating that mint marks on U.S. coins were mandated by law (see Charles and Joel Anderson). I never received an answer from her, and I did not expect one. But mint marks are still part of U.S. coinage today.

I also got to know Dorothy Andrews Elston Kabis, who was U.S. treasurer from 1969 to 1971. Her signature first appears on U.S. paper money of that era as Dorothy Andrews Elston, but it changed when she married Walter Kabis. I would stop in to see her on some of my visits to Washington, and she also attended coin conventions. She was a very nice person.

Frederick J. Wenzel

"Fritz" is another fellow member of the Marshfield Clinic National Advisory Council. He was a lab technician at the clinic at the time Dr. Dean Emanuel was conducting his research on farmer's lung. I think Fritz got the worst of it, because he was actually in the mows pitching hay. From there, he worked his way into the front office and eventually became the clinic's executive director.

Fritz always had a sincere greeting for me at council functions and still does when we have the opportunity to meet. He also talked me into a substantial gift to the American Cancer Society Hope Lodge in Marshfield, where cancer patients can stay at no charge while undergoing treatments at the clinic. But I was happy to contribute, and Fritz's ensuing letter of thanks left no doubt that he was happy with the gift, too.

Index

Dear Chet

First you were my little brother and then you

grew up to be a sweet and caring man.

Progress?

Of course

Continue to Grow?

Of course!

What did you become?

That thing I had to learn to spell and speak...

A philanthropist.

You are it!

I thank you so much for being...

so generous

so caring

so thoughtful

so able to care for the whole family.

Love, Mary